Maintaining the Safety Net

Maintaining the Safety Net

Income Redistribution Programs in the Reagan Administration

John C. Weicher, editor

American Enterprise Institute for Public Policy Research
Washington and London

John C. Weicher, who has served with the President's Commission on Housing and as chief economist at the U.S. Department of Housing and Urban Development, holds the F. K. Weyerhaeuser Chair in Public Policy Research at AEI.

Library of Congress Cataloging in Publication Data
Main entry under title:

Maintaining the safety net.

    1. Income maintenance programs—United States—Addresses, essays, lectures. 2. Education and state—United States—Addresses, essays, lectures. 3. Manpower policy— United States—Addresses, essays, lectures. 4. United States—Economic policy—1981-   —Addresses, essays, lectures. I. Weicher, John C.
HC110.I5M24 1984   362.5′82   84-9259
ISBN 0-8447-3558-2
ISBN 0-8447-3549-3 (pbk.)

1 3 5 7 9 10 8 6 4 2

AEI Studies 401

Printed in the United States of America

Contents

Foreword

One of the most controversial areas of public policy during the Reagan administration has been its changes in the income security and redistribution programs. The administration has sought to restrain the growth, and in some cases to reduce the level, of expenditures in these programs. It has argued that this can be done while still preserving "the social safety net" that provides for the poor in this country. Critics, however, have charged that the administration's actions "reflect an abandonment of notions of social obligation." In this election year of 1984, further discussion and sharp debate are certainly likely.

Serious discussion of the changes in the income security programs, however, is hampered by their complexity and diversity. Income maintenance programs range from broad entitlement programs, such as food stamps, to those with limited participation, such as public housing; from programs that provide direct cash assistance, such as welfare, to those that help the poor buy only a single good or service, such as home heating fuel or vocational rehabilitation. The programs were originally enacted at different times to serve different purposes, and the differences persist.

To contribute to informed and dispassionate discussion of these recent policy changes, the American Enterprise Institute asked a group of experts to review and evaluate the changes that have occurred in their particular areas of interest. All the authors have previously studied extensively and written widely about the program areas they discuss here. Several have served in administrative and policy development positions in the federal government, where they were responsible for some of these programs. They use their knowledge and experience to describe the budgetary and programmatic changes that have occurred, beginning with the Reagan administration's original proposals of early 1981 and continuing through its submission of the fiscal year 1985 budget in February of this year. Each author thus has written a chronicle of the changes within a major component of the income security system of the United States during the last three years.

The papers are necessarily limited in scope. They attempt to provide a comprehensive view of the legislative and administrative

changes in the program. They cannot describe with any similar preci-
sion what the consequences of those changes have been. Many of the
authors take pains to point out that it is too early to evaluate the
effects of the changes on the poor and near-poor in America. Where
possible, they offer assessments, stressing that they are tentative and
provisional.

In addition to these discussions of specific program areas, we also
asked a former official of the Reagan administration and a critic of its
policies to write overviews of the changes from their differing perspectives. We believe that these papers complement the particular
studies and together help to define the broad issues of income security that the country will be addressing this year.

Nearly all of these papers were originally presented at a session
of AEI's Public Policy Week in December 1983. That session, entitled
"The Safety Net after Three Years," was organized by Dr. John C.
Weicher, who holds the F. K. Weyerhaeuser Chair in Public Policy
Research at AEI. Dr. Weicher has edited this book and contributed an
introduction, describing the overall patterns of program modifications
and expenditure changes.

The present volume can be regarded as the latest contribution by
AEI to the evaluation of the policies of the Reagan administration. We
have recently published a volume on *Disinflation* in our series on
Contemporary Economic Problems; that book is in part a discussion of the
macroeconomic policies of the administration and their consequences. We have also published the proceedings of a symposium on
the deregulation of economic activity in our *Regulation* magazine. And
we have evaluated the administration's efforts to change the roles of
the public and private sectors in assistance with respect to social problems in our book *Meeting Human Needs: Toward a New Public Philosophy*,
published in 1982. We believe that this book helps to round out our
assessment of the important changes that have taken place in domestic economic policy. We expect to continue to study and publish
studies of these changes in the future, as policy continues to evolve
and as the consequences of the recent changes become clearer.

WILLIAM J. BAROODY, JR.
President
American Enterprise Institute

Maintaining
the Safety Net

1

The Safety Net after Three Years

John C. Weicher

Almost as soon as President Reagan came into office, he proposed a major shift in the domestic income redistribution, or welfare, programs of the federal government. He asked Congress to make extensive changes in most of these programs, and extensive changes were made. The changes have been accompanied by passionate political rhetoric both from the administration and its supporters and from the programs' advocates. The rhetoric has often obscured the reality of the policy changes. After three years, however, the pace of change has slowed, if not come to a halt (though the rhetoric has not). Thus it seems appropriate to survey the changes at a time when we can see fairly clearly what has actually happened and what else is likely to happen in the near future.

This book is an attempt to do so—we hope dispassionately. It looks at both the overall pattern and the detailed changes in the most important program areas. All but two of the papers were originally written in late 1983 and presented at a session of AEI's Public Policy Week; they were subsequently revised in light of the fiscal year 1985 budget proposed by the administration in February 1984. They thus document the proposed and actual changes of the first three years of President Reagan's administration and the proposals for the fourth year.

The Concept of the "Safety Net." The theme of the book comes from a phrase coined and popularized very early by the Reagan administration, within a month of taking office. At that time the president submitted a fundamental revision of President Carter's last budget. In the area of social welfare programs, the new administration characterized its purpose as simultaneously "preservation of the social safety net" and "revision of entitlements to eliminate unintended benefits."[1] It identified the "safety net" as including "those programs, mostly begun in the 1930s, that now constitute an agreed-upon core of protection for the elderly, the unemployed, and the poor" and also veterans; "unintended benefits," by contrast, were primarily a problem in

1

"newer Federal entitlement programs and related income security programs that have undergone rapid growth during the last 20 years" but also to some extent in "certain aspects of social safety net programs that have been added unnecessarily or have grown excessively."

This original formulation suggests that the safety net includes social security (and perhaps Medicare), veterans' benefits, unemployment compensation, and welfare (Aid to Families with Dependent Children—AFDC), although, at the same time that it coined the term, the administration proposed modifications of all of these programs except veterans' benefits. The administration also sought substantial changes in a great many other domestic programs, including several that provide benefits specifically to the poor on the basis of income: subsidized housing, food stamps and other nutrition programs, and Medicaid. Thus the original concept seems to have comprised primarily programs for which eligibility does not depend on income. Except for AFDC, eligibility is based on criteria such as age or employment status, and benefits do not depend on current income. These programs reach middle-class families and individuals as well as the poor.[2]

In the 1985 budget, however, the administration has given a somewhat different definition to the term. It now includes, and apparently only includes, programs that provide benefits in cash or in kind to the poor and in which the value of the benefits is inversely related to the recipient's income. These programs are also identified as the "low-income benefit programs" in the budget; they consist of AFDC, Supplemental Security Income (SSI), public housing, Section 8 and other subsidized housing programs, food stamps and child nutrition, Medicaid, and a few smaller programs such as low-income home energy assistance and the earned income tax credit.[3]

This definition is probably more in line with common notions about what the safety net should be. It is also close to the definition used in this book. We include in addition most of the programs in the budget category of "education, training and employment, and social services." Like the low-income benefit programs, these are income conditioned, but they do not directly increase the income or economic well-being of the poor people whom they serve. Instead, they pay professionals, such as teachers and social workers, to provide services to the poor. These programs are intended to help their beneficiaries become more skilled and more productive in the future—the near future for manpower programs, the more distant future for elementary and secondary education. For convenience, we term these "human capital services programs." Our definition of the safety net thus includes a broadly defined set of "welfare" programs.[4]

2

The Organization of the Book. This book contains essays on all of these program areas except SSI—where no significant changes were proposed—social services, and some minor low-income benefit programs. It thus comes close to being a chronicle and evaluation of the full, broadly defined safety net. Some of the papers also look at programs that are not as directly related to income but that nonetheless provide substantial benefits to lower-income individuals, such as Medicare, unemployment compensation, community development block grants, and aid to college students. Any definition of the safety net is bound to be somewhat arbitrary; inclusion of these additional programs seemed warranted, in the judgment of the specialists in the subject areas.

The final two papers are overviews by a former official of the Office of Management and Budget during the Reagan administration and by an opponent of the present administration's policies who has long experience with income security programs. The differences between them, in perspective and emphasis, help to sharpen the issues that have divided the administration and its critics.

Expenditure Changes

The budgetary consequences of the policy changes can be simply summarized. When the Reagan administration came into office, outlays for income-conditioned programs had been rising rapidly for two decades, in both nominal and real dollars. Through 1985 they were projected to continue rising slightly in real terms. The administration sought to reverse the real growth of these programs and succeeded, although it achieved only about half of its initial goals. Instead of rising by about 4 percent, as projected by the Carter administration, real outlays fell by about 7 percent.

These are aggregate changes; there were substantial differences among program categories. In particular, the administration wanted to cut human capital services programs sharply, eliminating one—public service employment—altogether and cutting the others by about a quarter in real terms. It did succeed in getting rid of public service employment and achieved perhaps two-thirds of the other desired cuts.

It is difficult to be as precise about the relationships between the administration's goals and its achievements for the low-income benefit programs, because part of the changes in actual expenditures were a result of unexpected economic changes. Essentially the administration wanted to hold real benefits constant and apparently would have done so in the absence of the 1981–1982 recession. But because of the recession, actual outlays were close to the Carter administration's projections. Indeed, actual AFDC outlays in 1982 and 1983 were well above the 1981 projections of both administrations.

Program Growth before 1980. The rapid expansion of income-conditioned programs is shown in table 1–1. In 1960 the federal government was spending less than $4 billion for such programs, over half of it for AFDC. Expenditures roughly doubled in each succeeding five-year period, reaching $73 billion by 1980. Part of this growth resulted from inflation, particularly in the late 1970s. The real increases were less dramatic but still substantial. They were all well above the growth of the U.S. economy: Real gross national product rose at an annual rate of about 2.5 percent in the early 1970s and 3.7 percent after 1975. Thus the share of GNP going to the income-conditioned programs was rising, from 1.68 percent in 1970 to 2.46 percent in 1975 and 2.78 percent in 1980. Outlays were also rising as a share of the total federal budget—from 8.5 percent in 1970 to 12.7 percent in 1980. Real per capita expenditures also increased sharply, from $50 in 1960 to $320 in 1980; real outlays per person below the poverty level increased tenfold.

Table 1–2 shows the growth in both nominal and real outlays by program category. Most of the growth in the 1970s came in programs that were created in either the Johnson administration (Medicaid and

---

TABLE 1–1

EXPENDITURES FOR INCOME-CONDITIONED PROGRAMS, 1960–1980

	1960	1965	1970	1975	1980
Total expenditures (billions of dollars)					
Current dollars	3.8	6.9	16.7	38.1	73.3
1980 dollars	10.0	16.4	32.6	54.0	73.3
Annual growth rates (percent)					
Current dollars		12.3	19.5	17.9	14.0
1980 dollars		10.5	14.7	10.6	6.3

NOTE: Income-conditioned programs include Aid to Families with Dependent Children; Supplemental Security Income; low-income home energy assistance; earned income tax credit; housing assistance; food and nutrition assistance; Medicaid; elementary, secondary, and vocational education; training and employment; and social services.

SOURCE: Office of Management and Budget, *Budget of the United States Government,* various fiscal years.

TABLE 1-2
EXPENDITURES BY PROGRAM, 1960–1980
(billions of dollars)

	Current Dollars					1980 Dollars				
	1960	1965	1970	1975	1980	1960	1965	1970	1975	1980
Low-income benefit programs	3.8	5.4	10.1	25.5	50.1	10.0	12.9	19.8	36.1	50.1
Aid to Families with Dependent Children	2.1	2.8	4.1	5.1	7.3	5.3	6.7	8.1	7.3	7.3
Supplemental Security Income	1.4	1.8	1.9	4.8	6.4	3.7	4.3	3.6	6.8	6.4
Low-income home energy assistance	0	0	0	0	1.8	0	0	0	0	1.8
Earned income tax credit	0	0	0	0	1.3	0	0	0	0	1.3
Housing assistance	0.1	0.2	0.5	2.1	5.4	0.4	0.5	0.9	3.0	5.4
Food and nutrition assistance	0.2	0.3	1.0	6.6	13.9	0.6	0.7	1.9	9.4	13.9
Medicaid	0	0.3	2.7	6.8	14.0	0	0.7	5.3	9.7	14.0
Human capital services programs	0	1.5	6.5	12.6	23.2	0	3.4	12.8	17.9	23.2
Elementary, secondary, and vocational education	0	0.7	2.7	4.2	6.7	0	1.6	5.3	5.9	6.7
Training and employment	0	0.5	1.6	4.1	10.3	0	1.3	3.1	5.8	10.3
Social services	0	0.3	2.2	4.4	6.1	0	0.7	4.3	6.2	6.1
Total	3.8	6.9	16.7	38.1	73.3	10.0	16.4	32.6	54.0	73.3

NOTE: Detail may not add to totals because of rounding.
SOURCE: Same as table 1–1.

food stamps) or the Nixon administration (Section 8 housing and CETA). During the first half of the decade, growth in these program categories occurred largely because of increases in the number of beneficiaries as the programs matured; more recently this growth has slowed markedly and in some programs stopped. Real benefits per recipient, however, have risen all during the decade.

Proposals and Outcomes, 1980–1985. President Reagan was inaugurated during the fourth month of the 1981 fiscal year. Congress had already appropriated funds for the current year, and President Carter had just submitted his proposed budget for fiscal year 1982, to begin in October 1981. The new administration moved quickly to rewrite the 1982 budget substantially and even to make slight changes in the spending levels and patterns for the remainder of 1981. By April an extensive revision of the Carter administration's budget was submitted to Congress.

The income-conditioned programs were among those most affected. Table 1–3 compares the Carter and Reagan budget proposals for the next five fiscal years, beginning with the current one (1981). The differences are dramatic. Beginning in 1982, President Reagan

TABLE 1–3
PROPOSED AND ACTUAL EXPENDITURES FOR
INCOME-CONDITIONED PROGRAMS, 1980–1985
(billions of dollars)

	1980	1981	1982	1983	1984[a]	1985[b]
Current dollars						
Actual outlays	73.3	81.7	77.8	84.5	86.6	90.7
Carter fiscal year						
1982 projections	—	80.4	88.2	99.1	106.0	115.5
Reagan revised						
projections	—	78.8	72.2	75.1	76.6	80.2
1980 dollars						
Actual outlays	73.3	74.7	67.1	69.9	68.6	68.5
Carter fiscal year						
1982 projections	—	72.8	73.0	75.6	75.1	76.4
Reagan revised						
projections	—	71.7	60.6	59.0	56.7	56.4

a. Estimated.
b. Proposed.

SOURCES: Office of Management and Budget, *Budget of the United States Government,* fiscal years 1982 through 1985; *Additional Details on Budget Savings,* April 1981.

proposed to cut a large and steadily increasing share from his predecessor's planned budget: 18 percent in current dollars in 1982, rising to 31 percent by 1985. A small part of the difference—one percentage point in 1982, up to five points by 1985—reflected an expectation of lower inflation; the rest was a real reduction. President Carter had proposed to cut the rate of real increase in expenditures to less than 1 percent annually. This would itself have been a dramatic departure from the recent past. But President Reagan proposed to cut real expenditures by one-sixth immediately between 1980 and 1982 and to reduce them further by about 2.5 percent annually to 1985. By that time real outlays would be about the same as they had been in 1975.

Actual outlays through 1983 have proved to be about halfway between the two projections. Nominal outlays have been a little closer to the Reagan projections, real outlays to the Carter estimates. The difference occurs because the rate of inflation has followed a course much closer to the Reagan administration's initial assumptions; in fact, it has fallen more sharply than even the administration expected. Thus the constant-dollar numbers give a much sharper picture of the changes. There was about an 8.5 percent real decrease by 1982. That appears to be the high- (or low-) water mark of the Reagan administration's accomplishments, however; in 1983 real outlays increased instead of continuing to fall as the administration hoped. They may continue to rise; the administration's 1985 budget includes about $2.8 billion in reductions ($2.0 billion in 1980 dollars), nearly all of which Congress has rejected in the past. But it seems certain that real outlays in 1985 will be lower than in 1980, even if the administration's budget is not accepted in full.

The actual outlays for 1983 and the estimates for 1984 reported in table 1–3 include the effects of policy changes proposed in the 1983 and 1984 budgets and approved by Congress, as well as of the 1982 revision of the Carter budget. Thus comparison of the original proposals with the eventual outcome is not strictly appropriate. In some areas, such as food stamps, the administration made significant further proposals, building on its 1982 achievements; in a few, such as housing assistance, its 1983 budget sought much more fundamental reform than it initially asked. In nearly all cases, however, the administration has received very little of its 1983 or 1984 requests; what has happened is very close to what the administration was able to persuade Congress to accept during its first year. It therefore seems reasonable to compare the actual outcomes with the initial proposals for the purposes of this overview, even though there have been further proposals in most areas. Detailed discussions of subsequent proposals are contained in the papers on individual program areas.

Changes by Program to 1983. Tables 1–4 and 1–5 show the changes that have so far occurred for individual program categories, compared with the fiscal year 1982 budget projection of the two presidents. The tables bring out the political as well as substantive differences between the low-income benefit programs and the human capital services programs. Each administration had quite distinct plans for the two areas. President Carter proposed real increases for all low-income benefit programs (including substantial growth for food stamps and Medicaid) except AFDC and two minor programs, but real decreases, of 10 to 15 percent, for all three human capital service program areas. President Reagan, by contrast, proposed to hold most of the low-income benefit programs roughly constant in real terms (the major exception being substantial cuts in nutrition) and to cut the service programs much more sharply, by 35 to 65 percent. He proposed to cut almost exactly the same amount from the Carter budget in each of the two categories—about $8.3 billion—even though the low-income benefit programs were more than twice as large.

Economic versus Policy Changes. The actual outlays reported in tables 1–3, 1–4, and 1–5 reflect the combined impact of congressional action on the administration's policy proposals and unforeseen changes in economic circumstances. What actually happened was different from what would have occurred given the policy changes alone. The unexpectedly low rate of inflation tended to hold expenditures down; the unexpectedly high unemployment rate tended to drive them up.

The changing economic conditions make it difficult to formulate a precise scorecard of the Reagan administration's accomplishments in relation to its original goals. The most detailed effort to do so was prepared by the Congressional Budget Office in August 1983.[5] CBO compared actual outlays with those projected from the 1982 Carter budget, using CBO's most recent assumptions about the behavior of the economy rather than the economic assumptions used to derive the Carter budget. That is, the Carter budget was reestimated to reflect the changed economy and thus to be comparable to the conditions under which outlays were actually made or likely to be made in the near future. CBO did not calculate outlays for the 1981 Reagan proposals under the same assumptions, however, but only those for the policies actually adopted by Congress.

The projections covered all the low-income benefit programs except the earned income tax credit and about three-quarters of the service programs, including all the larger ones; about $9 billion of the outlays discussed in the previous section were excluded. It is unlikely

8

TABLE 1-4
ACTUAL AND PROPOSED OUTLAYS, BY PROGRAM, 1980–1983
(billions of current dollars)

	1980 Actual	1983 Actual	1983 Carter	1983 Reagan	1980–1983 Change Actual	1980–1983 Change Carter	1980–1983 Change Reagan
Low-income benefit programs	50.1	66.8	73.0	60.4	16.7	22.9	10.3
Aid to Families with Dependent Children	7.3	8.4	8.0	6.9	1.1	0.7	− 0.4
Supplemental Security Income	6.4	8.7	9.5	9.4	2.3	3.0	3.0
Low-income home energy assistance	1.8	2.0	1.9	1.4	0.2	0.1	− 0.4
Earned income tax credit	1.3	1.2	1.6	1.0	− 0.1	0.3	− 0.2
Housing assistance	5.4	9.6	9.5	9.2	4.1	4.1	3.7
Food and nutrition assistance	13.9	18.0	21.4	14.1	4.0	7.5	0.2
Medicaid	14.0	19.0	21.0	18.5	5.0	7.1	4.5
Human capital services programs	23.2	17.7	26.1	14.7	− 5.5	2.9	8.5
Elementary, secondary, and vocational education	6.7	6.3	7.5	5.4	− 0.4	0.7	− 1.3
Training and employment	10.3	5.3	11.5	4.8	− 5.0	1.2	− 5.5
Social services	6.1	6.1	7.1	4.5	0.0	1.0	− 1.6

NOTE: Changes in last three columns calculated from unrounded outlay numbers. Detail may not add to totals because of rounding.
SOURCES: Same as table 1–3.

TABLE 1-5

ACTUAL AND PROPOSED REAL OUTLAYS, BY PROGRAM, 1980–1983

(billions of 1980 dollars)

	1980 Actual	1983			1980–1983 Change (percentage points)		
		Actual	Carter	Reagan	Actual	Carter	Reagan
Low-income benefit programs	50.1	55.3	55.7	47.4	5.2	5.6	− 2.7
Aid to Families with Dependent Children	7.3	6.9	6.1	5.4	−0.4	−1.1	− 1.9
Supplemental Security Income	6.4	7.2	7.2	7.4	0.8	0.8	0.9
Low-income home energy assistance	1.8	1.6	1.5	1.1	−0.2	−0.4	− 0.7
Earned income tax credit	1.3	1.0	1.2	0.8	−0.3	−0.1	− 0.5
Housing assistance	5.4	7.9	7.3	7.2	2.5	1.9	1.8
Food and nutrition assistance	13.9	14.9	16.3	11.1	0.9	2.4	− 2.8
Medicaid	14.0	15.7	16.1	14.5	1.8	2.1	0.5
Human capital services programs	23.2	14.7	19.9	11.6	−8.5	−3.3	−11.6
Elementary, secondary, and vocational education	6.7	5.2	5.7	4.2	−1.5	−1.0	− 2.5
Training and employment	10.3	4.4	8.8	3.8	−6.0	−1.6	− 6.5
Social services	6.1	5.1	5.4	3.5	−1.0	−0.7	− 2.6

NOTE: Changes in last three columns are calculated from unrounded outlay figures. Detail may not add to totals because of rounding.

SOURCES: Same as table 1–3.

that their inclusion would greatly affect the analysis.

Table 1–6 contains the CBO figures for the major program categories for fiscal year 1983. Since the projections were made during that
year, the estimates do not exactly correspond to those reported in
previous tables for actual outlays, but they are close enough for com-
parative purposes. When the projected outlays are adjusted for
changing economic conditions, the effect of the 1981 legislative
changes becomes much more pronounced. The *growth* of real expenditures for the low-income benefit programs was essentially cut in half;
actual real expenditures for the service programs were cut in half.
Even if public service employment is omitted, actual expenditures for
service programs were cut by a third. The reductions were much
larger in each of the service program categories than in any of the
benefit areas: the smallest service cut was 18 percent for education,
the largest cuts in the benefit programs about 13 percent for both
AFDC and food stamps. Total real expenditures were essentially the
same in 1983 as in 1980, whereas they would have risen by almost 20
percent if the Carter budget had been enacted.

These figures differ sharply from those in table 1–5. Actual benefit outlays in 1983 were very close to those projected in the 1982 Carter
budget; in effect, the deterioration in the economy largely offset the
policy changes enacted in 1981. In food stamps, for example, the
Carter budget projected about a 5 percent increase in real benefits
between 1980 and 1983, and President Reagan asked for and received
about a 5 percent cut. Had his original economic assumptions proved
valid, the savings would have been about $1.0 billion. But the increase
in unemployment pushed outlays up by about $1.2 billion. Actual
service outlays were less affected by economic factors, and the policy
changes were more sweeping; outlays may have been almost a third
lower than the Carter budget projections (including the programs
omitted in table 1–6).

Although the CBO memorandum does not estimate the outlays
that would have occurred under the original Reagan proposals, it is
possible to derive a very rough approximation by adjusting the proposals for the effect of higher unemployment. This can be done by
adding about $2 billion to the benefit program projections of table
1–5.[6] The Reagan proposals would then have called for virtually constant real benefit outlays between 1980 and 1983. The additional outlays would have been concentrated in AFDC and food stamps.

With this crude adjustment, it appears that the effect of the 1981
policy changes, as distinct from economic conditions, was to "split
the difference" between the Carter and Reagan budget proposals for
the benefit programs. President Reagan appears to have achieved

TABLE 1-6

EXPENDITURE CHANGES RESULTING FROM POLICY CHANGES, 1983

(billions of dollars)

	1980 Actual	1983 (current dollars)		1983 (1980 dollars)	
		Carter policy	Revised policy	Carter policy	Revised policy
Total[a]	64.4	89.0	76.4	73.6	63.3
Low-income benefit programs	48.8	69.4	64.7	57.5	53.6
Aid to Families with Dependent Children	7.3	9.4	8.2	7.8	6.8
Supplemental Security Income	6.4	8.6	8.7	7.1	7.2
Low-income energy assistance	1.6	2.2	2.0	1.8	1.7
Housing assistance	5.5	9.3	9.4	7.7	7.8
Food and nutrition assistance	14.0	19.4	16.9	16.1	14.0
Medicaid	14.0	20.5	19.5	17.0	16.1
Human capital services programs	15.6	19.6	11.7	16.1	9.7
Education[b]	4.1	4.6	3.7	3.8	3.1
Training and employment[c]	7.5	10.3	4.1	8.5	3.4
Social services[d]	4.0	4.7	3.9	3.9	3.2

a. Excludes earned income tax credit.
b. Includes only Title I (Chapter I) and vocational education.
c. Includes only CETA (JTPA), public service employment, Work Incentive (WIN) program, and Job Corps.
d. Includes only social services block grant, community services block grant, and Head Start.

SOURCE: Congressional Budget Office, "Major Legislative Changes in Human Resources Programs since January 1981," staff memorandum, August 1983.

about half of his original aims. For the service programs, he was more successful; outlays were much closer to his projections than to President Carter's.

One major budgetary accomplishment of the administration is not reflected in these tables and deserves separate mention. The administration proposed to stop almost all subsidized housing construction and nearly managed to do so. This does not affect outlays for housing assistance, which are largely uncontrollable in the short run; they consist mostly of current interest and subsidy payments on past long-term bonds and contracts, issued to finance construction of public housing and Section 8 projects. But by stopping further new construction, the administration may have cut the total long-term costs of subsidized housing by about $100 billion, nearly one-third, over the course of the next thirty years. This is a major achievement, but it will not start to show up in budget outlays for a few years.

Policy and Program Changes

The Reagan administration has pursued budgetary savings partly by seeking systematic and generally consistent changes in the various program categories and partly by addressing particular problems in selected programs. Thus there is an overall pattern of policy change, overlaid by specific modifications in some areas.

Targeting Benefits. Perhaps the most pervasive policy has been to direct benefits more precisely to the lowest-income individuals and families. In nearly every program area, eligibility standards have been lowered to eliminate those who were relatively well off. Thus in housing the income limit was reduced from 80 percent of the local median (for a family of four) to 50 percent, which is roughly the poverty line. For food stamps the income limit for nonelderly households was cut less sharply, from 160 to 130 percent of the poverty line. Eligibility for AFDC was limited to those with incomes below 150 percent of a state's "standard of need." In addition, AFDC benefits were curtailed for recipients who were working or who began to work while receiving assistance. This amounted to a reduction on a different basis from income alone but with a similar effect, since the working poor tend to have the highest incomes of the program's beneficiaries. The AFDC limits on benefits for the working poor also affected Medicaid and food stamps. Consistent with this general approach, the administration tried to impose a means test and reduce eligibility limits for the college guaranteed student loan program and to limit Trade Adjustment Assistance, which benefits laid-off manufacturing workers, a relatively well-to-do group. Overall, a larger share of a smaller dollar amount of assistance is now going to the poorest part of the population.

Limiting Benefits. The administration also sought to cut benefits for those who remained in the various programs. Tenants in subsidized housing were required to contribute a larger fraction of their income toward their rent. In AFDC the exclusions of income for newly employed welfare recipients and of work-related expenses were limited. In Medicaid the administration sought a 5 percent ceiling on the growth in outlays, which was transformed by Congress into a reduction in the rate at which the federal government would match state outlays. In most of these programs, a number of small changes tightened administration and deferred adjustments of benefits.

Reducing Regulations. A recurrent theme of this administration has been to reduce federal regulation of the states and localities actually administering the programs. It proposed block grants for elementary and secondary education programs (two of them), for social services, for community services, and for low-income home energy assistance. It also converted the nutrition programs for Puerto Rico into a separate block grant. Most of these incorporated several or many programs—for the Title II education programs, the administration tried to include thirty-eight programs and succeeded in including twenty-nine. The block grant idea is, of course, not new; as a serious policy proposal, it dates back to the Nixon administration, when several grants were created. But the Reagan administration sought to extend the concept to new program areas.

One reason for consolidation was the belief that programs can be administered more effectively and less expensively by states or localities if there is less federal regulation; therefore, federal expenditures can be reduced without affecting the overall amount or quality of assistance that the poor actually receive. But the administration did not view block grants as a panacea; it did not propose one in the area of low-income housing, for example, even though President Reagan had suggested it during the campaign. And it was interested in reducing regulation in other ways: It offered states some freedom to try new approaches to controlling the cost of Medicaid, it tried to weaken the low-income targeting requirements of the community development block grant, and it proposed new regulations for bilingual education programs. In the last two areas, the administration was completely unsuccessful, but little budget saving would have been achieved even if it had succeeded; these were applications of a general approach that went beyond budget issues. At the same time the administration sought to curtail waste and abuse by providing new incentives to states and localities to reduce errors and by instituting new penalties for failing to do so.

Helping the "Truly Needy." Another reason for the administration's interest in block grants and reduced regulation seems to be the conviction that assistance should be given only to the "deserving poor" or the "truly needy," not to everyone who is poor according to some income criterion alone. Who is or is not deserving can best be determined by states or localities, not by the federal government. This may explain why the Reagan administration had no interest in the negative income tax approach to welfare reform, advocated by President Carter and considered seriously by earlier administrations and congresses. And it may also be the rationale for administration proposals to give states more freedom to experiment with Medicaid financing and delivery systems.

Programmatic Changes: A Mixed Record. The pattern of the administration's proposals and its accomplishments in structural reform is less clear. For some programs, such as CETA and AFDC, it came into office with clearly defined objectives and was able to persuade Congress to accept them quickly. For others its basic goal has been to cut costs, and the changes have been largely tailored to this purpose, as in food stamps, nutrition programs, and Medicaid. In housing it did not propose fundamental reforms until the 1983 and 1984 budgets; it has achieved one major success but has not been able to put most of its new ideas into effect. In education and social services its successes have been limited to the block grants; broader changes have received little attention, particularly in education. In SSI it has proposed virtually no change, budgetary or structural. These changes do not add up to a consistent pattern, but they may reflect the administration's priorities nonetheless. If they do, the administration has achieved most of what it probably thought was really important.

In addition, some programs were clearly politically vulnerable in 1981, and the incoming administration was able to seize on targets of opportunity: The Section 8 new construction housing program was recognized as extraordinarily expensive; public service employment had been heavily criticized during the Carter administration for providing payments to laid-off city workers rather than to new entrants to the labor force; the guaranteed student loan program was something of a scandal, with no limits on eligibility for below-market loans. The Reagan administration was able to terminate the first two and to impose income limits on the third, though not as stringent limits as it wanted. If President Carter had been reelected, he would in all probability have tried, or been forced by Congress, to modify these programs, but it is doubtful whether the changes would have been as dramatic as those actually put into effect. At the other extreme were some programs that the administration did not try to change, despite their incongruity with its basic philosophy, such as the Summer Youth Employment Program and the Section 202 housing program for the elderly. The administration's policy proposals have thus reflected political realities, producing some inconsistencies in the overall pattern.

Maintaining the Safety Net?

After all these budgetary and program changes, proposed and actual, one may wonder whether the safety net still holds. These are not the terms in which most social scientists would evaluate policy and program proposals, but they are perhaps the terms that will be used in political debates in 1984 and beyond and may therefore be worth a brief discussion.

This book addresses the question by examining the individual programs rather than by analyzing changes in the income distribution. Thus the answer to the question depends on the program, and the opinions of the authors vary. In nutrition, housing, and manpower, they conclude that it still does—though perhaps with some fraying. These assessments are noteworthy because criticism of the administration's changes has recently centered on the problem of hunger and because the largest budget and programmatic changes have occurred in housing and manpower. In welfare and Medicaid the working poor have clearly been adversely affected, a matter of concern to both authors; otherwise benefits have not been greatly reduced. (In both Medicaid and housing, it is worth noting, the safety net has never included all those who are eligible on the basis of income, so that the validity of the metaphor is open to question, but assistance has been targeted more toward those at the bottom of the income distribution.) In education the answer depends significantly on the states' response to the program changes, and it is too early to see what they will do; thus the authors withhold judgment. To some extent, this is also the case with AFDC, although many states have responded by raising their standards of need to offset the federal changes.

A different way of evaluating the changes is to measure the total amount of assistance being provided by these programs in relation to the number of people living below the poverty line. This criterion is apparently one that the administration itself is willing to use.[7]

As noted earlier, outlays per poor person rose dramatically before 1980; for the low-income benefit programs—the safety net as defined in the 1985 budget—they increased from $250 in 1960 to $1,400 in 1975 and $1,700 in 1980 (all measured in 1980 dollars). For 1984 and 1985 they are likely to be about $1,600, perhaps 5 to 10 percent below the 1980 figure but well above that for 1975. This ratio, however, does not measure actual benefits per poor person, because eligibility for many programs is not limited to those in poverty. The administration's efforts to improve targeting have probably offset part if not all of the reduction, so that benefits actually going to the poor have not decreased as much as the outlay figure. In the case of food stamps, for example, the share of benefits going to the poor increased from 72 to 81 percent between 1980 and 1982.[8]

All in all, both the budget and the program changes turn out to be smaller than much of the public discussion would suggest; the "safety net" has probably been maintained. But those who did not think the safety net was adequate in 1980 have reason to be at least as dissatisfied now—more dissatisfied, if they were anticipating continuation of the growth rates of the preceding two decades.

Whether the administration's specific proposals to modify the safety net programs should have been adopted is a somewhat different question. Many of the authors offer their own suggestions. In some instances, such as health and education, they favor more fundamental program changes than those proposed by the administration and are more concerned about these issues than about the effects of the expenditure reductions.

A Look into the Future

Although the Reagan administration has not achieved everything that it originally hoped for, it nonetheless seems to be satisfied with what has been done. The 1985 budget contains a retrospective discussion of the low-income benefit programs, which is largely written in the past tense.[9] It asserts that "one of the most intractable budget and social policy issues facing the Nation in 1980 has largely been resolved." The growth of these programs has been dramatically slowed, while the social safety net has been maintained. In constant dollars, outlays will be basically unchanged from their 1981 levels. This stability is now portrayed as the administration's goal. "Only modest additional reforms" are sought in the 1985 budget, amounting to $2.8 billion. If they are achieved, real outlays will decline slightly from their 1983 levels; if they are not, real outlays will rise slightly.[10]

17

This suggests that the administration's 1981 proposals were intentionally overambitious, that it did not expect to be able to reduce real expenditures as much as it proposed to do and was willing all along to settle for constant real outlays. Alternatively, of course, it may have changed its policy in the light of three years' experience of running the government, or it may merely be choosing to minimize the difference between its original proposals and the results. But whatever the explanation for it, the administration's present position suggests strongly that it does indeed intend to regard the changes in the low-income benefit programs as finished business. If that is true, then an evaluation of what it has done and not done is certainly appropriate now.

Notes

1. Office of Management and Budget, *Fiscal Year 1982 Budget Revisions*, March 1981, p. 8.

2. More recently some members of the administration have minimized the significance of the term "safety net." Martin Anderson, who served as director of the Office of Domestic Policy during 1981 and 1982, has since written that the phrase was "political shorthand that only made sense for a limited period of time," and David A. Stockman, director of the Office of Management and Budget, termed it a "happenstance list." It is ironic to note that these remarks appeared in the *Washington Post* two days before the AEI Public Policy Week session at which the papers in this book were originally presented. Thus the administration was apparently saying that it was not meaningful to talk about the safety net, just as we were about to do so. (See Milton Coleman, "More Reliant on Aid Than Whites, Blacks Hit Harder by Cuts," *Washington Post*, December 4, 1983, for the quotations from Anderson and Stockman.)

3. Office of Management and Budget, *Budget of the United States Government, FY 1985*, pt. 3, "Budget Program and Trends," pp. 3-27–3-30.

4. This broad definition of the safety net corresponds closely to the classification of "P" programs, "targeted primarily to lower economic groups," developed by Arthur L. Broida of AEI in "Social Programs and the Federal Budget," unpublished paper, August 1981. See also Jack A. Meyer, "Social Problems in the United States: Dwindling Federal Resources, Ongoing Needs, and the Case for New Initiatives," unpublished paper presented at AEI's Public Policy Week, December 1981. The present definition excludes some veterans' benefits and very small programs, which were not affected by the Reagan administration.

5. Congressional Budget Office, "Major Legislative Changes in Human Resources Programs since January 1981," staff memorandum, August 1983.

6. This figure is derived from an OMB Technical Staff Memorandum, "Sensitivity of Federal Expenditures to Unemployment," unpublished paper, April 18, 1980. Outlays for food stamps are calculated to rise by about $400 million

for each percentage point increase in the unemployment rate; outlays for AFDC, by a little less than $200 million. Other benefit programs are much less sensitive. Unemployment in 1983 was 2.9 percentage points higher than projected in the Reagan budget revision of 1981. I have not attempted to adjust the OMB figures for programmatic changes since 1980.

7. Office of Management and Budget, *1985 Budget*, p. 3-29.

8. These figures are calculated from G. William Hoagland, "Perception and Reality in Nutrition Programs," table 3-4.

9. "Budget Program and Trends," pp. 3-27-3-30.

10. The budget modifications being proposed in early 1984 both by the administration and the Senate Republicans and by the House Democrats involve only minor reductions in the low-income benefit programs and do not modify the trends of the last four budgets.

PART ONE

Evaluation of Specific Programs

2

Changing the Meaning
of Welfare Reform

Edward D. Berkowitz

After three years in office, the Reagan administration has done more to change the Aid to Families with Dependent Children program than any administration since that of Franklin Roosevelt. This achievement carries with it a sense of irony. Working at the federal level, the administration has reformed the AFDC program; yet it has proposed that responsibility for administering and funding the program be shifted completely to the states. Adding to the irony, Congress has rejected the administration's proposal to make AFDC a state program. Because Congress has acquiesced in almost all of the administration's other proposals for welfare reform, the administration's actions warrant close attention. This essay details the administration's proposals, searches for their intellectual origins, and comments on their significance. Although substantive judgments come hard in the field of welfare, some tentative assessments can now be made.

The Reagan Revolution

Welfare statistics have a numbing effect. Billions of dollars spent on particular programs fail to convey the situations of welfare recipients. They also project a misleading clarity. Often they jumble state, local, and federal expenses together and neglect the interrelationships among welfare programs. Gaining an overview, however, requires the use of statistics.

Expenditures for social security (old age, survivors', and disability insurance) overwhelm those for welfare programs (programs restricted to those who demonstrate that they are in financial need). As early as 1955, for example, social security expenditures reached $4.3 billion. In 1955 federal outlays for Aid to Families with Dependent Children remained below $0.5 billion, and federal outlays for welfare payments to the permanently and totally disabled, the blind, and the elderly amounted to $1 billion. A decade later the figures revealed an even wider disparity. The welfare programs accounted for less than $3 billion in federal outlays, the social insurance program $16.6 billion. The same series of statistics also reveal an important fact about the different types of welfare programs. Until about 1970 the federal government laid out more money for state-administered programs in aid of the needy blind, permanently and totally disabled, and elderly than it did for similar programs in aid of dependent children and their parents. After 1970 the program for dependent children consistently cost more than the other programs combined.[1]

This paper focuses on changes made by the Reagan administration in Aid to Families with Dependent Children. AFDC, however, needs to be considered in relation to the food stamp and Medicaid programs, each of which gives many welfare recipients added income in the form of coupons to purchase specified food items (food stamps) and reimbursement for medical care (Medicaid). Of the money spent by all levels of government on the various programs in fiscal 1981, AFDC amounted to $14.6 billion, Supplemental Security Income $9.2 billion, food stamps $11.8 billion, and Medicaid, by far the most expensive program of all, $30.4 billion. Some seventy programs that might be classified as welfare (not including social security) in fiscal year 1981 cost $116.7 billion, about three quarters of which came from federal outlays, amounting to 4 percent of that year's gross national product.[2]

These numbers underscore the magnitude and complexity of the social welfare system. Martin Anderson, a former member of the Nixon and Reagan administrations who worked on the Reagan welfare proposals, once noted wistfully that the federal government maintained only 40 major domestic programs at the close of the Eisenhower administration. When Anderson arrived in the Nixon White House, he found himself looking at over 400 and encountered great difficulty in "finding out exactly what was going on." "The domestic side of the federal government had gotten so big that it was literally impossible to grasp it, intellectually, in its entirety," Anderson noted.[3]

For all of this perceived complexity, the Reagan administration offered major proposals on welfare reform within months of its arrival in Washington. In the jargon of the day, the administration hit the beach running, hoping to exploit the advantage of surprise and resist congressional sniping. In February 1981 the administration unveiled its Program for Economic Recovery, and within a few more weeks it offered detailed proposals for changes in AFDC.

The contrast with the early days of the Carter administration could not have been more striking. Carter, like Reagan, came to office with a desire to move swiftly on a plan to reform the welfare system. Arriving in January 1977, he promised to have his plan ready by May. In May he admitted that the welfare system was "worse than we thought," that the welfare system's "complexity" made it "almost incomprehensible."[4] Not until August did the Carter administration reveal its plan. Throughout the rest of the administration, the plan unraveled until it faded from sight. Carter's plan would have moved the welfare system closer to providing universal income support. The debate over the plan never centered on whether it would increase welfare spending; the only question concerned the amount by which such spending would rise.[5]

President Reagan removed the guaranteed income from the agenda of presidential politics, and he promised to cut the rate of growth of the various welfare programs. Within a few months, a new politics of subtraction replaced the uneasy incremental politics of the Carter era. In presenting a rationale for this change, the Reagan administration seized upon the metaphor of the safety net. The federal government owed the nation's citizens a net to protect them against the most severe causes of misfortune. Certain programs already in place gave the net its strength. Social security, with its program of old-age, survivors', disability, and health insurance, led the list of safety net programs. Unemployment insurance and veterans' benefits also supported the net. These programs had strong political backing, in part because their benefits extended beyond the nation's poorest citizens and reached middle-class Americans.[6]

Since the details of the cuts proposed for the various welfare programs lay beyond most people's comprehension, the image of the safety net became a convenient shorthand to describe the administration's efforts. Later some members of the administration regretted the use of the term. Martin Anderson called it "political shorthand that only made sense for a limited period of time." He claimed that the administration made some early decisions about which programs could be cut and which needed to remain in place, at least during the first round of budget cutting. In order not to invoke a "torrent of passionate, often irrational criticism," the administration spared the programs in the safety net.[7] Politically vulnerable programs like AFDC attracted its attention. From the beginning, therefore, the administration laid itself open to the charge of being unfair by concentrating on social welfare programs restricted to the poor. These were not the most costly programs, only the most disliked.

Two of the administration's reforms held the most significance for the future of the AFDC program. One limited eligibility to families with gross incomes that were less than 150 percent of a state's standard of need; the other changed the program's work incentives.

Because states allowed welfare recipients to keep some of their income without being removed from the rolls, many states paid benefits to people whose earnings rose above 150 percent of that state's standard of need. At the time that Congress debated the Reagan administration's proposed change in the program, the Department of Health and Human Services estimated that about 20,000 AFDC families had incomes of more than $9,500 a year. As many as 200 families earned more than $18,000 and still collected welfare.[8] The change made it hard for such families to remain on the welfare rolls. In fact, a job that paid the minimum wage would leave a typical family of four with too much money to qualify for welfare and too little to live above the poverty level.

The administration's second major change in the AFDC program reversed a long line of incremental change. As a result of reforms enacted in 1967, the program featured a work disregard and work bonus. As these forms of Washington shorthand imply, the law gave welfare recipients a bonus by allowing them to work and receive welfare benefits at the same time. Federal law required state agencies simply to disregard the first $30 of income a month. A welfare recipient kept that money without penalty. Beyond $30, however, a recipient found his benefit reduced by two-thirds. If, for example, a recipient made $60 a month, his check would be reduced by $20. At this rate of taxation, it probably paid the recipient to accept a job. So the theory went. In reality, the situation was more complex because the recipient seldom received only AFDC. In all likelihood he also benefited from Medicaid and food stamps and perhaps from public housing as well. Unfortunately, the amounts by which benefits were reduced for working were not coordinated across the various programs, even though a welfare recipient regarded food stamps in the same way as he did money. The resulting confusion meant that work became more costly than the 1967 law, with its work disregard, implied.

The Reagan administration took the bold step of ending the system altogether. The administration came close to abolishing the work disregard and bonus. After four months a working welfare recipient lost the bonus and needed to wait a year before it could be resumed.[9] The change meant that a welfare recipient now had a trial work period. After this trial he either lost his welfare because his earnings took him beyond 150 percent of the state standard of need or found his grant greatly reduced—a reduction of one dollar for every dollar he earned.

In addition to these two major changes, the administration made numerous other reforms. Some of these went back to the unsuccessful efforts of the Carter administration to reduce the costs of the AFDC program. Both administrations, for example, called for basing grants on a family's financial condition in a previous month. Along with another accounting measure called periodic reporting, this change reduced errors in the system. Although Carter advocated this change, Reagan managed to pass it into law, along with changes that required states to count a portion of a stepparent's income as available for a stepchild and to treat food stamps and housing subsidies as income available to meet a family's needs.[10]

Perhaps the most significant of the changes first mentioned by the Carter administration and enacted during the Reagan administration concerned the way in which the AFDC program computed work-related expenses. The differences between the old and the new laws, though highly technical, constituted a major change in the program. Under the old law a welfare recipient could claim work-related expenses, such as the cost of taking the bus to work or of providing a dependent child with care during working hours. When it came time to reduce the AFDC benefit to reflect the income earned at work, administrators disregarded these work-related expenses, as well as the first $30 of earnings and one-third of the remainder. The new law limited the work-related expenses that the welfare recipient could claim and ordered the states to compute the deductions differently. The changes reduced a working welfare recipient's benefit even during his four-month trial work period.[11]

To these changes the Reagan administration added others of its own. Workers on strike, for example, were prohibited from receiving welfare benefits, and a woman pregnant with her first child could not receive benefits during the first six months of her pregnancy.[12] These items reflected social judgments of the sort that have pervaded welfare programs; the administration expected to gain only negligible savings from them.

The resemblance of the administration's changes to a shopping list hid their economic significance. Looked at individually, the changes appeared relatively inexpensive and inconsequential. Taken together, they formed part of a package that the Congressional Budget Office estimated would save the federal government about $1 billion in outlays for AFDC in fiscal 1982. Many of those savings would come about because, by the administration's estimates, 400,000 families would lose their benefits and another 258,000 families would have their benefits reduced. (When the cuts went into effect, 3.9 million families were on the rolls, and 11.1 million people were receiving welfare.) Of the dollars that would be saved, nearly half (44 percent) would come from reductions in the grants paid to the 13 percent of AFDC families who worked. Nearly 40 percent of those earning families would become ineligible, and 42 percent would have their benefits reduced.[13]

The numbers remain only educated guesses. They are also misleading. They give the impression that AFDC families stay on welfare rolls, instead of moving on and off the rolls, and they fail to convey the sensitivity of welfare programs to increases in the unemployment rate. Preliminary findings from a study conducted by Mathematica for the Congressional Research Service showed, for example, that changes in the unemployment rate have affected the AFDC program more than the changes made in 1981.[14]

The increase in the unemployment rate has increased the difficulty of measuring the effects of the changes. During the first month that the Omnibus Budget Reconciliation Act took effect (October 1981), the rolls dipped below 11 million people for the first time in more than a year. By October 1982 payments were down $35 million, or 3 percent, from a year earlier. Federal expenditures for AFDC declined from fiscal 1981 to fiscal 1982 by $0.5 billion, from $8.5 billion to $8.0 billion. The average number of recipients and the average expenditure per recipient also fell. In fiscal 1983 and 1984, however, the trends began to reverse themselves. In January 1983 payments stood 5 percent higher than a year earlier, in part because of the cumulative effect of the rise in the unemployment rate during the Reagan administration.[15]

By 1983 a round of 1982 budget cuts made determining the magnitude of the savings from the Reagan reforms even more difficult. The Tax Equity and Fiscal Responsibility Act of 1982 permitted states to prorate the shelter and utilities portion of benefits for welfare recipients living with other families. The administration originally estimated a savings of $174 million from this change. When the Congressional Research Service reported on the final law, it reduced the savings to $43 million. Other changes made in 1982 netted a smaller amount of estimated savings. Eliminating parental absence for military service as a source of welfare eligibility, for example, was expected to save $16 million, and rounding benefits down would save another $10 million. Compared with the magnitude of the cuts enacted in 1981, the 1982 cuts were less significant and saved less money. The *National Journal* used Congressional Budget Office data to estimate a 2 percent reduction in the cost of the program in fiscal 1983 as the result of cuts enacted in 1982. The cuts made in 1981, by way of contrast, reduced 1983 expenditures by 16 percent.[16]

The Intellectual Basis of the Cuts

For previous administrations, the complexity of the welfare system had proved to be the undoing of their plans for reform. Compared with the records of those administrations, the accomplishments of the Reagan administration appear all the more remarkable. The process by which the new administration completed the first legislatively successful reform of the welfare system since the New Deal requires further analysis.

President Carter's Program for Better Jobs and Income was the culmination of a generation of effort to create a guaranteed annual income. Carter proposed his plan only four years before President Reagan offered completely different proposals. The Carter program would have replaced AFDC, food stamps, and Supplemental Security Income with a federal program offering uniform cash benefits across the country. The plan diverged from other welfare reform plans by treating people expected to work differently from those not expected to work. In this one detail, it resembled Reagan's welfare reform plans. For the people who were expected to work, Carter envisioned the creation of a job search program that would help them find jobs. Failing to get a job in the private sector, a welfare recipient would receive a job in public service employment.[17] More than six years later, this Carter plan, like the other guaranteed income programs before it, appeared to be irrelevant to the course of welfare reform, an artifact of history.

To the advisers close to President Reagan, the previous plans failed because of the impossibility of designing a workable negative income tax. Robert Carleson and Martin Anderson, in particular, have argued that the negative income tax presents a logical puzzle with no good solution, a Rubik's cube that looks easy to twist into place but never quite comes together. The idea relies on a decent level of income for those who cannot work and must depend on the government (the government's guarantee), on low tax rates as welfare recipients begin to work and make money (the marginal tax rate), and on an implicit political promise of reasonable cost. Each of these three things depends on the other two. Halving the tax rate doubles the amount of income at which the government continues to pay benefits and therefore increases the cost of the plan. In short, "There is no way to achieve all of the politically necessary conditions for radical welfare reform at the same time." To this bit of logic, conservatives add pieces of empirical evidence that also cast doubt on the negative income tax and the guaranteed annual income. The Seattle-Denver negative income tax experiment revealed, for example, that a guaranteed income increased the rate of divorce among the working class.[18]

Anderson's rhetoric on the subject of a guaranteed annual income captures the conviction and fervor of the Reagan forces. "A small, largely liberal, intellectual elite" who have been seduced "by simplistic beauty" favor a guaranteed annual income. The members of this elite reside in the favored liberal haunts, "the universities, the welfare agencies that administer the program, the government, and the welfare rolls." Perhaps because of the privileges they enjoy, they have a desire to be free "of the constraints of reality, to soar off into the dream land of unlimited plenty." These "neo-romantics" believe that people "basically like to work . . . and that even mild incentives will encourage them to leave the welfare rolls." Those who oppose the idea see the world "as it is" and have a "realistic, traditional view of life." They realize that people with a guaranteed income will "simply cease working and loaf." They accept the conditions of a world of unequal income, wealth, power, beauty, and talent, a world in which "people need help from others and by this very fact are dependent." It is no wonder, then, that Anderson describes a central objective of the Reagan administration as "not to propose any disguised guaranteed income programs." Says Anderson, "No time has even been wasted in studying them." He therefore rejects what Palmer and Sawhill call the "egalitarian values" of previous administrations. He joins other members of the administration in not placing income redistribution high on the list of desired policy outcomes.[19]

The origins of these strong convictions lie in the late 1960s and early 1970s, when Richard Nixon proposed his Family Assistance Plan, a version of a guaranteed annual income, and Ronald Reagan formulated and implemented a different sort of welfare plan for California. In response to the same welfare crisis, the two leaders reached different conclusions and set the tone for the debate over welfare that stretched through the 1970s.

Nixon saw in the negative income tax a way to end the welfare mess, as people referred to the problem at the time, and to encourage the work ethic. As Milton Friedman had noted, the negative income tax held the appeal of substituting the market, an individual's own preferences, for the whims of a social worker. As Nixon came to realize, however, the negative income tax contained its share of political problems. When Friedman proposed the idea, he saw the negative income tax as the nation's only income maintenance program. With social security, Medicaid, and food stamps already in place and not likely to be abolished, a negative income tax became much more difficult to pass and implement. Nixon's plan died, and the welfare mess persisted.

Inside the Nixon White House, Anderson led the fight against the negative income tax. Arthur Burns, Anderson's boss, wrote a memorandum to Nixon in which he lamented "moving away from the concept of welfare based on disability-related deprivation and need to the concept of welfare as a matter of right."[20] In California plans were under way to return the welfare system to one based on just those things. A year after President Nixon decided to endorse the Family Assistance Plan, Governor Reagan sent a letter to his cabinet in which he announced the formation of a task force to examine public assistance. This task force hoped to produce a plan that would put a stop to the growth of the state's welfare rolls. The AFDC rolls alone were increasing at the rate of 40,000 people a month. The strategy for reducing the growth of the welfare rolls would be to "purify" the welfare system and limit welfare to those "strictly entitled." The task force plan should maintain welfare for the "truly needy," but others would have to work to survive. Calling the welfare system "a moral and administrative disaster," Reagan presented his welfare reform plan to the California legislature on March 3, 1971.

The California plan relied on trimming ineligible people from the welfare rolls, on forcing fathers and other relatives to assume financial responsibility for dependent children, and on making the able-bodied poor work for their grants. The California welfare statistics responded as the federal statistics would a decade later. In April 1971 the number of welfare recipients dropped, and it continued to drop for eight straight months. Meanwhile, benefits for those still on welfare increased, and a significant number of former welfare recipients entered the labor force. If the federal welfare plans appeared to be stalled, the California plan showed great vitality.[21]

The California plan soon gained national attention as an alternative to the creation of a negative income tax. On February 1, 1972, Governor Reagan made a rare appearance before a congressional committee. The subject was welfare, and the governor used his testimony as a vehicle for lauding the California program. Carleson, then a bureaucrat from the California Department of Public Works who had done much to formulate and implement the proposals, accompanied Reagan. Senator Russell Long of Louisiana, impressed with Reagan's performance, asked Carleson to spend some time in Washington advising the Senate Committee on Finance. In this manner an important connection developed between California and Washington. Reflecting on this connection, Carleson remarked that "on welfare, Long and Reagan are identical."[22] Soon Carleson left Sacramento to serve as commissioner of welfare under a fellow Californian, Caspar Weinberger. Carleson brought John Svahn, a California welfare official and later commissioner for social security under President Reagan, to Washington to serve in another important post in the Department of Health, Education, and Welfare. During the Nixon and Ford administrations, therefore, HEW became a battleground, divided between proponents of the negative income tax and supporters of the California approach.

These years of struggle sharpened Reagan's welfare ideology. This ideology began with the notion that, since resources are limited, welfare should be focused on the truly needy. If a person was capable of working, he had no business receiving aid from the state. Low-paying jobs were a fact of life, and the millions of Americans who accepted this fact resented those who chose to live at a subsistence level by doing nothing. Welfare belonged to those in a state of dependency. This was not the sort of dependency described by Daniel Moynihan and others as reinforcing generations of poverty or one that created an automatic association between a demographic characteristic and the state of poverty, as in the "feminization" of poverty. Instead this was an honest state of dependency. As Anderson has recently explained, "the very fact of being dependent, especially when that state occurs through no fault of one's own," is not something of which to be ashamed. By clearing some of the working poor from the rolls, the California approach reserved welfare for what an earlier generation called the "deserving" poor.[23]

Proponents of the negative income tax based much of their argument on using the benefit structure to create incentives for welfare recipients to work. To pay money only to people not expected to work, the argument went, risked increasing total welfare costs. People would stop working to get on welfare, and the number of people on welfare would rise. Reagan's welfare ideology rejected this notion. Svahn claimed that work incentives "don't work" and Carleson that they "suck up available funds. It may work for producers, but it just doesn't work for the low-income people."[24]

Instead of using economics to design costly negative income tax schemes, Carleson and the other Reagan ideologues believe that administrators should concentrate on maintaining strict eligibility standards and on requiring able-bodied welfare recipients to work. The elderly, blind, and disabled have a claim on welfare by the very fact of being in those circumstances. Supplemental Security Income, the welfare program that comes to their aid, requires less substantive change than Aid to Families with Dependent Children, which bears close watching to focus its resources on those who really need them. Separating the needy from the non-needy, the deserving from the nondeserving, has never been an easy task. But Anderson argues that "as in all judicial-type decisions, there are things that reasonable people can reach agreement on."[25]

For the Reaganites, agreement began with the notion that the closer a program was to the welfare population, the more effective and efficient it would be in reaching the needy and excluding those who could help themselves. Welfare programs that met their objectives depended on close human contact between the administrators and welfare recipients. Successful programs demanded a retreat from the automatic, check-cashing type of welfare represented by the negative income tax. Governor Reagan and his followers believed, therefore, that the states could administer the AFDC program more effectively than the federal government.

A final element of the Reagan ideology concerned the use of workfare. By this term Reagan meant something different from the manpower programs that blossomed in the 1960s and 1970s and tried to induce welfare recipients to gain skills and enter the labor force. Instead, Reagan advocated a program that forced the able-bodied to work in return for their welfare checks. In California's Community Work Experience Program, a recipient worked for as many hours as it took to pay back his grant at a rate of pay equal to the state's minimum wage. Because the program sought to encourage welfare recipients to look for work, it established a ceiling of eighty hours per month.[26]

Carleson and Joe Anne B. Ross, a former staffer for Senator William Roth of Delaware and now associate commissioner for family assistance, believe that workfare serves a deterring and transforming function. Administered correctly, it keeps able-bodied people from seeking welfare and also endows welfare recipients with a sense of dignity. In common with members of the labor force, welfare recipients earn their income under the California workfare plan. They also learn about the discipline that the world of work demands. Workfare reinforces such commonplace lessons as the need to show up on time for work.[27]

Although the Reaganites emphasized the transforming aspects of workfare, the deterring aspects also played an important role in their ideology. This side of the Reagan forces' beliefs went back at least as far as the 1834 English poor law. The English law mandated the construction of local workhouses that would sustain the poor at a subsistence level but make their conditions so forbidding as to discourage others from seeking welfare. Another precedent for workfare came from the New Deal model, which Reagan closely copied. For able-bodied, prime-age males, the New Deal advocated the provision of temporary jobs. Reagan's Community Work Experience Program was an updated version of the Works Progress Administration (WPA), expanded to embrace modern mores that sanctioned the labor force participation of women and members of racial minorities.

Although some aspects of the Reagan ideology appeared to be out of step with the times, the Reagan forces gained strength as the 1970s progressed. By 1975 conservatives in Congress had introduced legislation patterned closely on the California reforms, and by the end of the 1970s the coalition that favored the negative income tax began to unravel.[28] Three times the negative income tax passed the House of Representatives, but each time the Senate Finance Committee blocked its passage. Weary of the long struggle, liberals in both political parties began to retreat. They argued that the expansion of food stamps and the introduction of Supplemental Security Income were disguised forms of a guaranteed income that made the negative income tax politically disruptive and economically unnecessary. Richard Nathan, a prominent welfare expert, began to see virtue in having a wide variety of welfare programs. He argued that "different strokes for different folks" reflected the judgment of the American people and should be accepted. When President Carter sounded the call to battle on behalf of the negative income tax, Nathan repeated the despair and weariness of many. He asked the president to "abandon the search for a utopian solution to welfare problems and instead build on the programs we have."[29]

With the negative income tax forces already exhausted, Reagan's election boosted his approach to welfare from ideology to public law. In January 1981 Carleson met with the president-elect in Blair House. For two hours the two men discussed a proposal to reform the AFDC program. Reagan reacted to the proposals with enthusiasm. Said Carleson, "Reagan understands welfare." Reagan needed little prompting; the new federal proposals bore a direct relationship to the old California plan. Later Carleson approached David Stockman and told him, "Here is something that has already been approved. All you have to do is plug it in. It's like a cassette." The administration moved so quickly on welfare, therefore, because it had over a decade of preparation. It hit the beach running, but running on a course set a decade before.[30]

The Limits of the Reagan Revolution

When the administration moved beyond the present system and tried to achieve its own form of radical reform, it found the going difficult, just as previous administrations had. On two issues in particular it encountered political opposition. In the case of the new federalism the administration backed away from its original bold proposals, and in the case of workfare it settled on experiments in some states rather than permanent programs in all the states.

President Reagan's January 26, 1982, State of the Union message called for the withdrawal of the federal government from the AFDC and food stamp programs. Unlike the other welfare initiatives, this item stimulated no quick action on the administration's part. As the year ended, details of the proposal remained vague; as late as November 1982, no legislation had reached Congress on the subject. In the proposals that led to the Omnibus Budget Reconciliation Act of 1981, the administration showed a willingness to come to grips with the details of welfare programs, but the particulars of the federalism initiative were unclear. The administration failed to specify how the plan would operate in a particular state, such as Mississippi. It neglected to say whether Mississippi would be required to pay a mother with two children $22 a month, the amount of the current state payment; $96 a month, the total current state and federal payments; or $279 a month, the sum of state, federal, and maximum food stamp payments. As early as June 1982 the administration began a retreat from the plan, which was shaping up as an exchange of AFDC for Medicaid and food stamps. The federal government would pay for those two if the states accepted the burden of AFDC. A year later the entire matter had faded from sight. In a recent interview Svahn stated that the administration had no desire "to fight that battle again." Carleson continues to push for federalization but sees no action until 1985.[31]

The federalism proposal foundered in part because it required the states and the federal government to make major institutional changes. The previous initiatives had been self-contained and built on the workings of the AFDC program; the new initiatives required a major rethinking of how the welfare system would operate. In this sense, the federalism proposals were Reagan's version of a utopian scheme. Not only would the states receive new responsibilities, they would also receive new revenues. According to Anderson, this part of the proposal is as vital to the argument "as vermouth is to a good martini."[32]

The administration also considered the new federalism the best strategy for breaking down the forces of incremental growth within the welfare system. Although the administration applauded the creation of welfare programs to reflect the special conditions of needy groups, it resented the way in which transfers could be hidden in a fragmented system. It deplored the strength of the iron triangles that pumped money straight from Washington to thousands of special interests. To replace this highly efficient system of income redistribution, it wanted to decentralize the authority to initiate the transfers.[33] For the major welfare programs, the effort failed. Instead the administration settled for having a major influence from Washington over state welfare programs. In the process it proved that a president, as much as a governor, could induce a decline in the rate of a welfare program's growth.

The administration sustained its second major failure when it tried to mandate a California-style workfare program in the states. Congress rejected the proposal and substituted one that permitted (but did not require) various forms of workfare in the states, including the Community Work Experience Program (CWEP) favored by the administration.

In advocating workfare, the administration believed that it had the public on its side. Just as the public supported the administration's other proposals, so it supported workfare: 93 percent of the respondents in a 1977 NBC News poll replied yes when asked if they thought that people who received welfare and were capable of working should be required to work at public service jobs to receive their checks. On workfare, however, the administration received less than it asked for from Congress.[34]

The reason may lie in the long history of unsuccessful efforts to mix work and welfare. Sar Levitan once wrote a book entitled *Work and Welfare Go Together*. If they did, their marriage proved remarkably difficult to arrange. Although the existing programs were far more permissive than those advocated by the administration, workfare still possessed a dismal record. Congress initiated the Work Incentive (WIN) program in 1967 and amended it in 1971 to provide welfare recipients with immediate employment. By 1980, 10.9 million people received AFDC; 3.4 million of them were adults, of whom 1.2 million were required to register for the program. If the number of potential jobholders appeared relatively large, the number of actual jobholders proved disappointingly small.[35]

When, for example, the Ford administration prepared a briefing for the president in 1975, it needed to look hard to find good things to say about the program. The data for fiscal 1974 showed 1,811,446 registrants; the program in that year and for the years to follow acted as an inefficient funnel to place the registrants in jobs. For one reason or another, only 534,885 people reached the stage of program participant, only 177,271 obtained employment, and only 51,627 left welfare. The cost-to-benefit ratio of such an effort left the Ford and Carter administrations with little to cheer about.[36]

WIN proved to be a loser. In fact, part of the administration's strategy was to replace WIN with new workfare programs. The results of Governor Reagan's CWEP in California and of a similar program in Utah provided little basis for optimism, however. During 1974, for example, 182,735 people were eligible for CWEP, 5,712 were assigned to work sites, and 4,760 actually worked. The low numbers occurred partly because less than half the state's counties participated and many of the caseworkers in the counties that did participate lacked enthusiasm for the plan. They refused to regard it as mandatory. Utah established a Work Experience and Training Program that required an AFDC recipient to participate in ninety-six hours of unpaid work each month, regardless of the size of his grant. This program established higher rates of participation and job placement, although the training proved to be rudimentary: On-the-job training consisted of being shown "how to mop and wax a floor, clean windows, run a copy machine." Surveying the pre-1981 workfare experience, two researchers found that none of the programs had established a "smoothly functioning system."[37]

By June 1983 about half the states had accepted President Reagan's challenge to create some form of CWEP. Three states discontinued the program, and all states discovered that even when people worked at the minimum wage, it took them few hours to "earn" their welfare grant. In September 1983, to take a hypothetical case, a four-person family in Alabama received a maximum of $147 from the AFDC program. At a wage of $3.50 an hour, such a grant bought forty-two hours of work a month. Furthermore, a workfare participant received only his welfare benefits. Although those benefits may have included health care, they did not contain many other fringe benefits. Nor did the worker have much incentive to improve his job performance. Not only did he perform the job on a very temporary basis, but he had no hope of ever getting a raise since his wage remained pegged to the minimum wage.

The administration points with pride to Michigan. Despite the high unemployment in the state (or maybe because of it), Michigan has initiated a statewide CWEP and managed to place 11 percent of its caseload in jobs. In general, the administration remains optimistic about workfare, claiming that its approach constitutes a substantial improvement over the old WIN program. Visits by staff members of the Office of Family Assistance to the projects initiated in the various states reinforce the sense of optimism. Despite a new flexibility in the administration's workfare proposals, Congress remains unconvinced.[38]

Some Final Thoughts

It appears that the administration has approached some aspects of welfare with hardheaded realism and other aspects with a desire to change the world. The contrast between the two approaches merits comment. Legislative changes enacted in 1981 and 1982 in AFDC and child support legislation reduced federal outlays by an estimated $875 million (10 percent) in fiscal 1982 and $1,222 million (13 percent) in 1983 and will continue to reduce outlays by about the 1983 proportion for the foreseeable future. By contrast, outlays for Supplemental Security Income actually rose in 1982 as a result of the new laws and will be reduced by less than $100 million annually (1 percent) in 1983 and later years.[39] According to the Congressional Budget Office, the workfare program would not have saved any money in 1982 and would have yielded a modest $20 million in 1983.[40] The federalism plan presents too many imponderables even to guess at its future cost. The point that emerges from these figures is that the administration has taken certain actions that match its ideological preconceptions and that have yielded immediate cost reductions. It has taken other actions that conform to its ideological preconceptions even though the actions will produce no substantial short-run savings and contradict some of its stated policy objectives in areas outside welfare.

The workfare and federalism initiatives stand out. Even though the administration has reduced costs significantly through the leverage of federal grants, it still wishes to entrust the states with the program. Carleson argues that one action necessarily precedes the other. States do not want to accept responsibility for a program that is out of control. Although the administration claims to encourage diversity in welfare programs, it still despairs of state caseworkers who refuse to take workfare seriously. The administration responds by saying that once the states gain complete control of the program, they can do as they wish. Even though the administration wants to reduce government regulation, it has increased federal regulations that apply to the AFDC program. Here the administration's response is more pragmatic: The AFDC program needs to be brought under control, whatever the consequences for deregulation.

On balance, this administration has produced a series of reforms that focus welfare payments on those unable or unwilling to work. The strategy, successful in changing the welfare programs, raises questions about the fairness of the administration's social policy across income levels. The wealthy have received tax cuts; welfare recipients who work have received tax increases. Supply-side economics applies to the rich but not to the working poor. The administration resolves this contradiction by pointing to the results. By reducing inflation, the administration has helped the poor. Besides, the Reagan administration does not seek to make incomes equal. It merely wishes to maintain incentives for all to work and to provide income maintenance for the very poor.[41]

This administration, unlike its predecessors, places no faith in the statistical validity of the poverty line and makes no claim to raise everyone above it. Its actions appear to have increased, at least in the short run, the number of the nation's poor. In nearly every state, maximum AFDC and food stamp benefits still leave the typical welfare family below the poverty line (for an urban family of three, the poverty line was $7,690 in 1982). One avenue for rising above this level has been the receipt of other welfare benefits combined with wages from private employment. The administration's actions make it more difficult for the poor to travel along this avenue; many benefits have been cut, and working carries with it the possibility of losing welfare altogether. According to an econometric simulation performed by the Urban Institute, the administration's 1981 cuts moved 137,156 families below the poverty line and increased the nation's poor families by 1.5 percent.[42]

Such results need to be accepted with more than the usual caution. The welfare system is dynamic. Since things change over time and individual parts of the system react in unpredictable ways with other parts and with the economy, the effects of the administration's actions become very difficult to trace.

One is left with impressionistic evidence on the workings of the welfare system in individual states and counties. Examining the 1982 caseload, the Pennsylvania Department of Welfare found that more than half the cases that were closed because of the Omnibus Budget and Reconciliation Act were closed because of the eligibility limit of 150 percent of the state's standard of need. Of the cases in which benefits were reduced, the new work provisions accounted for more than half. The study serves as a reminder that states may react to the Reagan changes in unforeseen ways. In the first year of the Reagan cuts, for example, twenty-seven states raised their needs standard to avoid terminating some of the working poor.[43]

Despite these difficulties, the outlines of the administration's initiatives now become clear. Exploiting a moment of congressional consensus with maximum efficiency, the administration made incremental changes in the AFDC program. These changes reduce benefits for the working poor. On this point there appears to be little dispute. The changes also may pave the way for significant benefit increases for the "deserving" poor. The evidence on this point remains ambiguous. In fiscal 1982 twenty-four jurisdictions increased their welfare benefits, but the median maximum benefit fell slightly.[44]

In taking these actions, the administration has accepted age-old judgments about the membership of the deserving poor. A poor blind person receives benefits without submitting to workfare; so does an elderly or disabled person, despite constant demands on the part of these groups that they be integrated into the labor force. A welfare mother with children over six years old faces far different treatment.

In sum, the administration has not made the welfare problem go away. As good conservatives, the members of the administration do not expect it to go away. Nor has the administration radically altered the existing set of welfare programs. It has, however, changed the terms of the debate. One hears less these days about the guaranteed annual income and the negative income tax. Ronald Reagan and his administration have chased those concepts from the political agenda. For the time being, the California approach to welfare reform has triumphed over its rivals.

Notes

1. James R. Storey, "Income Security," in John L. Palmer and Isabel V. Sawhill, eds., *The Reagan Experiment* (Washington, D.C.: Urban Institute Press, 1982), pp. 364–65.

2. This statistical overview comes from the Congressional Research Service. For a succinct summary of the sizes of the various programs, see Vee Burke, *Welfare Reform: Issue Brief 77069* (Washington, D.C.: Congressional Research Service, 1983), p. 1. See also U.S. House of Representatives, Committee on Ways and Means, *Background Material and Data on Major Programs within the Jurisdiction of the Committee on Ways and Means,* WMCP 98-2 (Washington, D.C., 1983), pp. 3–12.

3. Martin Anderson, *Welfare: The Political Economy of Welfare Reform in the United States* (Palo Alto, Calif.: Hoover Institution, 1978), p. 7.

4. Austin Scott, "Carter Endorses Tentative Plan on Welfare Reform," *Washington Post,* May 27, 1977.

5. Congressional Budget Office, *The Administration's Welfare Reform Proposal: An Analysis of the Program for Better Jobs and Income* (Washington, D.C., 1978).

6. Storey, "Income Security," p. 383.

7. Martin Anderson, "The Objectives of the Reagan Administration's Social Welfare Policy," unpublished paper, August 1983, p. 5.

8. Data reported by the Congressional Research Service in Vee Burke, *Aid to Families with Dependent Children: FY 82 Budget Cuts, Issue Brief 81051* (Washington, D.C.: Congressional Research Service, 1982), p. 5. See also U.S. Department of Health and Human Services, Social Security Administration, Office

of Policy, Office of Research and Statistics, *Quarterly Public Assistance Statistics* (Washington, D.C., 1982).

9. Public Law 97-35, Title XXIII, subtitle A, chap. 1, secs. 2301-7, Omnibus Budget Reconciliation Act of 1981, signed into law on August 12, 1981.

10. Ibid.; Burke, *Issue Brief 81051,* also contains a good discussion of the similarities in the Reagan and Carter requests; Congressional Budget Office, *Reducing the Federal Budget: Strategies and Examples, FY 1982–1986* (Washington, D.C., 1981), pp. 175–76.

11. Congressional Budget Office, *An Analysis of President Reagan's Budget Revisions for Fiscal Year 1982* (Washington, D.C., 1981), pp. A72–A75.

12. Public Law 97-35, Title XXIII; Burke, *Issue Brief 81051,* p. 10.

13. Congressional Budget Office, *Analysis of Budget Revisions,* pp. A72, 93; U.S. Department of Health and Human Services, Social Security Administration, Office of Policy, Office of Research, Statistics, and International Policy, *Quarterly Public Assistance Statistics July–September 1981* (Washington, D.C., 1983), pp. 1–3.

14. U.S. House of Representatives, Committee on Ways and Means, Subcommittee on Oversight and Subcommittee on Public Assistance and Unemployment Compensation, *Background Material on Poverty* (Washington, D.C., 1983), p. 68.

15. Committee on Ways and Means, *Background Material and Data,* pp. 3–7; Burke, *Issue Brief 77069,* p. 5.

16. Public Law 97-248; Office of Management and Budget, *Major Themes and Additional Budget Details, FY 1983* (Washington, D.C., 1982), p. 51; Vee Burke, *Aid to Families with Dependent Children: Structural Change, Issue Brief 74013* (Washington, D.C.: Congressional Research Service, 1983), p. 7.; Joel Havemann, "Sharing the Wealth: The Gap between the Rich and Poor Grows Wider," *National Journal,* October 23, 1983, p. 1972.

17. Congressional Budget Office, *Administration's Welfare Reform Proposal;* "Welfare Reform: A Brief History and Analysis," briefing paper prepared for Secretary of Health and Human Services Patricia Harris, April 29, 1980, privately held.

18. Anderson, *Welfare,* pp. 135, 148.

19. Ibid., pp. 68, 70–80; Anderson, "Objectives," p. 18; John L. Palmer and Isabel V. Sawhill, "Perspectives on the Reagan Experiment," in *The Reagan Experiment,* p. 26.

20. Quoted in Anderson, *Welfare,* p. 82.

21. Ronald A. Zumbrun, Raymond M. Momboisse, and John H. Findley, "Welfare Reform: California Meets the Challenge," *Pacific Law Review,* vol. 4 (1973), pp. 739–85; Robert B. Carleson, "The Reagan Welfare Reforms," *Journal of the Institute for Socioeconomic Studies* (Summer 1980), pp. 1–13.

22. Interview with Robert Carleson, November 22, 1983.

23. Ibid.; Anderson, "Objectives," p. 4.

24. Interview with John Svahn, November 17, 1983; Carleson interview.

25. Anderson, *Welfare,* p. 162.

26. Judith M. Guerson and Richard P. Nathan, "The MDRC Work/Welfare Project: Objectives, Status, Significance" (Paper presented at the Fifth Annual

Research Conference of the Association for Public Policy Analysis and Management, October 20–22, 1983), p. 12.

27. Carleson interview; interview with Joe Anne B. Ross, November 21, 1983.

28. Anderson, *Welfare*, p. 157.

29. Ibid., p. 46; Richard P. Nathan, "No to Block Grants for Welfare," *Commonsense*, vol. 3 (1980), pp. 4–12.

30. Carleson interview.

31. "AFDC's Proposed Transfer to States—New Federalism," manuscript prepared by the Congressional Research Service, January 25, 1983; Svahn interview; Carleson interview.

32. Anderson, "Objectives," p. 6.

33. Claude E. Barfield, *Rethinking Federalism: Block Grants and Federal, State, and Local Responsibilities* (Washington, D.C.: American Enterprise Institute, 1981), pp. 24–26, 56; Palmer and Sawhill, "Perspectives," p. 11.

34. Cited in R. Royal Shipp, *Workfare in AFDC and Food Stamps: Issue Brief 81149* (Washington, D.C.: Congressional Research Service, 1983), pp. 7–8.

35. Ibid., pp. 4, 8.

36. "Briefing Paper: The Work Incentive Program," April 25, 1975, pp. 2–4, in Spencer Johnson Papers, Box 12, WIN File, Gerald R. Ford Library (Ann Arbor, Michigan).

37. Gueron and Nathan, "MDRC Work/Welfare Project," pp. 11, 12, 23.

38. Ibid., pp. 1, 30, 45; Carmen D. Solomon, "Community Work Experience Programs (CWEP)," July 15, 1983, Congressional Research Service white paper, pp. 1–2.

39. Committee on Ways and Means, *Background Material and Data*, pp. 11, 12.

40. Burke, *Issue Brief 81051*, p. 11.

41. Svahn interview; Storey, "Income Security," p. 386.

42. Storey, "Income Security," p. 382.

43. Center for the Study of Social Policy, "The Impact of Federal Budget Cuts on AFDC Recipients: A Compendium of Studies," January 1983, p. 21; Carmen D. Solomon, *Need and Payment Levels in the Program of Aid to Families with Dependent Children (AFDC): Legislative History and Current State Practices, Report 82-203* (Washington, D.C.: Congressional Research Service, 1982), p. 22. The most sophisticated study of the cuts is Research Triangle Institute, "Final Report: Evaluation of the 1981 AFDC Amendments," April 15, 1983, mimeographed.

44. Solomon, *Need and Payment Levels*, p. 22.

3

Perception and Reality in Nutrition Programs

G. William Hoagland

The Reagan administration's domestic food assistance proposals have proved to be some of the most controversial safety net policies. The polemics surrounding these policies are founded in an accepted tenet of civilized government: that some minimum standard of nutrition should be enjoyed by all members of the society. A society may have no minimum standard for income yet strive for minimum standards of health and nutrition for all its citizens.[1]

The administration's food assistance proposals have suggested, at least to some, that this government was beginning to question that established tenet. It has been politically difficult for the administration to assure the public of its commitment to a nutritionally adequate diet for all its citizens while at the same time proposing to reduce funding for programs that were established to meet that commitment.

In three short years the administration has become acutely aware of this political sensitivity. From significant budget reduction proposals in March 1981, which would have reduced domestic food assistance expenditures by over 25 percent and resulted in the president's being portrayed as a Dickensian hard-heart, it has moved to an expression by the president of disbelief over reports of increasing hunger in America.

On establishing the President's Task Force on Food Assistance in August 1983, the president reaffirmed this country's commitment to a

The views and opinions expressed in this paper are those of the author and do not necessarily reflect those of the Senate Budget Committee, its members, or its staff. The author wishes to express his appreciation to Hal Sider, of the Department of Labor, for his assistance in obtaining special tabulations of noncash benefits from the U.S. Bureau of the Census. The author is also indebted to Sidney Brown, of the Senate Budget Committee staff, and Roger Hitchner, of the Congressional Budget Office, for their assistance in providing background data. Any errors or conclusions obtained from these data are, of course, the responsibility of the author.

43

minimum standard of nutrition: "If even one American child is forced to go to bed hungry at night, or if one senior citizen is denied the dignity of proper nutrition, that is a national tragedy. We are too generous a people to allow this to happen."[2]

This paper attempts to analyze whether the food assistance policies of the administration and Congress in the last three years have reduced this country's commitment to some safety net standard of nutrition. First, the paper reviews the historical growth in food programs. The programs' rapid growth has clearly been a major impetus for the administration's proposals to reduce their budgets. Second, it presents a chronicle of proposals by the administration and final congressional action in three program areas—food stamps; child nutrition, including the women, infants, and children (WIC) program; and direct commodity distribution to needy persons.

Growth of Federal Food Assistance Programs, 1970–1980

It is somewhat ironic that another Republican president—Richard Nixon—announced in May 1969, "That hunger and malnutrition should persist in a land such as ours is embarrassing and intolerable. The moment is at hand to put an end to hunger in America itself for all time."[3] After this announcement the federal government began to expand domestic food assistance programs rapidly through both legislative and administrative changes.

In fiscal year 1970 the federal government spent $1.5 billion for domestic food assistance (table 3–1).[4] The primary programs at that time included the federal school lunch program, a direct food distribution program to needy families, and an embryonic food stamp program. During the 1970s new programs were added and older programs significantly modified, all for the purpose of meeting unique nutritional needs of selected groups.

By 1980 there were more than thirteen federal food assistance programs, many with specifically identifiable subprograms. The programs grew in complexity. There were over thirty-seven federal reimbursement schemes required to operate them. Federal benefits varied within programs with the particular type of food service provided, the income of the participant, the characteristics of sponsoring organizations, and other factors. Some benefits were fully financed by the federal government; others required that additional charges be levied against participants or that additional state and local resources be made available. Some programs received advance funding; some were traditional grants-in-aid; most were entitlements, such as food stamps; others were performance funded, meaning that grant funds were provided to states on the basis of the number of meals or individuals served. The programs involved state agencies of welfare, social services, health, and agriculture.

As important as the programs' growing complexity were their rapidly growing costs. By 1980 federal expenditures exceeded $14.0 billion, reflecting an annual growth rate of 25.2 percent for the period 1970–1980. Corrected for food price inflation over this period, federal food expenditures grew at a 15.7 percent real annual rate. That real growth rate was over twice that of total federal expenditures during this period (6.7 percent) and five times that of the total economy as measured by real GNP (3.1 percent).

Participation in the programs similarly grew rapidly between 1970 and 1980 (table 3–2). The federal government subsidized approximately 47 million meals daily in 1970; by 1980 this figure had grown to 97 million. The programs with the largest growth in participation included the food stamp program, the free and reduced-price school lunch program, subsidies for preschool children in child care centers, and a newly created special supplemental food program for women, infants, and children (WIC).

In retrospect, the rapid increase in expenditures for domestic food assistance was probably unjustified by the actual documented malnutrition at the time. Overt clinical cases of severe malnutrition, which served as the initial catalyst for the programs' growth, appear to be quite rare in the United States.* Indeed, after the initial concern with the availability of food 1969 and 1970, the decade of food assistance evolved in two directions: (1) general income maintenance programs (such as food stamps) and (2) programs (such as WIC) designed to address specific marginal nutritive intake that could eventually result in symptoms of subclinical nutritional deficiency.

Toward the end of the decade, a new awareness of inefficiencies in some social welfare programs stimulated proposals to slow public welfare expenditures. Food stamp legislation adopted in 1979 and 1980 eliminated the semiannual adjustment of benefits, slightly reduced income and asset eligibility standards, and strengthened antifraud provisions. In 1980 major changes were adopted in child nutrition programs. The Omnibus Budget Reconciliation Act changed child

---

*The term "malnutrition" refers to a condition characterized by an intake of one or more nutrients at insufficient levels such that the individual is placed in high risk of developing specific clinical signs of deficiency or abnormal physical development. "Severe malnutrition" usually refers to a clinical syndrome arising from long-term protein-calorie malnutrition—kwashiorkor. It should be noted that despite some specific documented cases of severe malnutrition by the Senate Subcommittee on Employment, Manpower and Poverty in the Mississippi Delta in 1967, the extent of severe malnutrition nationwide was never estimated.

TABLE 3-1

FEDERAL EXPENDITURES FOR FOOD ASSISTANCE PROGRAMS, FISCAL YEARS 1970–1983, AND ESTIMATED EXPENDITURES UNDER BUDGET RESOLUTION FOR FISCAL YEARS 1984-1986

(dollars in millions)

Fiscal year	Child Nutrition Programs			Family Feeding Programs					
						Commodities			
	School lunch, other school programs	Nonschool programs	WIC/ CSFP[a]	Food stamps[b]	Needy families, institutions	Elderly	Emergency food	Total[c]
1970	583	7	8	577	304	0	0	1,479
1980	3,651	350	726	9,138	92	75	0	14,032
1981	3,732	434	912	11,081	117	94	0	16,369
1982	3,297	407	980	11,047	153	99	180	16,163
1983	3,630	436	1,188	12,653	306	100	960	19,273

1984[d]	3,580	453	1,423	11,823	306	100	960	18,730
1985[d]	3,752	490	1,390	12,106	306	100	960	19,189
1986[d]	3,940	530	1,390	12,700	306	100	0	19,051
Annual rates of change								
1970–1980	20.1	47.9	57.0	31.8	−11.3	71.4[e]	—	25.2
1981–1983	−1.4	0.2	14.1	6.9	61.7	3.1	—	8.5
1984–1986	4.9	8.2	−1.2	3.6	0.0	0.0	−100.0	0.9

NOTE: Detail may not add to totals because of rounding.

a. WIC: Women, infants, and children program; CSFP: commodity supplemental food program.

b. Includes Puerto Rico nutrition assistance.

c. Includes federal funds for food program administration not shown in table.

d. Includes estimated bonus commodities of $340 million annually and $115 million annually in section 32 commodities.

e. Growth rate FY 1976–FY 1980.

SOURCES: See note 4. Estimates of commodity assistance 1984–1986 are those of the author.

TABLE 3–2
PARTICIPATION IN MAJOR FEDERAL FOOD ASSISTANCE PROGRAMS,
FISCAL YEARS 1970, 1980, AND 1983

Program	Average Participation[a] (millions)			Average Annual Rate of Change	
	1970	1980	1983	1970–1980	1980–1983
Food stamps[b]	4.3	21.1	23.3	17.2	3.4
National school lunch					
Paid	17.8	14.7	11.2	−1.9	−8.7
Free/reduced	4.6	11.9	11.9	10.0	0
Total	22.4	26.6	23.1	1.7	−4.6
School breakfast					
Paid	0.1	0.6	0.3	19.6	−20.6
Free/reduced	0.4	3.0	3.1	22.3	1.1
Total	0.5	3.6	3.4	21.8	−1.9
Supplemental food program (WIC)	0	1.9	2.5	—	9.6
Commodity supplemental food program	0.1	0.1	0.1	0	0
Child care food program	0.1	0.7	n.a.	21.5	n.a.
Summer food service	0.2	1.6	1.1	23.1	−11.7
Special milk[c]	16.1	10.0	1.2	−4.7	−50.7
Nutrition education and training	0	6.0	3.3	—	−18.1
Food distribution, needy families[c]	4.1	0.1	0.1	−31.0	0
Elderly feeding programs[c]	0	0.7	0.7	—	0
Emergency food assistance	0	0	n.a.	—	—

n.a. = not available.
a. Average monthly participation except for school programs, which are nine-month averages, and summer food program, which is a three-month average; 1983 figures preliminary.
b. Food stamp participation for FY 1983 includes Puerto Rico nutrition assistance block grant program, which began in July 1982. Participation in Puerto Rico estimated to be 1.7 million persons monthly.
c. Author's estimates.
SOURCES: U.S. Department of Agriculture, *Annual Historical Review of FNS Programs FY 1982*, Fall 1983, and *Food Program Update for September 1983*, December 1983.

nutrition legislation by temporarily reducing income eligibility standards, reducing reimbursement rates for school meals, and, for one year, eliminating the semiannual adjustment in reimbursement rates. Permanent changes in the child nutrition programs adopted in this legislation included eliminating high reimbursement rates for some reduced-price meals, eliminating the Job Corps from participation in the child care feeding programs, slightly reducing reimbursement rates for child care program supplements, establishing a flat five-cent reimbursement rate for milk served in the special milk program, and prohibiting the distribution of commodities to school breakfast programs.

These legislative changes in food assistance programs set the stage for the incoming Reagan administration. Some of the policies of the new administration were simply an extension of the 1980 policies made permanent.

Domestic Food Assistance Policies, 1981–1983

The administration proposed legislative changes in the food assistance programs in each of its four years in office. Its food assistance policies were designed to reduce or slow budget outlays while addressing issues of targeting, equity, and administration. Essentially none of the recommendations of the final report of the President's Task Force on Food Assistance were offered in 1984. A number of the task force recommendations had been proposed before and rejected by the Congress, such as holding states totally responsible for error rates and giving states the option of continuing current categorical programs or creating nutrition block grants.

The policies included proposals to (1) reduce and standardize income eligibility standards across a wide array of food and income maintenance programs, (2) reduce or eliminate food assistance subsidies for persons determined to be above a safety net income standard, (3) eliminate actual and perceived duplicative or multiple food assistance subsidies regardless of the safety net income standard, (4) reduce federal regulatory requirements and increase state and local administrative discretion by converting some existing programs into broadly defined block grants, (5) reduce program error and fraud rates through modified administrative provisions, primarily through improved income reporting requirements, and (6) strengthen work and job search requirements for able-bodied recipients.

A number of these objectives were judged to be worthwhile, and, during the 1981–1983 period, Congress acted in four major pieces of legislation (three times for food stamps and once for child nutrition) to accommodate some of the proposals. Some of the objectives were judged to be internally inconsistent, however, such as strengthening work requirements while eliminating earning disregards in determining benefits, and others were flatly rejected because of the potential threat to the safety net concept.

Food Stamp Program

The Administration's 1981 Proposals. One of the first proposals of the new administration was not to reduce food stamp funding but to increase the statutory ceiling on food stamp spending by $1.2 billion in fiscal year 1981—from $9.7 billion to $10.9 billion. Under existing law a food stamp obligational ceiling is established, which is designed to trigger benefit reductions when the program grows beyond the amounts projected in the statute. The reduction provision has never been triggered, although it has been used as a political device to focus attention on the program's growth and, by the Reagan administration, to force congressional action on longer-term program reforms.

Had the administration's 1981 food stamp proposals been adopted, they would have reduced the program's costs by $1.8 billion in 1982 and by about $5.5 billion cumulatively from 1982 to 1984—a 14.6 percent reduction from 1981 current policy spending levels (table 3–3).

The 1981 food stamp proposals included savings of $0.4 billion proposed by the outgoing Carter administration, which effectively deleted cost-increasing provisions yet to go into effect in 1982. In addition, the Reagan administration proposed to establish as a monthly gross income standard for determining eligibility for food stamps 130 percent of the poverty-line income. Since eligibility was based on a net income standard (gross income minus a number of deductions), it was possible for some families to qualify for food stamps with gross incomes well above the poverty line (160 percent for a family of four). It was estimated that this provision would reduce participation by 350,000 households (1.1 million persons) and save $270 million in 1982.

The largest budget savings provision—$520 million—and probably the most controversial in 1981 was a proposal to eliminate duplicative nutrition benefits by reducing food stamp allotments for households that included children receiving free school lunches. It was argued that the thrifty food plan (used to establish food stamp allotments) was designed to cover all meals served a family and that free school lunches duplicated the food stamp allotment. This proposal would have reduced food stamp benefits by about $11.50 per child per month for over 35 percent of all food stamp households. On the average the total benefits of food stamp households with school-age children would have been reduced by over 14 percent.

Other major proposals of the administration in 1981 included freezing deductions permanently at their 1981 levels (they had been indexed for inflation), prorating food stamp benefits in the first month (so as not to provide a full month's benefits for households applying in the second half of the month), mandating monthly reporting of income and using retrospective instead of prospective income-accounting procedures, and replacing the program in Puerto Rico with a nutrition assistance block grant program, with reduced funding of about 25 percent.

Congressional Action in 1981. Congress responded favorably to most of the administration's food stamp proposals in 1981 and adopted major legislative changes in the Omnibus Reconciliation Act of 1981 and the Agriculture and Food Act of 1981. Whereas the administration had proposed savings of $5.5 billion for 1982 through 1984, Congress achieved estimated savings of $6.0 billion over the same period—a 16 percent reduction from current policy spending levels (table 3–3). Congress, however, achieved these savings very differently.

Congress adopted both the Reagan and the Carter administrations' proposals to repeal certain cost-increasing provisions yet to go into effect. A 130 percent gross income standard was established for income eligibility, except for households containing an elderly or disabled member. A daily prorating of first-month benefits (to the day of application), monthly reporting and retrospective income accounting, and the Puerto Rico nutrition assistance grant program were all adopted.

After flatly rejecting the proposal to reduce food stamp benefits in households with children receiving federally subsidized free school lunches, Congress achieved comparable budget savings by reducing an earnings disregard provision from 20 percent to 18 percent, delaying the annual benefit increases from January to October of each year, and delaying increases in deductions until July 1983.

The Administration's 1982 Proposals. In 1982 the administration again recommended major legislative changes in the program. Most of its proposals, however, were more controversial, and a number of them would have reduced benefits for persons with incomes below the safety net standard.

Included in the 1982 proposals were provisions to increase the rate by which benefits were reduced as net income increased (mar-

TABLE 3–3

FOOD STAMP SPENDING POLICIES: CURRENT POLICY, ADMINISTRATION PROPOSALS, AND CONGRESSIONAL ACTION, FISCAL YEARS 1982–1985

(millions of dollars)

Budget Policies	1982	1983	1984	1985	Total	Change from Current Policy (percent)
1982						
Current policy (1981)	12,298	12,598	12,945	a	37,841	—
Administration proposal	−1,799	−1,638	−2,078	a	−5,515	−14.6
Congressional action	−1,658	−2,046	−2,334	a	−6,038	−16.0
1983						
Current policy (1982)	NA	12,435	13,077	13,968	39,480	—
Administration proposal	NA	−1,778	−2,562	−2,850	−7,190	−18.2
Congressional action	NA	−548	−635	−756	−1,939	−4.9

Current policy (1983)	NA	NA	11,425	11,720	23,145	—
Administration proposal	NA	NA	−1,024	−1,181	−2,205	−9.5
Congressional action	NA	NA	0	0	0	0
Summary						
Current policy (1981)	12,549	13,882	14,281	14,606	55,318	—
Legislative action	−1,535	−1,343	−2,031	−2,061	−6,970	−12.6

NA = not applicable.
a. Not estimated.

SOURCES: 1982 policies, Congressional Budget Office, estimates June 9, 1981; final summary reconciliation savings, July 29, 1981. 1983 policies, Congressional Budget Office, estimates May 6, 1982; conference agreement reconciliation savings, August 17, 1982. 1984 policies, Congressional Budget Office, *An Analysis of the President's Budgetary Proposals for FY 1984*, February 1983, and unpublished memorandum. Summary, Congressional Budget Office analysis for Senator Robert C. Byrd, April 15, 1983; the 1981 current policy reflects technical and economic reestimates from the original current policy estimates made in 1981.

ginal tax rate) from 30 to 35 percent; to eliminate a $10 minimum monthly benefit for all eligible participants; to include all federal, state, and local energy assistance in the definition of income for determination of eligibility and benefits; to round all calculations down; to eliminate the 18 percent earnings disregard; and to penalize states for error rates exceeding 3 percent in 1983, 2 percent in 1984, and 1 percent in 1985, with no federal responsibility for erroneous payments after 1985. (The current error rate is approximately 9–10 percent.)

The 1982 proposals would have reduced net federal costs by $1.8 billion in 1983, allowing for increased food stamp costs because of proposed reductions in Aid to Families with Dependent Children (AFDC) and Supplemental Security Income (SSI). Over the period 1983 to 1985, $7.2 billion would have been saved, an 18.2 percent decrease from current policy levels (table 3–3).

Congressional Action in 1982. After the significant savings achieved in 1981, Congress reacted somewhat negatively to the administration's 1982 proposals. The proposals would have reduced household food stamp benefits on the average $23 a month, or nearly 20 percent. Households with earnings would have lost nearly $50 a month, a 42 percent reduction. Over 920,000 households, 1.8 million persons, would have been terminated from the program, twice the number estimated in the administration's 1981 proposals.

Modest budget savings were achieved by the Congress in the Omnibus Budget Reconciliation Act of 1982. Instead of the administration's proposed $7.2 billion savings for 1983 through 1985, Congress adopted changes totaling $1.9 billion, a reduction of 4.9 percent (table 3–3).

Once again most of the savings were achieved through delaying increases in deductions from July to October of each year; modifying the definition of a filing unit to include all parents and children or siblings living together; giving states the option of requiring applicants as well as recipients to search for jobs; establishing target state error rates of 9 percent in 1983, 7 percent in 1984, and 5 percent in 1985 and thereafter, with state penalties based on a reduction in their share of federally funded administrative expenses; and for 1984 and 1985 reducing food stamp allotments by 1 percent to achieve additional savings.

The Administration's 1983 Proposals. In 1983 the administration once again recommended budgetary savings that would have totaled about $1.0 billion in 1984 and $1.2 billion in 1985. These savings would have been achieved by simplifying and standardizing certain program calculations. Among the changes were replacing the 18 percent earned income deduction with a flat $75 a month deduction for full-time workers and a lesser amount for households with part-time workers (comparable to the AFDC earnings disregard), eliminating an income deduction for shelter expenses while increasing the standard income deduction from $85 to $140 a month, and delaying for six months the annual cost-of-living increase from October to April. States also would have been required to establish a workfare program for all able-bodied recipients.

Congressional Action in 1983. Congress adopted none of the administration's 1983 food stamp proposals. Although an approximately equal percentage of households receiving food stamps would have had increased benefits as would have lost benefits (excluding the six-month delay in benefit increases) and the proposals would have eliminated a provision that has historically complicated administration (the excess shelter deduction), the desire for food stamp reform was waning.

The Administration's 1984 Proposals. Despite the recommendations of the President's Task Force on Food Assistance (released in January 1984) that would have increased food stamp spending by $160 million in 1985, the administration's 1984 proposals, if adopted by the Congress, would reduce funding by $375 million in 1985. The administration's proposals, however, were designed not to reduce program benefits to needy individuals but rather to hold states liable for food stamp overpayments exceeding 3 percent (a 1982 proposal) and to require states to establish workfare programs (a 1983 proposal).

Congress had not acted on these proposals at the time of this publication. But because of the task force's recommendation for increased funding, the shortened legislative schedule in 1984, and election year politics, it seems unlikely Congress will react favorably to the proposals.

Net Effects of Food Stamp Program Reform

Legislative changes reduced food stamp costs by approximately $7.0 billion over the period 1982–1985—a 12.6 percent reduction from what would have been spent if the policies of January 1, 1981, had remained in place over that period. In part because of benefit reductions in the AFDC program and increasing unemployment, food stamp participation grew throughout the period, reaching a historical peak of over 24 million persons in March 1983 (figure 3–1). Federal expenditures similarly reached a peak of $12.7 billion in fiscal year 1983.

56

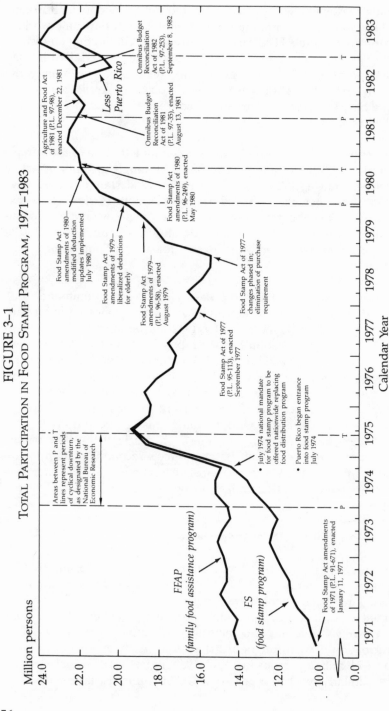

FIGURE 3-1

TOTAL PARTICIPATION IN FOOD STAMP PROGRAM, 1971–1983

SOURCE: Data provided by U.S. Department of Agriculture; graph by author.

Nevertheless, the changes adopted were successful in slowing the rate of growth in program costs (6.9 percent annually 1981–1983, down from 31.8 percent 1970–1980) and focusing program benefits on the lowest income groups. Using annual data from the Current Population Survey, table 3–4 shows that the number of people receiving food stamps at any time during the year increased by 2.1 percent from 1981 to 1982; the increase for those with incomes below the poverty threshold was 11.3 percent, however, while the population below that threshold increased by 8.1 percent. By far the greatest increases in participation took place in the lowest income categories, and the greatest decreases took place for persons whose annual incomes exceeded 130 percent of the poverty threshold.

Similarly, the distribution of food stamp benefits shifted toward the lowest income groups. In 1980, 27.6 percent of all food stamp benefits went to persons with annual incomes below 50 percent of the poverty line; by 1982 this had increased to 36.6 percent (adjusted for food price inflation). In 1979, 20.9 percent of all food stamp benefits went to persons with annual incomes above 130 percent of the poverty line; by 1982 this had decreased to 10.4 percent (table 3–5).

It is difficult to determine from this brief review what participation and benefit distribution would have looked like if all the administration's food stamp proposals had been adopted. It seems fair to conclude, however, that costs would have been significantly less and real food stamp benefits would have declined for those with incomes below the safety net standard.

Child Nutrition Programs and WIC

The Administration's 1981 Proposals. The administration's 1981 child nutrition proposals were the most far-reaching budget reduction proposals of any advanced that year. They would have reduced outlays by more than $2.0 billion in 1982 and by $7.3 billion over the period 1982 to 1984, a 43.4 percent reduction from policies in effect at that time (table 3–6). The major changes proposed in 1981 included the following:

• making permanent temporary changes of the Omnibus Budget Reconciliation Act of 1980, which would replace individual hardship deductions with a standard deduction, modify the Department of Agriculture's basis for updating poverty guidelines to make it consistent with that of other government agencies, make annual instead of semiannual adjustments in benefits, reduce by 2 cents commodity support for all meals, and reduce by 2.5 cents cash support for meal subsidies in non-needy schools

TABLE 3–4
Persons Receiving Food Stamps, by Poverty Ratio, 1979–1982

Calendar Year	Total	Less than 0.25	0.26–0.50	0.51–0.75	0.76–1.00	1.01–1.30	1.31–1.85	1.85+
				Recipients (thousands)				
1979	20,298	1,067	2,620	4,232	4,122	2,696	2,742	2,818
1980	22,338	1,403	3,414	5,056	4,233	3,063	2,803	2,367
1981	23,332	1,622	3,847	5,303	4,500	2,988	2,781	2,291
1982	23,823	2,099	4,549	6,001	4,343	2,949	2,087	1,795
				Percentage distribution				
1979	100.0	5.3	12.9	20.8	20.3	13.3	13.5	13.9
1980	100.0	6.3	15.3	22.6	18.9	13.7	12.5	10.6
1981	100.0	7.0	16.5	22.7	19.3	12.8	11.9	9.8
1982	100.0	8.8	19.1	25.2	18.2	12.4	8.8	7.5

					Annual rates of change			
Food stamp recipients								
1979–1982	5.5	25.3	20.2	12.3	1.8	3.0	−8.7	−14.0
1981–1982	2.1	29.4	18.2	13.2	−3.5	−1.3	−25.0	−21.7
Population with poverty ratio less than 1.85								
1979–1982	9.7	13.5	15.3	10.4	4.6	5.1	3.7	n.a.
1981–1982	8.1	14.4	33.6	10.6	−0.5	2.4	−1.6	n.a.

n.a. = not available.

NOTE: Poverty ratio is the ratio of income to the poverty-threshold income. Data exclude Puerto Rico. Detail may not add to totals because of rounding.

SOURCES: U.S. Bureau of the Census, unpublished tabulations. See *Current Population Reports*, Series P-60, No. 141, *Characteristics of Households Receiving Selected Noncash Benefits: 1982* (advance data from the March 1983 Current Population Survey), Washington, D.C., 1983.

TABLE 3-5
FOOD STAMP BENEFITS, BY POVERTY RATIO, 1979–1982

Calendar Year	Total	Less than 0.25	0.26–0.50	0.51–0.75	0.76–1.00	1.01–1.30	1.31–1.85	1.85+
				Benefits (millions of dollars)				
1979	2,449.5	151.0	425.9	588.0	498.5	271.9	241.0	273.0
1980	2,702.2	219.2	527.8	710.8	475.6	291.8	269.2	207.9
1981	2,727.7	243.9	592.5	689.5	448.5	253.3	316.2	183.8
1982	2,810.1	316.7	711.8	804.5	439.1	247.7	148.0	142.4
				Percentage distribution				
1979	100.0	6.2	17.4	24.0	20.4	11.1	9.8	11.1
1980	100.0	8.1	19.5	26.3	17.6	10.8	10.0	7.7
1981	100.0	8.9	21.7	25.3	16.4	9.3	11.6	6.7
1982	100.0	11.3	25.3	28.6	15.6	8.8	5.3	5.1
				Real annual rates of change				
1979–1982	4.7	28.0	18.7	11.0	–4.1	–3.1	–15.0	–19.5
1981–1982	3.0	29.9	20.1	16.7	–2.1	–2.2	–53.2	–22.5

NOTE: Poverty ratio is the ratio of income to the poverty-threshold income. Data exclude Puerto Rico. Detail may not add to totals because of rounding.

SOURCES: U.S. Bureau of the Census, unpublished tabulations. See *Current Population Reports*, Series P-60, No. 141, *Characteristics of Households Receiving Selected Noncash Benefits: 1982* (advance data from the March 1983 Current Population Survey), Washington, D.C., 1983.

- eliminating subsidies for meals served to students from families with incomes above 185 percent of the poverty threshold
- reducing subsidies for meals served to students with incomes between 136 percent and 185 percent of the poverty threshold
- eliminating subsidies for snacks served in the child care food program
- eliminating a $15 million nutrition education and training program
- eliminating the summer food program
- eliminating an equipment assistance program
- establishing procedures for verifying income
- limiting the special milk program to schools without any other federal food program
- reducing WIC appropriations by 20 percent to focus the program on applicants with high nutritional needs

Congressional Action in 1981. Congress acted once in the 1981–1983 period on the proposed savings in the child nutrition programs. The Omnibus Budget Reconciliation Act of 1981 adopted a number of the administration's 1981 proposals but with some significant modifications.

Congress made permanent the temporary provisions of the Omnibus Budget Reconciliation Act of 1980, as requested by both the Carter and the Reagan administrations. These changes accounted for nearly one-fourth of the final savings adopted that year.

Income eligibility standards were simplified by eliminating hardship and standard deductions and establishing a consistent safety net income standard at 130 percent of the poverty-threshold income for maximum federal subsidies—$1.2025 per school lunch. Children from families with incomes between 130 and 185 percent of the poverty threshold (reduced-price category) qualified for a lesser subsidy, $0.8025, and children from families with incomes above 185 percent of the poverty threshold continued to receive a further reduced subsidy, $0.215. Under previous policies maximum federal subsidies could have been paid for children from families with incomes up to 136 percent of the poverty threshold and reduced-price subsidies up to 205 percent of the poverty threshold. Subsidies were continued to non-needy students, on the argument that schools would not participate in the federal school lunch program, and would thus hurt needy students, if they did not continue to receive these subsidies.

The summer food program was continued with slightly more restrictive eligibility standards. Anticipated savings of $90 million in 1982 from these changes were not achieved, and the program con-

TABLE 3-6

CHILD NUTRITION SPENDING POLICIES: CURRENT POLICY, ADMINISTRATION PROPOSALS,
AND CONGRESSIONAL ACTION, FISCAL YEARS 1982–1985

(millions of dollars)

Budget Policies	1982	1983	1984	1985	Total	Change from Current Policy (percent)
1982						
Current policy (1981)	5,105	5,650	6,129	a	16,884	—
Administration proposal	−2,120	−2,436	−2,753	a	−7,309	−43.3
Congressional action	−1,480	−1,625	−1,751	a	−4,856	−28.8
1983						
Current policy (1982)	NA	4,274	4,669	5,072	14,015	—
Administration proposal	NA	−693	−1,018	−1,249	−2,960	−21.1
Congressional action	NA	+70	+30	0	+100	+0.7

1984						
Current policy (1983)	NA	NA	4,554	4,733	9,287	—
Administration proposal	NA	NA	−213	−388	−601	−6.5
Congressional action	NA	NA	+300	+300	+600	+6.5
Summary						
1982 current policies (1981)	5,328	5,743	6,030	6,342	23,443	—
Legislative action	−1,349	−1,292	−1,147	−1,197	−4,985	−21.3

NA = not applicable.
a. Not estimated.

SOURCES: 1982 policies, Congressional Budget Office, estimates, June 9, 1981; final summary reconciliation savings, July 29, 1981. 1983 policies, Congressional Budget Office, estimates, May 6, 1982; conference agreement reconciliation savings, August 17, 1982. 1984 policies, Congressional Budget Office, *An Analysis of President's Budgetary Proposals for FY 1984*, February 1983, and unpublished memorandum. Summary, Congressional Budget Office analysis for Senator Robert C. Byrd, April 15, 1983, including reestimates by author for subsequent congressional action; the 1981 current policy reflects technical and economic reestimates from the original current policy estimates made in 1981.

tinues to cost approximately the same today as before the 1981 legislation. The administration's proposal to limit the special milk program was adopted, funding for the nutrition education program was reduced to $5 million from the $15 million originally authorized, and the administration's 20 percent reduction in WIC spending was rejected.

Congress adopted two-thirds of the administration's 1981 proposals. Savings were estimated at about $4.9 billion over the period 1982–1985, or a 28.8 percent reduction from what would have been spent under policies in effect in 1981. The bulk of the savings was achieved from income groups above the safety net level.

The Administration's 1982 and 1983 Proposals. The administration's 1982 and 1983 proposals were quite similar. Major savings were to be achieved by consolidating the school breakfast and child care food programs and making grants to states to develop their own food assistance programs for needy children.

Proposals were again advanced to eliminate the summer food service program and the nutrition education program. In 1982 the administration proposed to consolidate the WIC program with the Maternal and Child Health Program administered by the Department of Health and Human Services.

The administration's 1982 proposals would have reduced child nutrition spending by 21.1 percent from 1983 to 1985; the 1983 proposals would have reduced spending by 5.0 percent from 1984 to 1985.

Congressional Action in 1982 and 1983. Congress chose not to act on the administration's proposals in 1982 and 1983 and, in fact, moved to increase funding by $100 million for the WIC program in the Emergency Jobs Supplemental Act of 1983. Similarly, fiscal year 1984 WIC spending will be increased by $300 million by the 1984 Agriculture Appropriations Act, made part of that year's continuing resolution.

The Administration's 1984 Proposals. The administration's 1984 child nutrition proposals recommended consolidating the summer food program and child care food program into a "nonschool" food program grant to the states. Funding for the grant would be equivalent to the projected benefits under the two categorical programs. Therefore, along with a previous proposal to strengthen income verification procedures for child nutrition benefits and to eliminate a nutrition education program, less than $25 million in savings would result from enacting these proposals in 1985.

Congress will probably act on some child nutrition proposals in

1984 because of the need to reauthorize some expiring programs this year. It is unlikely, however, that the administration's proposal for consolidating the two child nutrition programs will be accepted.

Net Effect of Child Nutrition Reforms

The child nutrition policies of the last three years have reduced spending by about 21.3 percent from what would have been spent with a continuation of 1981 policies. The savings were achieved almost entirely by reducing subsidies to families with incomes above the safety net standard.

Participation in the WIC program today is the highest in its history—2.8 million women, infants, and children. The WIC program, which was one of the fastest growing food assistance programs in the 1970s (a 57.0 percent annual rate of growth), continued to outpace the growth of all other food assistance programs in the three-year period 1981–1983 (a 14.1 percent annual rate of growth—see table 3–1). Recent analyses from the Center for Disease Control also show a continual improvement in anthropometric, hemoglobin, and hematocrit values for infants and children over the period 1981–1983.[5]

Approximately 1,700 schools did drop the federal school lunch program in 1982; but about 90 percent of all schoolchildren continued to have access to a federal school lunch program—down from 92 percent in 1981. In the 1981 school year approximately 25.8 million students participated in the federal school lunch program. This number declined to 22.9 million in 1982 but increased to 23.1 million during the 1983 school year. Almost all of the drop in participation took place in the non-needy category of students.

More important, table 3–7 provides data on the number of children five to eighteen years old reported in the Current Population Survey (CPS) as receiving free or reduced-price school lunches between 1979 and 1982. These data, unlike federal administrative data, include children who received free or reduced-price school lunches regardless of the schools' participation in the federal school lunch program.

The CPS data show an increase in the number of children below the safety net income standard (130 percent of the poverty threshold) receiving free or reduced-price lunches over the period 1979–1982. While the number of children in poverty increased 8.7 percent from 1981 to 1982, the number of children below the poverty line receiving free or reduced-priced lunches increased 12.6 percent. In contrast to this increase, federal school lunch statistics show free meal subsidies (for children below the safety net standard) declining by 7.5 percent.

65

TABLE 3-7
CHILDREN RECEIVING FREE OR REDUCED-PRICE LUNCHES, BY POVERTY RATIO, 1979–1982

Calendar Year	Total	Less than 0.25	0.26–0.50	0.51–0.75	0.76–1.00	1.01–1.30	1.31–1.85	1.85+
				Children 5 to 18 (thousands)				
1979	12,523	579	1,178	1,937	1,755	1,693	2,437	2,944
1980	12,378	690	1,462	1,936	1,751	1,723	2,257	2,562
1981	11,744	834	1,507	2,015	1,723	1,605	2,196	1,863
1982	11,994	971	1,871	2,262	1,740	1,626	1,975	1,550
				Percentage distribution				
1979	100.0	4.6	9.4	15.5	14.0	13.5	19.5	23.5
1980	100.0	5.6	11.8	15.6	14.1	13.9	18.2	20.7
1981	100.0	7.1	12.8	17.2	14.7	13.7	18.7	15.9
1982	100.0	8.1	15.6	18.9	14.5	13.6	16.5	12.9

Annual rates of change

Children 5 to 18 receiving free or reduced-price lunches								
1979–1982	−1.4	18.8	16.7	5.3	−0.3	−1.3	−6.8	−19.3
1981–1982	+2.1	16.4	24.2	12.3	1.0	1.3	−10.1	−16.8
All children 5 to 18 in poverty								
1979–1982	10.1	11.8	16.4	−2.0	3.9	n.a.	n.a.	n.a.
1981–1982	8.7	14.3	14.8	13.0	−2.3	n.a.	n.a.	n.a.

n.a. = not available.

NOTE: Poverty ratio is ratio of income to the poverty-threshold income. Detail may not add to totals because of rounding.

SOURCES: U.S. Bureau of the Census, unpublished tabulations. See Current Population Reports, Series P-60, no. 141, *Characteristics of Households Receiving Selected Noncash Benefits: 1982* (advance data from the March 1983 Current Population Survey), Washington, D.C., 1983.

Although there are some inconsistencies in the various data sources, the CPS statistics tend to support the hypothesis that school-age children below the safety net standard continued to receive school lunches despite the budget reductions of 1981. Schools that dropped the federal program probably found alternative means to provide meals to needy children.[6]

Direct Food Distribution Programs

Finally, it is obvious that there has been a significant resurgence in providing surplus agricultural commodities directly to needy persons. The administration's attitude toward reestablishing direct distribution programs for individuals was initially cool. Such programs had always existed for schools and institutions and for individuals where the food stamp program was not in operation.

In the Agriculture and Food Act of 1981, however, the administration supported a provision authorizing a new category of eligible outlets—food banks serving needy persons. Shortly thereafter, on December 22, 1981, President Reagan ordered the Department of Agriculture to donate 30 million pounds of surplus Commodity Credit Corporation cheese to states. Over the next two years, surplus butter, nonfat dry milk, flour, rice, and honey were added to the list of commodities to be made available to needy persons.

Congress has promoted this food assistance policy through special provisions of the Agriculture and Food Act of 1981 and the Emergency Jobs Supplemental Act of 1983 and most recently by extending the emergency feeding program through 1985. In the 1983 fiscal year nearly $1.3 billion in surplus commodities (approximately 780 million pounds) was made available to needy families, charitable institutions, and the newly created emergency food assistance program. This $1.3 billion contrasts sharply with less than $200 million in commodities provided less than two years earlier.

The Department of Agriculture has found itself caught between mounting surplus price-supported commodities and advocate groups calling for an immediate release of government-held stocks. The administration and the Congress have approached the return to a direct food distribution program cautiously, with the intent that such a program be temporary. It is generally recognized that the difficulty of administering such a program in the 1960s and the relative lack of nutritional benefits from it led to its replacement by the food stamp program.

The administration has become more involved in the business of distributing surplus food commodities not because of a clear food assistance policy but because of the inability to correct seriously flawed agricultural production policies. In the long term, efforts of this and previous administrations to correct farm policies could prove more useful to the low-income population than the direct distribution of some limited price-supported commodities.

There is, however, a major public policy lesson to be learned from the direct food distribution program of the last two years, and that is simply that the low-income population is not homogeneous. As Richard Nathan and others have observed: "The focus is now on an underclass. To a far greater degree than in the past, the groups with deep social needs constitute a residuum not aided by the social programs of the post–World War II variety."[7] A large proportion of those receiving assistance in the emergency feeding programs no doubt generally feel excluded from society and, as one student of the underclass has observed, "suffer from *behavioral* as well as *income* deficiencies." The American Psychiatric Association recently estimated that about half of the homeless are persons who have been released from state mental institutions.[8] The good intentions of the past to provide a community setting for these patients may have become a major tragedy today.

The emergency food programs have helped to identify a major weakness in our nation's past food assistance programs. A large portion of the participants in emergency food programs today constitute a subset of the poverty population that was increasing throughout the 1970s but never received food assistance from the more traditional, bureaucratic programs. Their identified presence now should not lead to an inference of an increase in hunger or a failing of this administration's nutrition safety net policies but rather should be seen as an indication of broader failures in all our social programs of the past twenty-eight years to deal with this defined underclass.

Summary and Overview

Has there been a reduced commitment to a safety net standard of nutrition? This admittedly brief analysis suggests that current federal policies continue to support substantial nutrition assistance to those with incomes below 130 percent of the poverty threshold.

Federal expenditures and resources made available for domestic food assistance grew from $16.4 billion in 1981 to $19.3 billion in fiscal year 1983, an average annual rate of growth of 8.5 percent. Although this clearly constitutes a slowing of the rapid rate of growth experienced during the 1970s—25.2 percent annually—that could hardly be sustained on arguments of program, nutrition, or economic efficiency.

The legislative changes adopted by the Congress in 1981 and 1982 reduced food assistance expenditures by approximately 14 percent from what would have been spent without those changes. The changes were also successful in better focusing federal nutrition assistance on those with annual incomes below the safety net standard. But a large portion of the saving was achieved by adopting policies that slowed the rate of growth through delays or modifications of annual benefit adjustments. Given that inflation in food prices fell rapidly in 1982 and 1983 (from 4.5 percent in 1982 to 2.4 percent in 1983), these legislated delays produced less savings (and therefore less harm to recipients) than would have occurred under more rapid inflation in food prices.

Although the available data do not permit a careful analysis, it seems fair to conclude that if the administration's food stamp proposals of 1981–1983 (particularly 1982) had been adopted, a significant reduction of food assistance benefits for those with incomes below the safety net standard could have occurred. The administration's child nutrition proposals, however, could probably have been adopted with no serious violation of the safety net standard. Those proposals were designed primarily to reduce federal subsidies to children from families with incomes above 130 percent of the poverty standard or would have permitted states to design nutrition assistance programs for needy children only.

The perception of an issue sometimes becomes a reality. The recent perception of growing hunger in America because of food assistance budget cuts is probably unfair. The growth of state, local, church, and private charity food assistance programs has in fact been stimulated by federal food assistance policies designed to make surplus agricultural commodities available to those organizations. Unlike the conventional wisdom, I conclude that food assistance policies, both current policies and those preceding the Reagan administration, probably never addressed the food needs of a large sector of the low-income population who are now being served by the direct commodity distribution programs. If this conclusion is validated through further research, then, if anything, there has been an increased commitment to a safety net standard of nutrition, not a lessened commitment.

Notes

1. Shlomo Reutlinger and Marcelo Selowsky, *Malnutrition and Poverty: Magnitude and Policy Options*, World Bank Staff Occasional Papers, No. 23 (1976).

2. Memorandum for Edwin Meese III from the president on Task Force on Food Assistance, August 2, 1983.

3. *Public Papers of the Presidents of the United States: Richard Nixon*, "Special Message to Congress Recommending a Program to End Hunger in America, May 6, 1969," (Washington, D.C., 1971).

4. Expenditure and program participation data used in this paper were obtained from U.S. Department of Agriculture, Food and Nutrition Service, *Fiscal Year 1975 Statistics and Historical Tables, Annual Historical Review of FNS Programs,* and *Food Program Update for July 1983.*

5. U.S. Department of Health and Human Services, Public Health Service, Center for Disease Control, *Nutrition Surveillance, Annual Summary 1980,* and preliminary tabulations October 1983 for period 1976-1983.

6. This hypothesis is supported in part by media reports. See *Washington Post*, September 14, 1983; *New York Times*, September 14, 1981; *Omaha World-Herald*, October 24, 1983; and *Daily News*, September 16, 1981.

7. Richard Nathan, "The Underclass Challenge to Social Scientists," *Wall Street Journal*, June 14, 1983.

8. Robert E. Jones, "Street People and Psychiatry," *Hospital and Community Psychiatry*, vol. 34, no. 9 (September 1983).

4

The Unfinished Agenda in Health Policy

Jack A. Meyer

The purpose of this paper is to assess the health care policy changes proposed and enacted by the federal government in the early 1980s. The paper begins with a statement of the problems in health care cost management facing the federal government and the nation at the beginning of the decade. A set of guiding principles for reform is offered as a blueprint of the author's notion of a sensible set of policies to address those problems. Changes made by the government during the 1981–1983 period are evaluated in light of the extent to which they have moved public policy from its stance in 1980 toward this blueprint.

This paper is primarily an assessment of policy changes that were actually put in place, not simply a scorecard on the Reagan administration's "game plan" for health policy. Where possible, however, differences between what the administration proposed and what Congress enacted are highlighted, and several recent administration proposals are explained and evaluated even though their acceptance by Congress is uncertain.

The main focus of the paper is on Medicare, Medicaid, and the tax expenditure associated with the exclusion from employees' income of the full value of employers' contributions to health insurance. These three areas account for roughly $110 billion of budget exposure for the federal government in fiscal year 1984. Other federal activities in health care, such as the $4 billion flowing to the National Institutes of Health or Defense Department health-related programs, are not discussed here.

The emphasis in this paper is on the health policy of the federal government, including budget outlays covering health insurance for elderly and low-income citizens as well as federal regulations covering providers of care. In addition, the relation of these policies to state government activities (a direct link through the jointly funded Medicaid program) and private sector trends is noted.

Background and Statement of the Problem

The federal government must not renege on its commitment to assist elderly and low-income individuals in protecting themselves against outlays for health care that are beyond their means. But meeting this obligation does not mean that current federal health-related tax, reimbursement, and regulatory policies must be left untouched. Indeed, these features of federal health policy have been feeding spiraling health cost increases; fundamental structural reforms in federal policy are a precondition for a truly economical deceleration in cost increases, rather than one that simply cuts costs by cutting benefits.

The total cost of Medicare and Medicaid has been roughly doubling every four years and now accounts for about one of ten dollars in federal outlays (see tables 4–1 and 4–2). In an effort to contain this cost escalation, the federal government has reached for unwieldy, ineffective controls and, more recently, has tried to shift the cost to lower levels of government, patients, providers, and employers. With a few recent exceptions, meaningful reforms in government health policy have been sidestepped; as a result, costs have been not so much controlled or reduced as hidden and shifted.

This was the situation facing the new administration in 1981: Medicare and Medicaid had both inefficient and inequitable features that were widely recognized. Under Medicare hospital costs were shared at the "back end," when people had already incurred huge medical bills, but hardly shared at all for routine services at the "front end." Federal aid to the poor was inequitable, systematically excluding

TABLE 4–1

GROWTH IN OUTLAYS FOR FEDERAL HEALTH PROGRAMS, FISCAL YEARS 1970–1985
(billions of dollars)

	1970	1975	1980	1983	1985[a]
Medicare	7.1	14.8	35.0	56.8	74.9
Medicaid	2.7	6.8	14.0	19.0	24.2

a. Estimated.
SOURCES: Congressional Budget Office, estimates for FY 1985 based on January 1983 base-line projections; Office of Management and Budget, *Payments to Individuals*.

TABLE 4-2

FEDERAL SPENDING FOR HEALTH CARE AND ALL SOCIAL PROGRAMS AS
A SHARE OF TOTAL FEDERAL SPENDING, FISCAL YEARS 1970-1985
(percent)

	1970	1975	1980	1983	1985[a]
Medicare and Medicaid	5.0	6.6	8.5	9.4	10.7
All social programs	38.0	52.9	54.1	54.0	50.9

a. Estimated.
SOURCES: Congressional Budget Office, estimates for FY 1985 based on January 1983
base-line projections; Office of Management and Budget, *Payments to Individuals*.

millions of people on the basis of family status. Open-ended tax subsidies encouraged first-dollar insurance coverage for a wide variety of
health services, which in turn increased the demand for services. We
had handicapped innovative health care delivery systems that promised to compete with the dominant delivery system, and we had
entangled the health care system in a labyrinth of largely ineffective
government regulations. Federal reimbursement policies under Medicare and Medicaid were characterized both by generous retrospective,
cost-based payments to doctors and hospitals that rewarded ineffi-
ciency and by a penurious stance toward care in noninstitutional settings. These policies were also prevalent in private insurance plans.

Indeed, there were several bills pending in Congress in 1981 that
were designed to correct the major flaws in the health care finance
system.

Proposed Solution

The following principles are offered here as a blueprint or guideline
for correcting these problems, and I will assess recent policy changes
in light of their consistency with these criteria for reform: (1) a system
of sharing costs that encourages people to economize on the use of
routine health services while offering greater protection for serious
illnesses; (2) federal aid to low-income people that increases with
increasing need and vice versa; (3) within a given category of need,
fixed-dollar instead of open-ended federal subsidies to aid those unable to purchase adequate health insurance; (4) fair competition
among alternative health care plans for the consumer's dollar, rein-
forced by antitrust activity where necessary; (5) less reliance on gov-

ernment regulation; and (6) a change in the bias toward care in institutions. Incorporating these changes into government policy requires a major overhaul of federal programs.

With reforms in the current system of retrospective cost reimbursement, a ceiling on open-ended tax subsidies, and less reliance on planning and regulation, health cost increases might abate over time without jeopardizing the quality of care or access to it. The essential ingredients for reform are *greater choice of health plans* and *a more equitable system of subsidies.*

The general principles for reform traced here could be implemented through the following specific changes in government policy:

• Place a ceiling on the chief open-ended tax subsidy for health care—the tax-free status of employers' contributions to employees' health insurance; the revenues raised from this cap on tax-exempt benefits should be earmarked specifically for providing health care coverage on a poorest-first basis to those citizens living below the poverty line but currently ineligible for Medicaid.

• Build protection against expenses associated with catastrophic illness into Medicare through a stop-loss provision, combined with a greater amount of cost sharing for routine services; this would include a measure of cost sharing for relatively short-term hospital stays (not just a one-day per diem). Such cost sharing should be related to income so that low-income elderly patients would be exempt from the requirement. The hospital and physician portions of Medicare (parts A and B) should be merged into one fund, with a single premium for beneficiaries that is also related to income.

• Convert Medicare to a program of premium subsidies to be used for Medicare coverage or any qualified alternative plan.

• Accelerate deregulation in areas such as certificate-of-need and flexibility for states to alter reimbursement policies under Medicaid.

• Use existing antitrust laws to encourage fair competition among alternative health care plans and providers; encourage providers of care to offer more information to consumers about their charges for an array of standard services.

• Convert Medicaid to a system of sliding-scale premium subsidies in which the very poor would be fully subsidized.

An Assessment of Progress toward These Goals

Medicaid. Medicaid is jointly funded and administered by the federal government and the states, with a federal contribution rate to each state that is based primarily on its per capita income. In FY 1981 the

75

federal contribution ranged from 50 percent to 78 percent of total outlays and averaged 55.2 percent (see table 4–3).[1]

The Omnibus Reconciliation Act of 1981 called for reductions in the federal matching contribution rates of 3 percent in 1982, 4 percent in 1983, and 4.5 percent in 1984. These scheduled cutbacks, however, could be reduced in the following ways:

• A state receives a one-percentage-point increase in federal payments if it has a qualified hospital cost review program, or if it has an unemployment rate 50 percent higher than the national average, or if the recoveries from fraud and abuse are greater than or equal to 1 percent of the federal payments to the state.

• States were also allowed to receive relief from the 3 percent reduction by keeping federal Medicaid reimbursement in FY 1982 from growing more than 9 percent over federal FY 1981 levels. If federal reimbursement grew less than 9 percent, a state qualified for a dollar-for-dollar offset of the difference between actual federal spending and the 9 percent target growth rate.

As shown in table 4–3, the federal share of Medicaid is estimated to fall by about 1.4 percentage points between 1981 and 1984.

The administration's FY 1982 budget had proposed a flat "cap" of 5 percent on the growth of the federal Medicaid share for 1982, and the cap would thereafter have been set in line with the growth of GNP. Congress rejected this approach, and the three-year package of percentage reductions, with offsets, described above was a compromise position. Congress also reduced the number of people who automatically qualify for Medicaid by changing eligibility and benefit rules for

---

TABLE 4–3

PROJECTED FEDERAL AND STATE MEDICAID EXPENDITURES, 1981–1984
(billions of dollars)

Fiscal Year	Federal Expenditures	State Expenditures	Federal Expenditures as a Percentage of Total Expenditures
1981	17.1	13.9	55.2
1982	18.3	15.5	54.1
1983	19.9	17.0	53.9
1984	21.9	18.8	53.8

NOTE: As of the Omnibus Budget Reconciliation Act of 1981.
SOURCE: U.S. Office of Management and Budget.

Aid to Families with Dependent Children (AFDC); gave states greater freedom to determine eligibility and benefits for recipients other than the categorically eligible; and permitted states to depart from cost-based reimbursement and seek competitive bidding for services in some circumstances.[2]

The groups made vulnerable by the changes affecting those outside the automatically eligible AFDC group include near-poor households judged to be medically needy because unusually high health care outlays cause them to "spend down" into the poverty category, unemployed parents in the AFDC-U program, and people eighteen to twenty-one years of age. Nursing homes were barely affected by the 1981 legislation despite the fact that they account for about two-fifths of Medicaid outlays. Federal payment policies for nursing homes, however, had departed earlier from the retrospective, cost-based reimbursement that still characterized the acute care hospital sector under Medicaid in the early 1980s, and the tightness of the market for nursing homes may have led to fears that payment cutbacks would jeopardize access to care or quality of care.[3]

AFDC changes affecting Medicaid eligibility. A generation ago welfare recipients who took jobs lost their benefits on a dollar-for-dollar basis. In effect the "tax rate" on earned income was 100 percent. In the late 1960s Congress put into effect a new rule called "$30-plus-a-third," which lowered this effective tax rate to about two-thirds for recipients of AFDC. Under this rule the first $30 per month of earnings plus one-third of the rest of earnings were disregarded from income in determining the AFDC benefit. In addition, AFDC beneficiaries were allowed to deduct certain work expenses from earned income. This deduction further lowered the effective tax rate on earnings.

The $30-plus-a-third incentive was effectively repealed in 1981. At the urging of the administration, Congress placed a time limit on the work incentive bonus and a dollar limit on the work expense deduction. The $30-plus-a-third rule may now be applied only to the first four months of employment. After four months every penny of net earnings is subtracted from welfare benefits. The work expense deduction was limited to $160 per month per child for day-care expenses and $75 per month for other work-related expenses.

Eligibility standards were also tightened, denying AFDC assistance (and often Medicaid benefits) to many working poor families. States were authorized to institute workfare programs requiring welfare recipients to take jobs.

A similar trend is evident in the food stamp program, where in 1981 a gross income standard for eligibility was established at 130 percent of the poverty-line income and the earnings disregard was lowered from 20 percent to 18 percent. This disregard would have been eliminated entirely in 1983 under President Reagan's proposed budget. Congress balked at this recommendation, however, and also did not enact the administration's proposed increase in the benefit reduction rate (marginal tax rate) from 30 to 35 percent.

The Reagan administration's alternative to lower effective tax rates on earnings is to require AFDC applicants to seek work during and after the application stages; an able-bodied recipient who failed to find a job would be required to participate in a Community Work Experience Program. States would be allowed to develop job programs reflecting both their own needs and the needs of program participants.

The changes adopted by Congress seem to be unfair to the working poor and to worsen adverse work incentives facing our lowest-income households. These changes target benefits to the *dependent* poor, while others who have the ability to work and are deemed *independent* get no help, even if their means are about the same.

The administration contends that those dropped from the welfare rolls are the relatively less needy among low-income households, and this contention is valid. The cutting was generally from the top down. Within this slightly better off poor or near-poor group, however, those with earnings are treated more harshly than those not working at all. The administration suggests that it would be a waste of society's scarce public dollars to give "permanent" help to the working low-income households. Yet it has made little effort to withdraw the wide array of special tax breaks and other equally permanent subsidies flowing to middle- and upper-income households. The unique treatment of the working poor is a source of unfairness in the administration's policy.

It must be admitted that there is little evidence of any strong positive effect on labor supply from a lowering of the effective tax rate over this range. In fact, some studies suggest that such a lower tax rate, by raising the break-even level of income where households no longer qualify for welfare benefits, leads to an offsetting decline in the labor supply of newly qualified households with somewhat higher incomes.[4] Thus, even though there is research evidence suggesting a significant relationship between earnings and tax rates for welfare mothers,[5] it is difficult to detect such a relationship in the experience to date, and it is not clear that the government would save money through lowering the effective tax rate.

In my view, the possible offset effect does not mean we should discard the incentives. Even if such an effect cancels the predicted positive stimulus to work among AFDC recipients, society could experience a net gain because of a possible break in the cycle of dependency plaguing the welfare class. Even if the disincentives to work are not penny wise and pound foolish from the perspective of the federal government, they are likely to be dispiriting to beneficiaries whose sense of self-worth and usefulness would often be enhanced by voluntary participation in the work force. Moreover, basic fairness should be taken into consideration here. Our society should assure people that when they work they will have higher incomes than when they do not.

Regulatory changes in Medicaid. Although the Medicaid system of paying health care providers is still in need of a fundamental overhaul, there are signs of some meaningful reforms. Changes initiated by the Reagan administration and incorporated in the Omnibus Budget Reconciliation Act of 1981 permitted states to apply for waivers from federal and state laws that had previously blocked reforms in the financing mechanism. One such waiver allows states to restrict Medicaid recipients' free choice of provider, thereby allowing the states to channel recipients to low-cost providers and also avoiding unnecessary use of emergency rooms for nonemergency care, a problem that has plagued the Medicaid program throughout the country. The act also allows states to apply for waivers to set up case management systems for reimbursing long-term-care services provided in a lower-cost community-based setting rather than in an institutional setting.

The initial response of the states in 1981 to the combination of rising program costs, diminished tax revenues, and federal cutbacks was to stiffen the eligibility criteria by making income standards lower or by letting inflation cut into existing standards. In addition, about thirty states limited the scope of health services covered under Medicaid. Other states have been shortsighted by paying physicians well below their average fees for an office visit, which has discouraged their participation in the voluntary program. As a result, the states have ended up paying for other, more costly kinds of care—such as emergency room care—where providers do not have a whole picture of a patient's medical care needs.

By 1982, however, states realized that these short-term changes would do little to control their Medicaid costs. With the increased flexibility accorded by waivers from the Department of Health and Human Services, about thirty states began to design long-run structural changes in Medicaid that offer the possibility of enhancing access and efficiency in health care delivery and financing.[6]

Some states have begun to steer Medicaid patients toward economy-minded health care providers or even to cut profligate providers from the program entirely. Other states are acting as "prudent purchasers" of the various laboratory services and medical devices that they pay for under Medicaid.

California has been particularly active in attempting to promote increased competition among providers in its Medicaid program (known as Medi-Cal). In June 1982 the state legislature passed a bill (AB 799) that allows the state to restrict Medi-Cal beneficiaries' choice of provider by negotiating contracts for the provision of the covered services. The state immediately began negotiating service contracts with hospitals, a policy that has been highly controversial.

States are also introducing more cost discipline in their coverage for their own employees, and some states are taking rather bold steps in attempting to reform private sector health care markets. Although California's AB 799 received the greatest publicity, for example, a companion bill, AB 3480 (also passed in June 1982), has brought about a far greater change in the way health care services are provided in the state. AB 3480 allows health insurers to develop or negotiate with closed-panel delivery systems, which, like Medicaid's freedom-of-choice restrictions, serve to steer patients toward low-cost providers. These closed-panel delivery systems, often referred to as preferred provider organizations (PPOs), have developed rapidly, so that the traditional fee-for-service system has, in many areas of the state, been turned on its ear as providers scramble to maintain or increase their patient loads.[7]

Last year the Utah state legislature debated a measure that would allow restrictions on freedom of choice of provider in the interests of fostering the growth of PPOs and other more cost-conscious forms of care. The bill failed to pass. The federal government, however, has shown some interest in assisting states such as Utah in their efforts to facilitate the development of PPOs. U.S. Representative Ron Wyden of Oregon, a proponent of PPOs, has introduced a bill (H.R. 2956) in the House of Representatives that, if passed, would supersede any state law requiring the "free choice of provider." The Wyden bill again indicates an interest at the federal level in giving states the necessary freedom to design and implement their own reforms, rather than dictating to the states how their programs should be structured.

Medicare. In 1981 both the Reagan administration and Congress largely ignored Medicare, and no significant changes were made in the program in the 1981 Omnibus Budget Reconciliation Act. The administration proposed a 2 percent across-the-board cut in Medicare reimbursement of hospitals in its FY 1983 budget, but this proposal was rejected by Congress. The proposal illustrates, however, how little progress had been made toward addressing the basic causes of increases in health care costs as late as early 1982, a full year into the administration. Such an across-the-board cut would have ratified or even rewarded past inefficiencies. By seeking the same percentage cut from all hospitals, however costly their operations, the government would effectively have punished hospitals for holding down costs in the past.

In the same FY 1983 budget, the administration also proposed a one-year freeze on physicians' fees under the Medicare program, a move that was rejected then but revived in late 1983 in the House Ways and Means Committee. These proposals, seemingly totally at variance with the Reagan administration's philosophy emphasizing incentives instead of formulas and ceilings, suggest the lack of progress toward a market-oriented approach to health care reform in federal policy before 1983.

In its FY 1984 budget, the Reagan administration endorsed several major reforms in Medicare, along with a proposed ceiling on the tax subsidy. The administration proposed redesign of Medicare benefits, featuring catastrophic illness protection and more cost sharing for shorter-term hospital stays, and a voucher system for Medicare. None of these steps would be immediately politically popular, and the administration deserves credit for proposals that begin to address the causes of our problems of health care financing instead of the symptoms.

Regrettably, the administration withdrew its plan for redesigning Medicare benefits in the FY 1985 budget. A similar proposal, however, was introduced by Senator David Durenberger of Minnesota (S. 2163). The Durenberger bill is an improvement over the Reagan proposal a year earlier in the sense that it relates the added cost sharing for short-term hospital stays to beneficiaries' income.

My concern is that the more promising proposals from the administration and Congress will remain on the back burner while the more regulatory health care provisions of the Tax Equity and Fiscal Responsibility Act of 1982 (TEFRA) and the complex version of a new prospective payment plan embodied in the 1983 social security legislation occupy the front burner of public policy concerns. The TEFRA provisions for health care cost containment typify the "Band-Aids over broken bones" approach characterizing both administration proposals and congressional action in 1981 and 1982. The statute is a collection of measures that shift costs to employers and patients, extend the grip of federal regulation in a vain attempt to close loopholes, cut back reimbursement to providers, and reduce benefits.

The 1982 law extended the federal controls on doctors' fees and hospital room charges under Medicare to such ancillary costs as laboratory tests and X-rays. It also set a complex formula for determining "target" increases in hospital rates for Medicare patients, adjusted by an index of hospital wages and prices.

Moreover, there are new regulatory plans that would substitute new government formulas and cumbersome controls for the more promising negotiations between the purchasers of health care (primarily employers and governmental units) and those who provide it. Several states have adopted hospital rate-setting schemes, and legislation recently introduced by Senator Edward Kennedy of Massachusetts and Congressman Richard Gephardt of Missouri constitutes a complex regulatory approach to health care cost containment at the national level (see the Medicare Solvency and Health Care Financing Reform Act of 1984).

In my view, only two of the many provisions relating to Medicare enacted in the 1980s even begin to address the basic problem in our health care finance system, and these two steps in the right direction need to be extended or modified significantly if they are to hold real promise of improving the efficiency of the system.

Prospective payment. The 1983 Social Security Amendments directed the Department of Health and Human Services to establish a prospective payment system for Medicare reimbursement of hospitals. Prospectively set rates or spending amounts will reverse some of the inherently cost-generating incentives associated with retrospective, cost-based reimbursement and are a step in the right direction. In practice, however, many prospective systems retain few elements of "prospectivity" once they are implemented and end up being tied to the same allowable cost system that has characterized federal reimbursement policy for years.[8] Moreover, prospective payments to providers may put some pressure on each provider to cut costs but may not so much encourage true economies as lead to service cutbacks. Prospective payment per se is just a better way, in theory, of financing insurance coverage *under* a given health plan. In a world where there is still either no choice *between* traditional health plans and other plans with altered incentive structures or a biased choice that favors the traditional plan and handicaps the innovators, prospective budgets cannot substitute for multiple choice.

The federal government, after dragging its feet for years on developing a new reimbursement mechanism, is now rushing into a very complex version of a prospective payment system based on diagnostically related groups (DRGs). Medicare is now setting payment rates for 470 categories of illnesses, with an elaborate set of exceptions, adjustments, appeals, and phase-in formulas. The basic concept of prospective payment is an improvement over the retrospective, cost-based payment system that has characterized Medicare and Medicaid since these programs were inititated. It is easier, however, to *describe* a process of separating patients on the basis of diagnosis than to *implement* such a system. There is evidence that individual diagnostically related groups will contain patients with widely differing needs (for example, the severity of the condition may differ substantially), and such differences would be associated with widely varying price tags.[9] This will lead to a process of continuous refinements and appeals from hospitals that feel the system has not adequately controlled for their particular mixture of cases. And it could encourage cream skimming and penalize providers who treat a disproportionate share of complicated cases.

Furthermore, despite its complexity and detail, a DRG system is still, ironically, incomplete as a cost control mechanism. As long as hospital admissions are not brought into the loop, cost containment will prove elusive. As currently structured, the system encourages both more than one hospital admission for a medical problem that could be treated in one hospital spell and an upward creep in discharge diagnoses to increase revenues. These trends are particularly problematic in view of the evidence suggesting that rates of hospital admission are very important in explaining the cost advantage that prepaid plans have over traditional health plans.

Even if the DRG system works exactly as planned (an outcome that I consider highly uncertain, at best), it could not prevent a massive shortfall in revenues in Medicare. A recent report by the Congressional Budget Office highlights in stark terms the magnitude of expected deficits in Medicare funding under current law in the next decade. The CBO projects a deficit in the Hospital Insurance Trust Fund of at least $300 billion in 1994.[10] To meet this challenge, we must make major changes in the current cost-generating incentives in our health care system. We may also have to trim benefits for those who can best afford it. To the extent that such changes fall short of reconciling our commitments with our available resources, we will have to augment those resources by raising taxes.

As indicated earlier, the administration proposed a voucher system for Medicare and first proposed, but then withdrew, a plan to redesign benefits. The administration does not seem to be pushing for the incentives-based proposals that are still on its agenda, including vouchers and the tax subsidy ceiling. Moreover, it is clear that all of these proposals, if enacted, would make only a small dent in the expected shortfall in the Medicare Hospital Insurance Trust Fund. In the near future the government will have to give serious attention to such proposals as a major (income-related) increase in patients' contributions to their insurance coverage, an increase in taxes on alcohol or tobacco, or payroll tax increases to avoid the deficits looming in Medicare.

General revenue financing of the expected shortfall in Medicare funds should be avoided; federal deficits are too large as it is without swelling them further. Interfund borrowing that would drain the temporary surpluses expected in the social security retirement fund (OASI) should also be shunned because it would jeopardize the fragile stability introduced into social security by the 1983 legislation. Reform of the payment system is desirable and may delay the day of reckoning briefly, but it will not avert the massive deficits expected in the next decade.

Medicare payment to health maintenance organizations (HMOs). The Tax Equity and Fiscal Responsibility Act of 1982 authorized prospective reimbursement by Medicare under risk-sharing contracts with competitive medical plans (such as HMOs). The government would pay 95 percent of what is termed the adjustéd average per capita cost (AAPCC) in each area of the country. The new provisions, in effect, would share savings associated with lower HMO costs between the federal government and HMOs. Ultimately, the savings of HMOs should translate into benefits for HMO patients in the form of either expanded benefits or lower premiums.

Greater use of HMOs by the elderly may have only a small favorable effect on health care costs. Although HMOs have a cost edge at present, they may well have that edge because their members are younger and healthier than average. A system of medical vouchers for Medicare patients might do much more than the recent legislative change affecting HMOs, by allowing a variety of new health plans—including case management or preferred provider organizations—to compete with HMOs and the traditional Medicare plan for taxpayers' dollars. (Congress considered but dropped a proposal of this sort in 1981–1982.)

Comparison of Budget Trends in Medicare and Medicaid

In 1981 and 1982 percentage cuts were greater in Medicaid than in Medicare. The Omnibus Budget Reconciliation Act of 1981 (OBRA) made little change in the Medicare program but cut about $0.5 billion from Medicaid in FY 1982, or about 2.7 percent of federal outlays for this program.[11] The corresponding percentage cut for Medicare was 1.2 percent. The cumulative effect of the OBRA Medicaid cuts through FY 1984 has been estimated at $2.0 billion. And the administration's proposed budget for FY 1983 envisioned percentage cuts for Medicaid that were twice as great as for Medicare (10 percent and 5 percent, respectively).[12]

Table 4-4 provides further indication of the Reagan administration's different approaches to Medicare and Medicaid during the early 1980s. Whether actual outlays are compared with the Carter administration's final projections or with the Reagan administration's initial estimates, Medicare outlays continually exceed the estimates. In contrast, Medicaid outlays have been held below these projections.

In the past year, however, there has been a gradually tightening grip on Medicare and a corresponding easing—at least relatively—of the cutbacks in Medicaid. The cumulative 1982–1985 percentage reductions in outlays for Medicare and Medicaid from baseline projections were roughly equal—5.0 percent and 4.5 percent, respectively.[13] But these totals hide a turnaround in the middle of this administration. After a 4.7 percent reduction from baseline projections for Medicaid and a 1.1 percent reduction for Medicare in 1982, the relationship began to reverse, as table 4-5, based on CBO data, illustrates.

Other Proposed Federal Policy Changes

While decelerating cost increases in the Medicare and Medicaid programs have been a major focus of federal policy in recent years, there has also been considerable debate over two other proposals. One is a proposed ceiling on the open-ended federal tax subsidy; the other is

TABLE 4-4

EFFECT OF FEDERAL POLICY CHANGES ON MEDICARE AND MEDICAID
OUTLAYS, FISCAL YEARS 1981–1984
(billions of dollars)

| | Budget Outlays | | | |
	1981	1982	1983	1984
Medicare				
Final Carter projections	38.4	44.3	50.8	59.2
Initial Reagan projections	40.1	47.0	53.6	61.2
Actual Reagan outlays	42.5	50.4	56.8	66.5[a]
Medicaid				
Final Carter projections	16.5	18.1	21.0	24.1
Initial Reagan projections	16.6	18.3	20.8	23.6
Actual Reagan outlays	16.8	17.4	19.0	21.1[a]

a. Estimated.
SOURCE: FY 1984 projections obtained from Congressional Budget Office.

85

TABLE 4-5

CHANGE FROM BASELINE PROJECTIONS IN MEDICARE AND MEDICAID
OUTLAYS AS A RESULT OF LEGISLATIVE ACTION SINCE 1981, 1982–1985
(percent)

	1982	1983	1984	1985	Total 1982–1985
Medicare	−1.1	−4.8	−5.9	−6.9	−5.0
Medicaid	−4.7	−5.0	−5.9	−2.8	−4.5

NOTE: CBO uses a 1981 baseline, revised to reflect February 1983 economic assumptions, as the basis for computing percentage changes.

SOURCE: Congressional Budget Office, "Major Legislative Changes in Human Resources Programs since January 1981," p. 47.

the extension of government-assisted health care coverage to unemployed workers.

For both efficiency and equity reasons, I favor proposals to cap the open-ended tax subsidy associated with the exclusion from employees' income of the full amount of employers' contributions to health insurance. Such a step would foster a more efficient health insurance market by encouraging greater choice of health plans and by giving consumers an incentive to steer away from plans exercising little cost control and toward more cost-conscious health plans. I see this incentives approach as preferable to more controls on the providers of health care. The Reagan administration has proposed a cap of $175 per month on the tax-excludable status of employers' contributions for family health insurance and $70 per month for individual coverage. Legislation introduced in Congress during the last four years has also incorporated a cap on the open-ended tax subsidy (see, for example, H.R. 850, introduced by Representative Gephardt).

The debate over whether the anticipated savings in health care costs from the proposed tax subsidy cap would actually occur has diverted us from another, and in my view a larger, issue—the fairness of our health subsidies. Market effects aside, how fair is it to continue an open-ended subsidy to well-paid workers and executives while cutting people (mainly the working poor) from Medicaid?

It is in this light of fairness considerations that I believe the issue of government-assisted health insurance for the unemployed should be assessed. Under this proposal a new group of government beneficiaries—only some of whom are in or near the poverty category—would become entitled to assistance at the same time that some low-income households are being dropped from the Medicaid program.

The U.S. House of Representatives passed a bill (H.R. 3021) in spring 1983 providing health insurance for the unemployed, and the Senate is considering a similar measure (S. 951). Under this proposed legislation, the federal government would make grants to the states to permit the continuation of health insurance coverage and also impose certain requirements on employers for the extension of coverage. In the interests of fairness, such insurance assistance should be provided to the poorest first, regardless of their present labor force attachment, and funded progressively (as through a tax subsidy cap or a change in the federal income tax affecting upper- and middle-income households). It should not simply be an addition to the deficit. The Reagan administration has supported the idea of financing the proposed extension of coverage through a ceiling on the tax subsidy and has also proposed that states be allowed to determine eligibility through the use of a means test that would make income and assets, not current labor force status, the key to eligibility for federal health insurance assistance. The Senate bill mandates that each state impose a means test for eligibility at 150 percent of the state's median income and gives states the option of lowering this level if they choose. The House bill, however, explicitly forbids the use of a means test. A proposed amendment to the House bill that would have accomplished this objective (offered by Congressman Thomas Tauke of Iowa) was defeated. The administration's position appears to be that it would not oppose this legislation if it did not add to the deficit.

The problem with the legislation as it currently stands can be dramatized by the following comparisons: A family with low income but a working household head (holding, for example, a minimum wage job) would effectively be subsidizing the health coverage of a family with an unemployed household head, even where the resources of the latter household, including unemployment compensation and employer-provided supplemental unemployment benefits, exceed those of the working poor household. Working households would be paying taxes at the same time that those who were not working and were at least as well off were receiving tax-free benefits. These are benefits that many of the unemployed would lose if they returned to a lower-wage job providing no health insurance. Thus this legislation could provide an additional work disincentive on top of the already punitive effective tax rate on earnings facing many low-income households.

The working poor are not the only ones who fall between the cracks of public assistance and the ability to afford private health insurance. Many low-income single individuals and couples without dependent children in the home lack health insurance coverage; under this proposal they would continue to be uncovered if they are out

of the labor force at the same time that those with labor force attachment, and equal or greater means, received subsidized insurance coverage. For example, a fifty-five-year-old woman who may be out of the
labor force because of a chronic illness or a commitment to caring for
an aged parent will typically be ineligible for Medicare (too young)
and Medicaid (no dependent children in the household). To put this
woman *behind* a skilled and temporarily unemployed manufacturing
worker in the queue for government-assisted health insurance is a
strange and seemingly unfair twist in public policy. While I am sym-
pathetic to the unfortunate circumstances of the so-called new poor,
some of whom have skills no longer in demand, I am reluctant to see
them leapfrog over the "old poor" with longstanding and still unmet
needs.

Another equity problem that would be created by the proposed
health insurance for the unemployed is the unequal treatment of
equally situated unemployed workers. The House-passed bill would
distribute federal assistance to states (with a small amount of state
matching and a small measure of cost sharing by the insured) according to a formula based, in large part, on state unemployment rates.
On the surface a payment system providing more federal funds to
states with high unemployment might appear equitable, but a closer
examination reveals that states with relatively low unemployment
rates (particularly in the South) are also states with a relatively high
incidence of poverty. If federal funds for health insurance coverage
were not linked to labor force status and were apportioned according
to a strict need standard, they might be allocated in a way opposite to
the method envisioned under current proposals.

Summary and Conclusion

The decade of the 1980s began with the federal government's health
policies characterized by an inflationary retrospective, cost-based reimbursement system under Medicare and Medicaid that made providers' earnings a direct function of their spending. A few cost items
were excluded by the government from "allowable cost"—such as
some outlays for research and the bad debts of other payers—but,
basically, the federal government followed a "you buy it, we'll pay for
it" approach. Similar policies were pursued by many private payers.

Open-ended tax subsidies give workers an incentive to select the
most comprehensive insurance coverage and dampen workers' incentive to compare the advantages and disadvantages of alternative
health insurance plans. The combination of a cost-generating reimbursement system in the public and private sectors and open-ended

tax subsidies created a distortion in the health insurance market that led consumers to spend more on health care than they would have spent if they were balancing costs and benefits.

While government tax and reimbursement policies were saying "more," government regulatory policies were saying "less." With a heavy blanket of regulations on the allowable price and quantity of health services, the government sought to restrain through formulas and caps the spending increases that it was feeding with its tax and reimbursement policies.

Both Medicare and Medicaid policies also had serious inequities. Medicare's hospitalization plan required no cost sharing by patients, regardless of income, from the second to the fifty-ninth day of a hospital stay, but exposed patients to one-fourth of the hospital bill between the sixtieth and ninetieth days (and to even higher cost sharing beyond that point). Medicaid provided extensive coverage to a little over half the poor, no coverage to the rest of the poor, and some assistance to near-poor households. There was also little flexibility in the Medicaid program for states to experiment with innovative payment systems.

There was little effort in 1981 and 1982 by the Reagan administration or the Congress to address these fundamental problems. Budget cuts in health care fell most heavily on Medicaid, with tax subsidies flowing mainly to middle- and upper-income households untouched and Medicare subjected to only minor tinkering. This disparity within the health care sector was a microcosm of the broader tendency of the federal government to make disproportionately larger cuts in means-tested programs than in the larger social insurance programs providing benefits to all economic groups, as well as to leave tax expenditures untouched.

The Medicaid program is still basically intact, and it would be wrong to conclude that the health care component of the federal safety net has been ripped apart. It is important to recognize, however, that this safety net has always had some holes in it: Certain segments of the poor are systematically excluded from both welfare and medical assistance through categorical restrictions based primarily on family status. Moreover, these longstanding holes in the net were widened somewhat as a result of changes proposed by the Reagan administration and adopted by Congress.

There were some favorable developments during this period, such as the relaxation of regulation embodied in the waiver process established under the Omnibus Budget Reconciliation Act of 1981. In one sense this relaxation could be viewed as a potential compensation for the marginal increases in the size of the holes in the safety net, since opportunities for cost-saving financing reforms have enabled some states to avoid further eligibility restrictions. Some federal rules governing hospitals were also eased by the Reagan administration. But new formulas for allowable cost increases were added in the Tax Equity and Fiscal Responsibility Act, and no serious effort to reform the payment system, the tax system, or the fairness of the major government programs was mounted.

This policy drift began to change in early 1983. First, Congress adopted a prospective payment system for Medicare in the 1983 social security amendments. Second, the Reagan administration proposed major reforms in the FY 1984 budget, including a cap on the tax subsidy and a voucher system and benefit redesign for Medicare.

At this writing the proposed reforms are languishing and are not being vigorously pursued by the administration, while the phase-in of the new Medicare payment system—DRGs—promptly began in September 1983. The government appears preoccupied with refining the details of this new payment system and is postponing other reforms. Even if the DRG system works as planned, it could not possibly reconcile Medicare's current benefits with expected revenues. Tax and benefit changes will have to accompany payment system reforms.

Health care costs will continue to escalate as technological break-throughs and the aging of our population lead to higher spending. The challenge is *not* to shrink the system through more controls—federal or state—that would jeopardize the advances, innovation, and modernization needed to maintain or enhance the system's quality. Rather, we need some new incentives that would help sort out and reduce the inefficiencies built into our health-financing system. Such favorable incentives should dent the growth curve of health spending somewhat (but not flatten it), freeing some resources for alternative uses.

The recent proposals by the Reagan administration and Congress involving subsidy ceilings, benefit redesign, payment system reforms, and further deregulation offer a kind of blueprint for reforms that could shrink these inefficiencies. Similar proposals are embodied in legislation that has been pending in Congress for several years (see H.R. 850, Representative Gephardt; S. 580, Senator Durenberger).

In summary, after years of vainly flogging providers with government controls, we seem to be embarked on a change in course. Whether this initial redirection is a steppingstone to a wholesale new approach or a brief interlude followed by massive new controls remains to be seen. It remains a challenge, and an unfinished agenda, for public policy makers.

Notes

1. See Rosemary Gibson, "Quiet Revolutions in Medicaid," in Jack A. Meyer, ed., *Market Reforms in Health Care: Current Issues, New Directions, Strategic Decisions* (Washington, D.C.: American Enterprise Institute, 1983), pp. 78–81.

2. Ibid., pp. 79–80.

3. See Judith Feder, John Holahan, Randall R. Bovbjerg, and Jack Hadley, "Health," in John L. Palmer and Isabel V. Sawhill, eds., *The Reagan Experiment* (Washington, D.C.: Urban Institute, 1982), pp. 285–91.

4. See, for example, Frank Levy, "The Labor Supply of Female Household Heads, or AFDC Work Incentives Don't Work Too Well," *Journal of Human Resources*, vol. 1, no. 1 (Winter 1979). For an analysis of experimental studies, see Robert A. Moffit, "The Effect of a Negative Income Tax on Work Effort: A Summary of the Experimental Results," in Paul M. Somers, ed., *Welfare Reform in America: Perspectives and Prospects* (Boston: Kluwer-Nijhoff Publishing, 1982).

5. See, for example, Irwin Garfinkel and Larry Orr, "Welfare Policy and the Employment Rate of AFDC Mothers," *National Tax Journal*, vol. 24, no. 2 (June 1974), pp. 275–84; Robert Williams, "Public Assistance and Work Effort," Industrial Relations Section, Princeton University, 1974; and Daniel H. Saks, "Public Assistance for Mothers in an Urban Labor Market," Industrial Relations Section, Princeton University, 1975. For a thorough review of the literature on this subject, see Sheldon Danziger, Robert Haveman, and Robert Plotnick, "How Income Transfer Programs Affect Work, Savings, and the Income Distribution," *Journal of Economic Literature*, vol. 19 (September 1981), pp. 975–1028.

6. See Gibson, "Quiet Revolutions," pp. 75–102.

7. See Joan B. Trauner, *Preferred Provider Organizations: The California Experience* (San Francisco: Institute for Health Policy Studies, University of California, 1983).

8. For a review of the evidence on the effectiveness of prospective payment and state hospital rate setting, see Michael A. Morrisey, Frank A. Sloan, and Samuel A. Mitchell, "State Rate Setting: An Analysis of Some Unresolved Issues", *Health Affairs* (Summer 1983), pp. 36–47.

9. Susan Horn, "Prospective Payment: The Concept and Practice in Medicare and State Health Programs" (Paper presented at conference held at the American Enterprise Institute, Washington, D.C., March 3, 1983).

10. See Congressional Budget Office, "Prospects for Medicare's Hospital Insurance Trust Fund," February 1983, p. 3.

11. See Feder et al., "Health," pp. 279–81.

12. Ibid., p. 281.

13. See Congressional Budget Office, "Major Legislative Changes in Human Resources Programs since January 1981," August 1983, p. 47. CBO uses a 1981 baseline, revised to reflect February 1983 economic assumptions, as the basis for computing percentage changes.

5

Halfway to a Housing Allowance?

John C. Weicher

When the Reagan administration came into office, it was confronted by rapidly rising costs in the low-income housing subsidy programs; and the programs were widely regarded as defective on grounds of both equity and efficiency. The administration quickly began to restrain the rate of cost increase in these programs while it developed an alternative approach that was potentially a fundamental redirection of housing policy. In these efforts it has been fairly successful—more in cost cutting than with the new policy—but a new housing bill approved by Congress at the end of 1983 suggests that the administration has passed the high tide of its success and is beginning to lose ground.

The substantive policy proposals are generally consistent with the recommendations of housing economists in both parties.[1] But the administration has received less credit for them than might be expected. The rather unfavorable tone of public discussion appears to stem from three causes: the administration is not adding to the stock of subsidized housing fast enough; some of its cost-cutting measures fall on the recipients of subsidies and are thus considered inequitable; and it has proposed a few changes that are controversial out of all proportion to their real importance.

Background: The Development of Housing Policy before 1980

Housing policy has always had some features not commonly found in other income redistribution programs, partly because of its particular historical development. A brief description of these features provides a basis for understanding both what the Reagan administration has tried to do and how its proposals have been received.

Public housing was originally part of public works. It was seen as a way of stimulating the economy, particularly in the depression. Housing subsidies were therefore in the form of federal payments for the construction of new apartments specifically for lower-income families.[2] The macroeconomic purpose has been deemphasized as evidence accumulates that subsidized construction is an ineffective countercyclical policy tool, but it has had important lingering effects on attitudes toward housing policy.

• Program activity is usually measured by additional units subsidized each year rather than by the total number of assisted households or individuals. Other income redistribution programs are seldom evaluated on this incremental basis.

• Housing subsidies have usually been tied to the unit, not to the individual. In most programs a tenant who moves out of a subsidized apartment no longer receives the subsidy; the new tenant does, if he or she is eligible. The major exception is the Section 8 Existing Housing Program; if a subsidized family moves, it retains the subsidy in its new house or apartment, provided the unit meets program standards.

• Subsidized housing has never been an entitlement program, because it would be inordinately expensive to build new units for all low-income families. In fact, the poorest families were typically excluded from public housing for many years, because the subsidy mechanism required tenants to pay the operating costs without spending more than 20 percent of their incomes. At the beginning of 1981, just over half of all subsidized units were occupied by households below the poverty line.[3]

• Conversely, income limits for subsidized housing have often been set higher than for other redistribution programs. Public housing was originally aimed at the lowest-income full-time workers, thereby often excluding those who did not work. In 1974 the limit for the Section 8 program was set at 80 percent of the local median income, which is usually somewhat higher than 160 percent of the poverty line.

The policy of new construction also reflected the widespread belief that the existing housing stock, particularly that part of it available to the poor, was seriously substandard and could not easily be upgraded. Just before World War II, nearly half the occupied housing stock was substandard, largely because it lacked indoor plumbing. The postwar period, however, saw a rapid reduction in the number of substandard housing units, partly through demolition but also through upgrading; by 1970 fewer than 10 percent were still substandard. This fact gradually began to affect housing policy. In the mid-1960s public housing was extended to the existing privately owned housing stock. In the early 1970s the Department of Housing and Urban Development (HUD) began an extensive experiment with "housing allowances," in which low-income households were given vouchers—commitments from the federal government to make payments for housing that the households found for themselves in the private housing market.[4] The Section 8 program, established in 1974, has subsidized both new and existing housing. Throughout the 1970s there was increasing discussion of whether housing policy should continue to adhere to the traditional approach of building apartment projects or should place primary reliance on the existing privately owned inventory as the source of housing for the poor.

This argument exemplifies another feature of American housing policy. We have never been very satisfied with our housing programs. The oldest one, public housing, was created in 1937 and has been through rather violent cycles in popularity and activity; it has been stopped and revived several times. Moreover, since 1961 there have been three successive major new programs, intended either to substitute for public housing or to supplement it: Section 221 in 1961, Sections 235 and 236 in 1968, and Section 8 in 1974.[5] Each of these in turn has proved unsatisfactory and has been superseded. Thus there has been continuing political controversy about housing, perhaps on a more extensive scale than in other income redistribution programs; certainly none has been more frequently redesigned. The actions of the Reagan administration can be seen as the latest chapter in this debate.

Section 8

Program Description. When President Reagan took office, Section 8 was the major program to provide decent housing for the poor. Between its inception in 1974 and the election of 1980, it had grown rapidly. At the end of 1980 more than 1.1 million units were in the program, almost as many as in public housing (1.2 million) after more than forty years and more than the 900,000 units in all the other subsidy programs combined.[6] Two-thirds of the Section 8 units were existing housing. Table 5-1 shows the growth of subsidized housing programs since Section 8 was enacted. Including some new public housing, there had been a 50 percent increase in the number of subsidized units in just six years. This still left many low-income and other eligible households out of the program, but the proportion assisted had been rising. In 1976 about one-sixth of all renters below the poverty line lived in subsidized housing; by 1981 the proportion had risen to one-quarter.[7]

By 1980, however, the growth in the program was slowing. Its cost had been rising faster than the funds budgeted for it. From 1976 through 1981 annual subsidies per unit rose about 67 percent.

Meanwhile, the total budget authority approved by Congress did

TABLE 5-1
HUD Subsidized Housing Programs, 1975–1985

	1975	1976ᵃ	1977	1978	1979	1980	1981	1982	1983	1984ᵇ	1985ᶜ
Additional commitments (thousands)	92	517	388	326	325	206	178	146	147	203	151
Conversions from other programs	—	—	—	—	—	—	—	60	63	48	37
Net additional subsidized units	92	517	388	326	325	206	178	86	84	155	114
New construction (percent)	40	39	52	55	61	63	43	42	22	40	11
Budget authority ($ billions)ᵈ											
New authorization	e	16.6	27.3	30.6	23.4	23.7	20.1	11.5	6.1	8.5	4.7
Amount obligated	e	16.6	28.6	30.1	30.7	24.0	24.8	14.8	10.3	12.6	7.6
Total households assisted (millions)	2.1	2.3	2.6	2.8	3.0	3.1	3.3	3.5	3.7	3.8	4.0

a. Includes transition quarter.
b. Estimated; includes Housing Development Grants Program.
c. Proposed.
d. Excludes public housing modernization funds. Amounts obligated in one year may be recaptured and subsequently reobligated; therefore obligations may exceed authorizations.
e. Not comparable to later years.

SOURCE: U.S. Department of Housing and Urban Development, *Summary of the HUD Budget*, annual volumes, fiscal years 1977 through 1985.

not rise as rapidly. After an abrupt increase from $17 billion in 1976 to $27 billion in 1977, it fluctuated only slightly around that amount over the next three years.[8] This meant that fewer additional units could be subsidized each year, and the situation was further exacerbated by an increasing emphasis on new construction. During the first two years of the program, the Ford administration favored using the existing stock, and just over 60 percent of the units approved for subsidy ("reserved") were existing housing. By 1980 the Carter administration had shifted the proportions to 63 percent new construction (or substantial rehabilitation, which was even costlier). In addition, costs per unit were consistently underestimated, so that fewer units could be financed with each year's budget authority than were originally planned. For all these reasons, the number of newly subsidized units dropped from 388,000 in 1977 to 206,000 in 1980.

Rising costs also created political dissatisfaction with the program. Costs per unit had risen markedly faster than either rents or apartment construction costs. For fiscal year 1981, beginning in October 1980, the contract authority—the maximum annual amount the government will spend—was budgeted at about $5,400 for new units, or $450 per month, and $3,000 for existing units, or $250 per month. The cost for a newly constructed unit was about 50 percent more than the typical rent for a new private apartment and almost double the median rent for all units in the private market.[9]

The annual program costs differed so much because separate subsidy mechanisms were established for new and existing housing. For existing housing the maximum monthly subsidy—known as the fair market rent, or FMR—was based on rents actually paid in the private market for housing of standard quality. The FMR for new construction was based on rents for recently built unsubsidized apartment projects. These were supposed to be equivalent in quality, but the new private projects were typically much better than the average existing rental apartment. Moreover, a variety of adjustments were added to compensate for special factors that raised construction or financing costs. Indirectly if not officially, then, the FMRs for new construction were based on the cost of construction, rather than on the actual market rental of modest, decent housing, and were substantially higher than the FMRs for existing housing, even though both were supposed to be measuring the same concepts.

The federal government also undertook to subsidize new projects for a longer period. Commitments ranged from twenty to forty years, depending on the nature of the developer and the character of the project; the average was twenty-three years. In the Existing Housing Program, the commitment ran for only fifteen years. The rationale for the longer new construction commitment was to enable the developer to obtain a long-term mortgage with a guaranteed income stream.

The 1981 budget was the first to present explicitly the annual and total budget outlays per unit for each Section 8 program category. Because the full amount of the commitment is authorized in the budget for the fiscal year in which it is made, the budget authority was almost three times as large for each new construction unit as for existing housing—$123,000 versus $45,000. Annual costs per unit were nearly double, and the commitment ran half again as long. The total long-term federal budget obligation for Section 8 amounted to $130 billion over the next thirty years, of which two-thirds was for new construction, although far more existing housing units were receiving subsidies. In addition, some $71 billion was obligated for public housing projects and $45 billion for other low-income housing programs, for a total of nearly $250 billion. In 1975, by contrast, the long-term obligation was less than $90 billion.

It seems clear that, at the beginning of 1981, dissatisfaction with Section 8 new construction was sufficiently widespread that the program would have been terminated or drastically modified regardless of the outcome of the election, primarily if not exclusively because of its cost. For the fourth time in twenty years, the federal government, including both Congress and the administration, was seeking a new way to provide housing assistance for the poor.

Short-Run Goals: Reducing Program Costs. The Reagan administration initially focused on the cost of Section 8 new construction while it considered alternative policy approaches. During 1980 Congress approved $27.3 billion for subsidized housing in fiscal year 1981 to fund about 255,000 additional units, split 55/45 between new units (140,000) and existing units (115,000). President Reagan submitted a rescission of $4.7 billion of this authority as part of his revision of the Carter budget for 1982. This reduced the number of additional subsidized units to 210,000, split 49/51 between new and existing units (103,000 and 107,000). Congress approved the rescission.

For 1982 President Carter wanted $27.6 billion in budget authority for 260,000 additional units, split 50/50. President Reagan asked for another rescission of $9.4 billion, cutting the number of additional units to 175,000, split 45/55 (79,000 new and 96,000 existing). This rescission also passed. In September 1982 the president obtained a still further rescission as part of his across-the-board domestic spending cut. With all these changes, the actual number of reservations was only 145,000, split 28/72 (40,000 new and 105,000 existing units).

These figures overstate the change in the total units receiving subsidies from the federal government because they include units transferred from older subsidy programs to the Section 8 existing housing program, which are treated as additional Section 8 units in the budget. In 1981 President Carter proposed to convert the rent supplement program, consisting of about 175,000 units, to Section 8. He received approval to transfer 10,000 units in that year's budget and sought an additional 20,000 in 1982. President Reagan proposed to accelerate this process by transferring all units within three years beginning in 1982. Congress approved the transfer, and about 60,000 units were actually converted in 1982. They accounted for more than half the additional Section 8 existing housing reservations that year.

Thus, for the first two fiscal years of his term, President Reagan achieved a $14 billion cut in budget authority for additional units, about 25 percent; a reduction in the number of assisted units of about 160,000; and a much greater cut in new construction (127,000) than in existing housing (33,000). Taking conversions into account, President Reagan cut about 200,000 units, over 60 percent of them new.

At the same time that it cut the number of additional subsidized units, however, the administration was willing to raise the subsidy on those that it assisted. Conversion from rent supplement to Section 8 was accompanied by an increase of more than $500 in the annual subsidy, though for a shorter term.

Similarly, while it sharply cut the number of new Section 8 units, the Reagan administration institutionalized a mechanism for increasing the subsidies for those that were approved. It permitted new construction FMRs to be increased because interest rates were unusually high. The FMRs could be calculated on the basis of a 12 percent mortgage rate, rather than 8 percent. This financing adjustment factor (FAF), first used by the Carter administration in 1980, further reduces the relationship between actual market rents and the subsidy payments under the new construction program.

It should also be stressed that these large budgetary changes represent only reductions in the number of additional housing units to be subsidized, not reductions in the total number of subsidized units or in the number of households being subsidized. That number actually grew by about 400,000 between 1980 and 1982.

The significance of all these changes is that, although they did not constitute a fundamental redirection of housing policy, they did move the Section 8 program toward a much greater reliance on the existing housing stock, whether on ideological grounds or merely from a desire to reduce the budget. They thus set the stage for a more important program change, which was formulated in the administration's 1983 budget.

Long-Run Goals: Using Existing Housing. The new proposals had two major features: they virtually ended construction of new subsidized housing, terminating both Section 8 and conventional public housing; and they modified the Section 8 Existing Housing Program to provide more freedom of choice for assisted tenants, moving the program in the direction of a housing allowance, with less government involvement in the decision of the household. They also sought to reduce the effect of subsidized housing on the budget.

The most important change allows subsidy recipients—housing certificate holders—to select housing that rents for more than the FMR (or "payment standard," as it is called in the proposal) if they wish to spend more than 30 percent of their income for housing. It also gives a certificate holder an incentive to shop for the best bargain, by allowing him or her to keep any difference between the payment standard and the actual rent; in the original Section 8 program, households kept only part of the saving, and even this incentive was later eliminated. The proposed changes were features of the housing allowance experiments that had proved successful.

In other important respects, however, the program was unchanged from Section 8 existing housing. The minimum quality requirement was retained; subsidized households were not free to choose substandard housing. And the subsidy was to be paid by the local housing authority to the landlord, once the unit had been approved and the lease signed, rather than to the tenant. This meant that the landlord would automatically know that the tenant was being subsidized. Thus the administration's name for the new program—Modified Section 8 Housing Certificate Program—seemed entirely appropriate, although it was widely but erroneously termed a voucher program.

By themselves, these changes would not result in budgetary savings; indeed, they would, if anything, increase costs by permitting households to keep any difference between the payment standard and the rent. But the administration also proposed to reduce the term of the budget authority per unit from fifteen to five years. This change, while cutting the budget by two-thirds, would not necessarily lower long-term costs. Instead, it would require more frequent authorization to continue subsidizing the same number of households. Its most important effects might be to compel future administrations and congresses to reconsider housing programs regularly, to minimize the costs of unanticipated and undesirable outcomes, and to provide more flexibility to change programs. It might also have negative consequences, in that landlords would have less assurance of receiving a guaranteed income stream over fifteen years (assuming their tenants remained and their units continued to meet standards) and might therefore be less able to obtain mortgages.

The total budgeted cost of the program was more of a departure from the past and more controversial politically. The administration asked for funds for about 122,000 units, close to the number in the preceding two years. Only 10,000 were to be new construction; 106,000 were proposed for the new program. About 61,000 of the certificates, however, were to be used to convert units already in the Section 8 Existing Housing Program to the modified program; with other conversions, there would be a net increase of only 55,000 assisted units, 45,000 of them existing housing.

Even more startling was the total dollar amount of the program, $7.5 billion—less than half the figure for 1982 and less than a third of that for 1980. Moreover, the administration sought no new budget authority for additional subsidized housing units. It proposed to fund the entire amount needed out of recaptured funds from previously approved Section 8 new construction and public housing projects that the developer had subsequently decided not to build. Recaptures have not been uncommon; in 1981, for example, they amounted to $5.3 billion, for 42,000 units. But in the past the funds have been recommitted to other projects. HUD now projected recapture of $9.9 billion in 1983, proposed to use $7.5 billion of it for the new modified certificate program, and submitted a rescission for the remaining $2.4 billion. For good measure, it also asked for a rescission of the $7.5 billion that it expected to recapture in 1982 and an additional $1.9 million, virtually eliminating new construction from the 1982 budget.

The magnitude of these fiscal changes has obscured the fact that the substantive differences between the original Section 8 existing housing program and the modified certificate program are not actually very great. In addition, some of the smaller components of the administration's program further reduce the extent of the difference. The budget contained a proposed new rental rehabilitation grant, for example, which would have given $150 million to states and local governments for the rehabilitation of 30,000 rental houses and small apartment buildings. These units would also have received Section 8 certificates, so that in effect the government would guarantee the rent for five years in addition to paying for the rehabilitation. This explicit double subsidy is something new in low-income housing programs, although it was implicit in the Section 8 rehabilitation programs developed by the Carter administration. Further, as in the new construction programs, the rental subsidy was tied to the unit, not to the family.

The budget continued one new construction program, Section 202, which provides direct loans from the Treasury, at a below-market interest rate, to nonprofit sponsors (usually religious groups) of housing projects for the elderly. This popular program was established in 1959; in the late 1970s it averaged about 20,000 units annually, all in conjunction with Section 8, because the interest rate reduction is not large enough to bring the rents within reach of the low-income elderly. The administration cut the program to 10,000 units in the 1983 budget but did not propose to end it.

Congressional Action. In essence, the administration's proposal was accepted in the Senate but rejected in the House. The deadlock continued throughout 1982 until the postelection session, when a continuing spending resolution provided $13.1 billion for some 173,000 subsidized housing units—65,000 conversions and 108,000 additional units. Of these, only about 16,000—less than 10 percent—were new construction (14,000 Section 202 and 2,000 public housing units on Indian reservations). The remainder were Section 8 existing housing. No funds were provided for conventional public housing or Section 8 new construction. The administration thereby achieved one major goal—virtual elimination of new construction. The rental rehabilitation grant was not approved, however. Moreover, the program was larger than the administration had asked for by some 50,000 units, and Congress voted an additional $6.1 billion in budget authority to finance it. (Separately, Congress approved a rescission of $4.1 billion for 1982, instead of the $9.4 billion requested by the administration.) The amount of recaptured authority was projected as $4.6 billion instead of $9.9 billion.

1984 and 1985. For 1984 the administration essentially resubmitted its 1983 proposal, with only minor substantive modifications and a minor name change—it was now the Housing Payment Certificate Program. The main difference was that the annual subsidy could increase as market rents rose or household income fell during the five-year term of the certificate. Again it proposed to fund the program without new budget authority, projecting more in recaptures ($4.4 billion) and deferrals from 1983 ($3.1 billion) than the cost of the program ($6.5 billion). The total number of assisted units was about 130,000, of which 10,000 were again Section 202 new construction, 40,000 were conversions, and 80,000 were units not previously subsidized. The rental rehabilitation grant was again proposed for 30,000 of the additional units. The total was almost exactly the same as in 1983, but the number of incremental units, excluding conversions, was 35,000 more. Costs per unit for the certificates were projected at $2,000.

This time the administration was less successful. In midyear Congress passed an appropriation bill providing $8.4 billion for 100,000 additional units, of which 16,000 would be new Section 202 or Indian public housing units and 45,000 would be Section 8 existing housing. But it also set aside $1.5 billion for another 38,000 units, to be subsidized under whatever new program might subsequently be enacted. The recapture projection was cut to $2.5 billion; $5.9 billion was new budget authority.

At the end of its 1983 session, Congress created a new subsidized rental construction program, which differs from past subsidies in that the federal government will make direct grants to the local housing authority, rather than making the payments on long-term bonds. It will therefore require much less budget authority per unit. It is a small program—$615 million over two years—which may fund about 10,000 new construction or substantial rehabilitation units and 30,000 moderate rehabilitation units each year. Housing certificates will be tied to about half of the latter as a "demonstration" of the certificate program. The net effect is that Congress has not approved the Housing Payment Certificate Program but has approved the rental rehabilitation grant and called it a housing payment certificate.

The bill is a partial success for the administration. It halts new public housing projects, at least while the pipeline is cleaned out, and terminates altogether the statutory authority for Section 8 new construction even as it creates another construction program. It is somewhat, though not dramatically, larger than the budget request, more in new authority than in additional units. But it does not contain the major program changes sought by the administration.

For 1985 the administration will try again for the same program, at about the same unit and budget levels: 111,500 units, of which 12,500 will be new and 87,000 in the voucher program, at a total cost of $9.1 billion, of which $2.8 billion will be recaptured.

The Problem of Transition. The issue of recaptured authority illustrates the problems that the administration confronts in trying to achieve a major policy change. It became important as a result of the 1983 budget proposal. HUD's regulations have limited the time allowed between the reservation and the start of construction on a project, but the limits have traditionally not been enforced. HUD wanted to stop granting extensions for projects exceeding the time limits, which would have enabled it to recapture the budget authority; but the developers, the local housing authorities, and Congress opposed this. Instead, Congress directed HUD to make every effort to expedite construction of the units already in the pipeline. As part of this effort, the financing adjustment factor was increased; Section 8 new construction FMRs could now be set on the basis of a 14 percent mortgage rate. Some $655 million was also authorized to pay higher interest rates on public housing bonds. The cost per unit of subsidized new construction continued to rise.

HUD was also unable to recapture as much budget authority as it originally planned. For fiscal years 1982 and 1983, recaptures amounted to $6.1 billion, compared with the $17.4 billion projected in the 1983 budget. In 1984 this pattern is continuing; the $4.4 billion initially budgeted is now estimated at only $2.5 billion. Most, but not all, of the difference results from congressional insistence on cleaning out the pipeline. In fact, the pipeline is being reduced. The number of units not yet started declined from 290,000 at the end of 1980 to 101,000 three years later. A small part of the decline was due to actual recaptures, about 22,000 units in 1982 and 19,000 in 1983; the rest has occurred because construction starts from past commitments have greatly exceeded new reservations. About half the units still in the pipeline were approved before 1981 and have taken at least three years, so far, without reaching the ground-breaking stage; they seem to be reasonable candidates for recapture. The administration has projected some 33,000 recaptures in 1984 and 1985, less than the number of these older units. But suspicion persists that it is trying to stop projects that really could be built.

Tenants' Benefits

Besides reducing the number of additional households to be subsidized each year, the Reagan administration has annually proposed modifications in the benefits received by individual households. These have affected present as well as future subsidy recipients.

The most important of the original proposals in 1981 was an increase in the maximum ratio of tenants' rent to income from 25 to 30 percent. This was approved by Congress, subject to the limitation that no tenant's rent could be raised by more than 10 percent in a year, and the administration began to phase it in, one percentage point per year, beginning in 1982. New tenants were required to pay 30 percent immediately. A second technical change required all local housing authorities to adopt the same standards for determining tenants' income. The previous system had allowed discretion and caused some horizontal inequities: households with the same income received different subsidies in different places. This change was also approved by Congress.

The next year the administration tried to cut costs per unit further, as part of its modified certificate program. Its proposals would have applied to tenants continuing in Section 8 as well as to the new program. First, it proposed to reduce the payment standard from the fiftieth percentile of the rent distribution to the forty-fifth percentile. Second, it wanted to include the value of food stamps in tenants' income. Third, it asked Congress to allow annual rent increases of up to 20 percent. These changes were expected to hold the average annual subsidy to $2,000, compared with a budgeted $3,600 for Section 8 existing housing in the previous fiscal year.

Congress rejected all these proposals, and the administration resubmitted them in its 1984 budget. It was partly successful, winning approval to lower the FMR. But at the same time it was forced to accept a partial rollback of the increase in the rent-income ratio that had been legislated in 1981. Indeed, the House wanted to return to 25 percent; the final bill retained the 30 percent ratio but raised the amounts to be deducted from income before the ratio is calculated. The higher deductions mean that about a quarter of the 1981 increase has effectively been repealed—more for the lowest-income tenants.

Income Limits. The administration has also proposed to target housing programs more narrowly to the poorest households. In this it has been consistently successful. In 1981 it was able to limit the number of "moderate-income" households (those with incomes between 50 and 80 percent of the local median). It then proposed to limit Section 8 (and also the modified certificate program) to families with incomes below 50 percent of the local median, which was also approved by Congress. These changes have possible implications for future housing policy, which will be discussed later.

Public Housing

The changes in the rent-income ratio and the uniform standards for determining income apply to public housing as well as to Section 8, as would the inclusion of food stamps. But the administration has also had to address several special issues concerning public housing subsidies.

Operating Subsidies. When public housing was started in 1937, the financial arrangements were straightforward. The federal government paid the cost of building the units, making principal and interest payments on tax-exempt bonds issued by local public housing authorities; the tenants made monthly rental payments, which covered the operating costs of the project, such as utilities and maintenance, and a payment to the local government in lieu of property taxes. Rents were limited by statute to 20 percent of tenants' incomes (with various

104

adjustments). This meant that the very poorest households were effectively excluded from public housing, since their incomes were not large enough to meet the operating costs. In 1959 the law was changed to allow local authorities to set their own income limits and rents. Initially most continued to set rents high enough to cover operating costs. But after about 1965 operating costs began rising more rapidly than tenants' incomes, chiefly because of the general inflation suffered by the economy.

Congress reacted by limiting tenants' rent to 25 percent of income, even if this was less than the operating costs of the unit. This made public housing affordable for the poorest households, and the program began to serve an increasingly lower-income clientele.[10] It also necessitated a further federal subsidy to cover the difference between operating costs and rents. And it removed the financial constraint on operating expenses that had effectively been imposed by the tenants' rental payments.

Operating subsidies began in 1969 and grew rapidly, as shown in table 5-2.[11] By 1974 they had increased to $276 million, or over $25 per

TABLE 5-2

Public Housing Operating Subsidies, 1969–1985
(selected years)

Fiscal Year	Budget Authority ($ millions)	Total ($ millions)	Outlays per Unit Month (dollars)	Percentage of Total Operating Costs
1969	15	13	1	2
1971	108	44	5	8
1974	320	276	25	35
1977	591	522	39	37
1980	862	824	60	42
1981	1,002	929	72	44
1982	1,350	1,008	69	41
1983	1,351	1,542	103	n.a.
1984[a]	1,558	1,180	77	n.a.
1985[b]	1,124	1,125	76	n.a.

n.a. = not available.
a. Budget authority approved by Congress; HUD is proposing $331 million rescission, included in outlay figures. Outlays estimated.
b. Proposed.
Sources: U.S. Department of Housing and Urban Development, *Summary of the HUD Budget*, annual volumes, fiscal years 1976 to 1985; and unpublished data from HUD Budget Office and Office of Housing.

unit month, and some analysts were beginning to speak of the "financial crisis" in public housing caused by the rapid rise in operating costs.[12] Both the Office of Management and Budget and Congress were increasingly concerned and insisted that HUD find some way to set operating subsidies that would encourage local authorities to manage projects more effectively and economically. In 1975 HUD therefore adopted the Performance Funding System (PFS), which is based on a statistical analysis of the operating costs of well-run projects, relating their expenses to certain characteristics of the projects (such as size of units, type of structure, and location). The analysis is used to estimate the operating costs that any project should incur if it were well run, and the operating subsidy is the difference between the estimate and the rents paid by tenants.

The new system was insufficient, however, to restrain the growth of operating subsidies. From 1974 to 1977 they increased by over 50 percent per unit, to $522 million, or about $39 per unit month; from 1977 to 1980 they rose by more than half again, to $824 million, or about $60 per unit month. They also increased dramatically as a share of total operating costs, to over 40 percent by 1980. At the same time, total operating costs more than tripled.[13]

Much of the increase in operating costs was due to the rise in energy costs after the 1973 oil embargo, but public housing utility outlays increased more rapidly than the utility component of the consumer price index. An important contributing factor is that tenants in public housing have no incentive to conserve, because their rents cannot rise when their energy consumption does. HUD has attempted to meet this problem by paying for only 75 percent of any increase in consumption and by permitting the local authorities to keep 25 percent of any savings in operating subsidies resulting from reduced consumption. It has also been providing funds through its modernization program (discussed in the next section) for energy conservation equipment.

Despite the rapid increase in operating subsidies, some public housing analysts were concerned that the PFS was increasingly underestimating the growth of operating costs and therefore providing inadequate funding. The annual adjustment was based on two factors: utility costs and wages of local government employees. It therefore omitted changes in the cost of physical maintenance inputs, which were supposed to be measured by the wage rate. A study undertaken for HUD in 1979 concluded that the omission seriously understated the inflation rate for operating costs. In addition, operating subsidies are funded in advance, and therefore the expected rate of inflation is used to estimate them in each year's federal budget. In the late 1970s inflation was consistently underestimated, so that local housing authorities were faced with a real decline in operating funds in relation to actual costs.[14]

As President Reagan came into office, operating subsidies were rising at an accelerating rate. For 1981 the Carter administration had received an appropriation of $862 million, or about $61 per unit month, and was asking for a supplemental appropriation of $100 million (about $7 per unit month) to meet rising utility costs. The Carter administration's budget for 1982 also incorporated a retrospective inflation adjustment for increases in nonlabor operating costs, as recommended by the HUD study of 1979. The total request for 1982 was $1.265 billion, or over $85 per unit month. This was an increase of $400 million in two years, over 35 percent for each unit.

The Reagan administration retained the inflation adjustment in its revision of the 1982 budget, thus accepting a large increase in operating subsidies. It sought, however, to restrain their growth in other ways. It withdrew the supplemental request for 1981, on the basis that the higher utility costs should be funded out of the separate Low-Income Home Energy Assistance Program. It also asked for the same structural changes as in Section 8. Congress passed the supplemental anyway but also approved the changes in the maximum subsidy per household, subject to the limitation that no tenant's rent could rise by more than 10 percent in a year. The one-percentage-point increase in the tenants' rent-income ratio for 1982 cut operating subsidies by $60 million.

For 1983 the administration proposed further changes, besides those already mentioned in connection with Section 8. To restrain utility cost increases and give tenants the incentive to conserve energy, it sought to require them to pay any utility costs in excess of 25 percent of their income. Because these changes might increase rents for some tenants by more than 10 percent, it also asked that the annual ceiling on increases be raised to 20 percent. Finally, it proposed a reduction in operating subsidies to $1.075 billion, or $72 per unit month, partly to reflect these changes and partly on the ground that modernization of the older units would achieve significant energy conservation. Congress rejected all these changes and voted operating subsidies of $1.350 billion, or $92 per unit month, implicitly also rejecting the argument that modernization expenditures in the past had resulted in energy conservation.

After two years of these relatively minor changes in the existing operating subsidies program, the administration proposed a new and radically different program for 1984. The new system used the same fair market rent concept as Section 8. Operating subsidies would be based on the rents charged for private housing, not on the costs of operating public housing. The public housing FMR would be set at the fortieth percentile (rather than the forty-fifth) of the rent distribution for private, standard-quality housing at least two years old. The tenants' rent and the cost of debt service on the public housing bonds would be subtracted from the FMR to determine the operating subsidy. This plan would have lowered subsidies for some units and raised them for others; however, the administration proposed to give the latter only the amount that they would receive under the PFS, rather than the FMR-based subsidy. HUD estimated that about 5 percent of all authorities, managing 5 percent of all units, would have faced subsidy cuts of 10 percent and proposed to limit those cuts to 5 percent annually.

Under the FMR system, operating subsidies would have been $1.33 billion in 1984, or $90 per unit month,[15] instead of $105 per unit month, as under the PFS. In future years subsidies would have remained about 15 to 17 percent below those projected under the old system. They would have continued to rise; the projected 1988 FMR-based operating subsidy was $112 per unit month.[16]

This proposal attracted favorable comment among some advocates of public housing[17] but received short shrift in Congress. Congress appropriated $1.558 billion for operating subsidies, the full amount projected under the PFS, and very nearly legislated the continued use of the PFS, which had been adopted by HUD administratively.

In its 1985 budget proposal, the administration abandoned the FMR-based system and reverted to the PFS. It also asked for a rescission of $331 million of the 1984 funds and a reduced appropriation for 1985 of $1.124 billion; both figures reflect operating subsidies of just over $75 per unit month. These proposals are based largely on lower increases in utility costs than previously projected. Congress has typically voted the full amount required under the PFS; so it is questionable whether these cuts will be accepted.

Thus the administration's attempts to reform the system fundamentally have been unsuccessful. Its efforts to restrain the growth of operating subsidies have fared better but have come under increasing attack. For the four fiscal years from 1981 through 1984, it initially sought about an $800 million reduction in operating subsidies and achieved only about $150 million; moreover, for 1983 and 1984 actual outlays are above the Carter projections. This has occurred despite the favorable inflation performance. In real terms, the actual outlays are 7 percent above the Carter projections and 23 percent above the original Reagan proposals. Even if the 1984 rescission is approved, actual real outlays will be slightly higher than President Carter's last budget projection.

Modernization. Since 1968 the federal government has also provided subsidies for the modernization of older deteriorating or obsolescent public housing projects. Modernization funds are supposed to be used for major repairs or alterations that extend the life of the project and may therefore legitimately be regarded as capital outlays. Priority is also given to energy conservation.

The modernization program has several recognized problems. Normal maintenance is supposed to be financed out of operating revenues (including federal operating subsidies), but if maintenance is deferred until major repairs are necessary, modernization funds can be used. This is a perverse incentive for local public housing authorities. For this reason, some analysts and advocates of public housing have recommended that operating subsidies and modernization funds be combined.[18] This would confront public housing managers with the same incentives to allocate money between short-term maintenance and long-term major repairs that private landlords face.

A second problem is that funds are appropriated by Congress annually and then allocated by HUD to local authorities at its own discretion. Large year-to-year fluctuations have been common for individual housing authorities. This means that local authorities have trouble planning and conducting their repair programs on any long-term, comprehensive basis.[19]

Modernization is financed through the same mechanism as project construction. The local authorities issue bonds, for which the federal government provides the funds to make principal and interest payments over a twenty-year amortization period. Each year's budget contains an appropriation for the full term of the bonds to be issued in that year. Through 1980 about $6.6 billion in bonds had been issued, to finance about $3.6 billion worth of modernization.

The program has been growing rapidly, if somewhat erratically, since it was started, as table 5-3 shows. It grew particularly rapidly in the Carter administration. In the early 1970s about $250 million worth of modernization was financed each year; by 1977, the last year of the Ford administration, this figure had risen to $324 million; by 1980 it was up to $545 million.

These funds have not been enough to modernize public housing fully. A study conducted for HUD in 1979 estimated total catch-up costs of $250 million to bring all projects up to basic health and safety standards, $1.5 billion to meet HUD's minimum property standards for FHA-insured apartment projects, and $6.8 billion to make public

TABLE 5-3

PUBLIC HOUSING MODERNIZATION FUNDS, 1968–1985

(millions of dollars)

Fiscal Year	Budget Authority	Contract Authority	Capital Costs Financed by Contract Authority
1968–1970[a]	367	9	117
1971–1973[a]	800	20	240
1974–1976[a,b]	615	18	196
1977–1979[a]	875	43	439
1980	1,000	50	545
1981	1,700	85	927
1982	1,800	90	858
1983[c]	2,566	128	1,260
1984[d]	1,550	78	761
1985[e]	1,550	78	761

a. Annual averages.
b. Includes transition quarter funding.
c. Includes substantial rehabilitation set-aside.
d. Estimated.
e. Proposed.

SOURCES: Robert Kolodny, *Exploring New Strategies for Improving Public Housing Management* (Washington, D.C.: U.S. Department of Housing and Urban Development, Office of Policy Development and Research, July 1979), for years 1968–1974; and U.S. Department of Housing and Urban Development, *Summary of the HUD Budget*, annual volumes, fiscal year 1977 through 1985, for later years.

housing competitive with private rental housing.[20]

Thus the Reagan administration came into office confronting another rapidly growing program that was not effectively fulfilling its purpose and that was widely regarded as having significant structural and administrative flaws.

Here too its initial efforts were devoted to reining in the growth of the program, with mixed results. For 1981 Congress had doubled the 1980 appropriation, voting $2 billion in budget authority, enough to support about $1.1 billion worth of modernization; and for 1982 President Carter asked for the same amount. President Reagan sought and received a rescission of $300 million of the 1981 budget authority, which still left it 70 percent above that for 1980. He also cut the 1982 budget request to $1.5 billion, but Congress voted $1.8 billion. For

1983 the administration asked for $1.8 billion again; instead, Congress appropriated $2.6 billion.

In its 1984 budget the administration sought major structural reform. It wanted to combine operating subsidies and modernization funds, and it also proposed a new "transition modernization" program to bring all public housing projects up to the minimum property standards. The transition program was proposed to cover a four-year period, through 1987. The combination of funds would permit local authorities to make their own decisions about the proper maintenance strategies for their projects and would significantly reduce HUD's day-to-day involvement in the management of public housing. Thus the plan addressed the major conceptual problems in the current system.

The new replacement allowance was set at 20 percent of estimated operating costs excluding utilities. For 1984 this was budgeted at $340 million. In addition, $687 million worth of transition modernization would be financed by $1.4 billion in budget authority for twenty-year bonds. The total of $1.027 billion would be about 20 percent less than in 1983 but more than in any preceding year. Total modernization funds were projected to decline steadily until 1988, however, as the transition modernization program was phased out while the replacement allowance increased gradually to $437 million.

The adequacy of both the replacement allowance and the transition modernization funding has been questioned. The Congressional Budget Office (CBO) has noted that the replacement allowance is based on one year's experience of private rental projects and may therefore be an inadequate guide to long-term public housing needs; it has described an alternative that is about 20 percent more expensive.[21]

The transition modernization program would amount to $1.7 billion worth of repairs in four years, or about $1.1 billion in 1980 dollars. This is about two-thirds of the catch-up modernization needs estimated in HUD's 1979 study. The assumption of the administration's program that the worst 100,000 public housing units would be withdrawn from the stock accounts for much of the difference. That is about the number identified in the 1979 study as being distressed.

The program also assumed that recent modernization funding has not been spent on badly deteriorated units and that no further deterioration has occurred since 1980. The latter seems a reasonable assumption on its face, given the $2.5 billion in new modernization that has since been authorized; if that has not been enough to halt deterioration, on the average for the public housing stock if not for each unit, then one must wonder about the initial construction quality, the project management, or the administration of the modernization program. So large a sum should be adequate even if some of the money has been spent on projects that would be eliminated under the new proposal. But some experts have argued that more will be needed,[22] and Congress has ordered HUD to spend $4 million to repeat and update the 1979 study.

These modernization proposals, like the new operating subsidy mechanism, were not approved by Congress. There was support in the Senate for a more expensive replacement allowance, similar to that analyzed by the CBO, but the appropriation bill continued the present system, at a funding level of $1.550 billion.

In the 1985 budget, the administration has withdrawn the 1984 proposals. The budget makes no mention of a separate replacement allowance or long-range transition modernization program but merely asks for the same modernization funding as it received last year.

Thus over four years the Reagan administration has sought large reductions in modernization spending and achieved small ones. At the beginning of 1982 the Carter administration's budget projections amounted to $2.0 billion annually in budget authority, or $8.0 billion for 1981 through 1984. The Reagan administration's initial projections cut this to $5.6 billion. Its annual budget proposals have been higher, about $7.1 billion (including the twenty-year bond equivalent of the 1984 replacement allowance). Congress has actually voted about $7.7 billion. Thus there has been about a 4 percent cut from the Carter projections, but there has also been a doubling of the actual average level during the Carter administration.

Criticisms: Program Size

The structure of the Reagan administration's proposals has been supported by housing analysts from both parties, but strong criticism of their scale has created a more negative public impression than the proposals seem to merit. It may be useful to consider the question of scale separately.

Entitlement: Horizontal Equity. As part of its efforts to cut the growth in total program costs, the administration has reduced the number of additional units coming under subsidy each year and has considered a cap on the total number of units to be subsidized. This has concerned a number of analysts from both parties, who argue that the subsidized housing programs have been inequitable because they are limited and who believe that housing subsidies, like food stamps and

Medicaid, should be open to all households who meet the income eligibility rules.[23] The experience with the housing allowance experiment, which was operated as an entitlement in two metropolitan areas, suggests that the additional cost, for a program using the existing housing stock and similar to the housing allowance, would not be especially large. One recent estimate is about $6 billion in additional outlays each year, in 1984 dollars.[24]

An entitlement program is certainly preferable to either the present or the proposed program on grounds of equity. But housing programs have invariably cost more than originally expected and have developed unforeseen structural problems as they expanded. And an administration that has had to wrestle with the budgetary consequences of past entitlement programs may be forgiven for moving slowly on setting up a new one and for being skeptical—even unduly skeptical—about the validity of the findings of the housing allowance experiment about program participation. The administration has in fact made entitlement more feasible politically by lowering the income limit from 80 to 50 percent of the area median, even as it has expressed opposition to the concept.

At the same time, an entitlement housing program would have particular advantages for this administration as well as costs. It is not possible to address the continually rising costs of public housing operations systematically except on a piecemeal basis. With entitlement, public housing residents could be offered vouchers along with all other low-income households, and public housing authorities would be subject to the discipline of the marketplace, which would be consistent with the basic rationale for the administration's housing payment certificate program. The really "bad" projects could be identified easily and either upgraded or removed from the inventory.

Lower Subsidies for Tenants. The cost increases imposed on the poor, such as the higher rent-income ratio and the lower FMR, are more strongly criticized. It is distasteful to many people to see benefits reduced for the poor, particularly in a recession and particularly as taxes are also reduced for middle- and upper-income families. The most cogent argument for the changes is that housing costs have been rising for most Americans, as financial deregulation eliminates the protected position of housing in the capital markets and raises the mortgage rate, particularly for home buyers. If the real price of housing is indeed rising in the 1980s, as is often alleged, it is perhaps not unreasonable that housing subsidies should reflect its rise.

The lower FMR is a relatively minor change. Recipients of subsidies will spend the same amount for housing and have the same

113

amount for other goods and services. The quality of their housing will be somewhat lower, so that their overall level of economic welfare will be lower. But the new FMR should still be high enough to enable them to live in standard-quality housing.

The issue of horizontal equity is also relevant; if the present very large per-unit subsidies are cut slightly, there may be more money to help other equally poor families, and we may move to an entitlement program a bit more rapidly than we otherwise would. But so far, of course, we have not moved very far.

At the same time that it has tried to cut costs per unit, however, the Reagan administration has advocated or accepted changes that raise them. It has proposed to let housing certificate holders keep any difference between the payment standard and their actual rent. It approved the 1982 inflation adjustment in public housing operating subsidies and proposed a catch-up modernization program in 1984. All these changes were advocated before 1981; the administration has not received much credit either for actually accomplishing them or for trying to do so.

Criticisms: Symbolic Issues

Although the important policy issues have concerned the structure, scale, and funding of housing programs, other questions, more symbolic than real, have arisen and contribute to the impression that the administration is unsympathetic to the poor or is antihousing.

One of these is whether the administration wants to get rid of public housing. In the 1983 and 1984 budgets, as part of the modified Section 8 program, the administration proposed to set aside funds ($10 million) for tenants of 5,000 public housing units when the projects are sold or demolished. For 1985 it repeated the proposal but cut the number to 2,500. And in 1984, as noted, it proposed a modernization budget that anticipated the demolition of the worst 100,000 public housing units, which—according to the 1979 study—would cost about $10,000 per unit in current dollars to bring up to minimum property standards. This seems to be a defensible decision.

These proposals have symbolic overtones for public housing advocates, however, and perhaps for the administration as well. They bring back vivid memories of the demolition of the Pruitt-Igoe project in St. Louis in 1972, which has probably contributed more to the negative image of public housing than anything else. Eliminating even 2,500 public housing units could inflict further damage to the cause of subsidized housing, regardless of the specific reasons. I do not know if symbolism motivates the administration's proposals; it surely colors their reception and probably also the reaction to the administration's overall policy.

Another symbolic issue has arisen in the Community Development Block Grant program. The administration has proposed to change the requirement that the block grants be targeted to low- and moderate-income households, requiring instead only that they meet any one of three objectives, including the income criterion. This proposal has occasioned a great deal of concern, especially in Congress, and the housing bill approved at the end of 1983 required that over half the grant be spent on activities benefiting the poor. This action comes after two years of debate over such questions as what the statute actually means and what the purposes of the program really are. Much less attention has been given to the actual budget reductions in CDBG—about $200 million per year from the 1981 level of $3.7 billion.

My view is that the issue is trivial. Despite much ingenuity, we simply do not know very much about how the block grants are actually spent—what activities occur that would not occur without them. Some of the activities are "public goods," which confer benefits on all residents of a neighborhood or a whole city, and the benefits cannot meaningfully be assigned to individuals. Moreover, apart from housing rehabilitation grants and loans, where the income of the owner or tenant can be ascertained, the requirement is in practice more applicable to neighborhoods than to people: Benefits to an area consisting largely of low-income households are counted as low-income benefits. This means that creative accounting and creative cartography should enable a city to do much as it pleases with the money. It can be argued that the changes would have been consistent with the administration's overall policy of increasing local control and responsibility for local problems, but their effect would probably have been imperceptible.

Conclusion

The administration's most important policy initiatives have been at least partly successful. It has succeeded in terminating the Section 8 new construction program and halting new public housing projects. It has not quite stopped all new subsidized construction programs, but it has tried and come close. Its policies have sharply shifted the size and shape of subsidized housing, to an extent probably undreamed of four years ago. President Carter's last budget projected $118 billion in new authority for 1981 through 1984, to subsidize an additional 935,000 units; President Reagan initially cut this to $72 billion for

635,000 units. Then, as the administration made the decision to end subsidized new production in Section 8 and public housing, it was able to cut budget authority still further, to $46 billion for 500,000 more units. Two-thirds of the initial reduction was projected to consist of new construction; all the further realized cuts have been new units. Altogether, new construction has been reduced from President Carter's projected 530,000 to just under 200,000 units; existing housing, only from 405,000 to 305,000. These changes have not had much effect on budget outlays and were not expected to; in the short run of a few years, outlays are almost entirely determined by past commitments. They have, however, reduced the long-term budget obligation by about $100 billion, from the $340 billion inherent in President Carter's last budget to $240 billion as of President Reagan's 1985 submission to Congress. These are very large numbers.[25]

Although the administration has stopped the most expensive of the old programs, however, it has not been able to get its new one adopted. It has also tried to move cautiously in the direction of a housing allowance but has been unsuccessful in persuading Congress to go even as far as it has asked. The reluctance of Congress to approve the housing payment certificate and its insistence on a "voucher demonstration"—after ten years of a housing allowance experiment and nine years of the Section 8 Existing Housing Program—is a remarkable contrast to its willingness to vote a new subsidized production program, costing more than twice the demonstration program to start with.

Moreover, as the administration has tried to shift policy, it has run into transitional problems. Commitments made under the construction programs remain outstanding. Its attempts to minimize these commitments seem appropriate, given the high costs and other problems of the programs. But the result of all this is that the administration has been criticized by advocates of public housing, especially the local housing authorities, for terminating the construction programs and by advocates of the housing allowance for not going far enough.

The administration has some potentially important achievements in housing policy to its credit. But it is not yet clear whether they are merely temporary—like, for instance, the moratorium imposed by President Nixon in 1973—or whether they reflect a major change in housing policy. The 1983 housing bill suggests, unfortunately, that the former possibility is increasingly likely.

Notes

1. See, for example, Edgar O. Olsen and Stuart M. Butler, "Housing and Urban Development," in Richard N. Holwill, ed., *Agenda '83* (Washington,

D.C.: Heritage Foundation, 1983); and Raymond J. Struyk, Neil Mayer, and John A. Tuccillo, *Federal Housing Policy at President Reagan's Midterm* (Washington, D.C.: Urban Institute Press, 1983), chap. 6.

2. For an extended discussion of the history of housing policy, see John C. Weicher, *Housing: Federal Policies and Programs* (Washington, D.C.: American Enterprise Institute, 1980), chap. 3.

3. U.S. Bureau of the Census, *Characteristics of the Population below the Poverty Level: 1981*, Current Population Reports, Series P-60, no. 138 (March 1983).

4. For full discussions of the housing allowance experiments, see Raymond J. Struyk and Mark Bendick, Jr., eds., *Housing Vouchers for the Poor—Lessons from a National Experiment* (Washington, D.C.: Urban Institute Press, 1981).

5. Most housing programs are known by the section number of the National Housing Act or of the law that created them, probably because there are not many synonyms in the English language for "mortgage interest rate subsidy," which is the mechanism used in nearly all of them. This creates some confusion in the case of Section 8, which has quite different subsidy programs for new construction and existing housing, both created in the same section of the 1974 Housing and Community Development Act and therefore both known by the same title.

6. Unless otherwise indicated, all budget and program references are to fiscal years.

7. U.S. Census Bureau, Current Population Reports, Series P-60, nos. 115, 138.

8. All budget authority figures exclude public housing modernization funds but include amendments and lease adjustments.

9. This comparison overstates the relative cost of Section 8, because the budget figures are for future years, when the units being reserved in 1980 will actually be built and occupied. A rent inflation of 10 percent per year for three years would reduce the disparity to about 25 percent. The Section 8 units are typically smaller, however, than the units in the existing inventory; 77 percent were efficiency or one-bedroom apartments, compared with 38 percent of all rental units.

10. In the mid-1960s the typical family admitted to public housing had an income of about $2,500; by 1978 it had an income of $2,000, measured in 1967 dollars. The typical tenant in 1967 was in the tenth percentile of the income distribution, meaning that 90 percent of American families had higher incomes; the typical tenant in 1978 was in the fifth percentile.

11. Before 1969 subsidies were available on a small scale for units occupied by elderly and handicapped tenants.

12. Frank deLeeuw, *Operating Costs in Public Housing: A Financial Crisis* (Washington, D.C.: Urban Institute, 1974).

13. I am indebted to Robert Gair and Paul Gatons of HUD for these figures.

14. Roberta Drews, *Federal Subsidies for Public Housing: Issues and Options* (Washington, D.C.: Congressional Budget Office, June 1983), pp. 29–30.

15. These calculations omit the "replacement allowance," which is discussed in the next section.

16. Office of Management and Budget, *Major Themes and Additional Budget Details, Fiscal Year 1984*, pp. 48–50.

17. Struyk et al., *Federal Housing Policy*, p. 77.

18. Drews, *Federal Subsidies*, p. 47.

19. Raymond J. Struyk, *A New System for Public Housing* (Washington, D.C.: Urban Institute, 1980), pp. 97–98.

20. Perkins and Will and the Ehrenkrantz Group, *An Evaluation of the Physical Condition of Public Housing Stock: Final Report, vol. 1*; quoted in Drews, *Federal Subsidies*, pp. 16–20.

21. Drews, *Federal Subsidies*, pp. 49–51.

22. Raymond J. Struyk, *Reforming Public Housing: The Administration's Fair Market Rent Proposal* (Washington, D.C.: Urban Institute, 1983), p. 37.

23. Olsen and Butler, "Housing and Urban Development," pp. 172–75; and Raymond J. Struyk and John A. Tuccillo, "Defining the Federal Role in Housing: Back to Basics," *Journal of Urban Economics*, vol. 14, no. 2 (September 1983), pp. 219–22.

24. Jill Khadduri and Raymond J. Struyk, "Housing Vouchers for the Poor," *Journal of Policy Analysis and Management*, vol. 1, no. 2 (Winter 1981), pp. 196–208. Khadduri and Struyk estimate the cost in 1979 dollars; I have inflated them to 1984.

25. I am indebted to Kenneth F. Ryder of the OMB for the figures in this paragraph.

6

Ideology, Pragmatic Politics, and the Education Budget

Denis P. Doyle and Terry W. Hartle

The needs of the poor and the fate of government programs designed to help them are of special interest in 1984, both because of the impending election and because of the Reagan administration's efforts to provide a safety net to protect low-income individuals. But in the world of education the issue is not so clearly cast as it is in health, nutrition, and housing. Indeed, from a theoretical standpoint, one would expect to find only a limited set of education activities specifically geared to the needs of the poor. Poverty and educational problems are not on their face synonymous. Although the overlap between low academic achievement and low income is great, it is not complete.

In the abstract, then, education programs might have been designed around pedagogical criteria, only incidentally related to questions of poverty. Indeed, in the fifty states education programs are so designed, and emphasis on poverty criteria is slight.[1]

At the federal level, however, the pedagogical dimensions of education are of less importance than income and equity concerns. As it turns out, much of what the federal government does in education, though not means tested in a strict sense, is related to income. Indeed, the largest and best-known federal education programs are tied to income. For example, initial determination of eligibility for Title I of the Elementary and Secondary Education Act (ESEA) and for many postsecondary student aid programs, such as Pell grants and guaranteed student loans (GSLs), is means tested.[2]

Background

The Reagan administration entered office with the most ambitious domestic policy agenda in recent history. Substantial reductions were proposed in education programs, as in almost every domestic program. Breaking continuity with every president since Truman, the

119

administration proposed to decentralize much of what the federal government had historically done. To preserve local control and reduce federal "meddling," the administration proposed to do away with the Department of Education, reduce the central government's regulatory demands and burdens, rationalize and streamline those programs it continued to support, eliminate certain "objectionable" programs outright, and cut the education budget.

In contrast to the efforts to decentralize education, the Reagan administration advanced two federal initiatives: a constitutional amendment to permit prayer in the nation's classrooms and tuition tax credits for families whose children attend private schools.[3]

In short, the Reagan administration had mixed policy objectives in education; means-tested education programs did not figure prominently in its plans. Perhaps the most enduring impression is also the most appropriate, for it is the expression of a consummate political irony. Committed to returning education to its community roots and significantly diminishing the federal role, this administration has inadvertently made education a national issue of the first priority.

In this essay, however, we emphasize budgetary and policy changes in means-tested programs: what the Reagan administration has proposed, how Congress has responded, and how the changes have affected state and local governments and educational institutions. This is not a simple undertaking. What the administration has attempted to do in higher education is quite different from what it has sought to do in elementary/secondary, vocational, or bilingual education. Moreover, the programs themselves are diverse: some, such as Title I (now Chapter I) and Pell grants, are multibillion-dollar efforts while others are small, almost invisible, efforts aimed at very specific targets. As a result, before examining what the Reagan administration has done, it is necessary to summarize the contours of federal aid to education and review the criticisms that surrounded it when President Reagan took the reins of government.

Moving In: The Reagan Administration Sets Its Education Agenda

The origins of federal support for education can be traced to 1785, but most of the growth in federal aid has occurred in the twentieth century.[4] The Smith-Hughes Act of 1917 authorized appropriations for vocational education, and a number of subsequent enactments deepened the federal commitment.[5] The Serviceman's Readjustment Act of 1944, popularly known as the GI Bill of Rights, provided financial aid to encourage veterans to pursue higher education.[6] During the Korean War, Congress enacted a small program known as impact aid designed to compensate local school districts for property tax revenues lost and educational expenses incurred through the presence of federal military installations.[7] The passage of the National Defense Education Act in 1958 was designed to help America meet the challenges presented by the Soviet Union's launching of the first space satellite.[8]

Despite the importance of these measures, it was not until the 1960s that federal aid to education grew rapidly. In 1963, partly in response to President Kennedy's assassination, Congress passed both the Vocational Education Act and the Higher Education Facilities Act.[9] In 1965 Congress passed the Elementary and Secondary Education Act, which provided billions of dollars for economically and educationally disadvantaged children.[10] Later that year Congress enacted the Higher Education Act (HEA), which provided guaranteed student loans, work-study funds, and supplemental educational opportunity grants (SEOGs) to students enrolled in colleges and universities.[11] Both measures are landmarks: Title I of the ESEA is the centerpiece of federal aid to elementary and secondary education, and the HEA occupies a similar position with respect to postsecondary education.

More federal programs were established in the 1970s. The Higher Education Amendments of 1972 created the basic educational opportunity grants (BEOGs), which established the principle that the federal government would help any qualified but financially needy student meet the cost of college.[12] Also in 1972, at President Nixon's urging, Congress created the National Institute of Education (NIE) to conduct education research and passed the Emergency School Assistance Act (ESAA) to help school districts meet some of the costs associated with desegregating their classrooms.[13] The Education of All Handicapped Children Act of 1975 mandated significant changes in the education of handicapped children.[14] The Vocational Education Amendments of 1976 expanded the federal role in vocational education and required that more attention be given to the needs of such special groups as handicapped persons, women, and other disadvantaged persons.[15]

Higher education programs were expanded sharply in 1978 when Congress, at President Carter's request, enacted the Middle Income Student Assistance Act.[16] Designed primarily to forestall enactment of a tuition tax credit bill, the act greatly broadened eligibility for federal financial aid by allowing any student, regardless of family income, to borrow money under the guaranteed student loan program. Access to federal financial assistance was further expanded when Congress passed the Higher Education Amendments of 1980.[17]

The most important feature of the federal education agenda as it emerged in the past two decades was its focus on equity, weaving together strands of race, poverty, gender, ethnicity, and handicapping condition. In traditional education terms, the federal agenda was "content free." Its purposes were to assist the dispossessed by using the school as the service delivery institution. And succeeding presidents shared this view: Presidents Nixon, Ford, and Carter faithfully put more money into education without significantly changing the shape or purpose of the basic programmatic structure. Indeed, the few exceptions further enlarged the federal role: President Nixon's commitment to research as a national strategy to improve education, President Ford's (reluctant) signature on the Education of All Handicapped Children Act, and President Carter's creation of the Department of Education, as well as his temporarily successful attempt to expand eligibility for postsecondary financial aid to the middle class.

Interestingly, each of these ventures proved controversial. Nixon's National Institute of Education was a conceptual breakthrough because it suggested that the federal government, by sponsoring research, could help find the answers to America's educational problems. Racked by problems throughout its existence, however, today the NIE is barely alive.[18]

The Education of All Handicapped Children Act, though an extension of earlier federal policies, constituted a giant leap in the prescriptiveness of aid to education. Alone among federal education programs, it is not conditional. Because the law is cross-referenced with a major civil rights mandate (Section 504 of the Rehabilitation Act of 1973), states and localities must comply whether or not they take federal money. Accordingly, states and localities must supply substantial funding and reorganize classroom practices to meet federal standards, because the federal government refused to fund more than a minimal portion of the law's costs.

Carter's Middle Income Student Assistance Act was doomed from the start. Created for the wrong reason (to derail the enactment of tuition tax credits), it was recognized even by its most ardent supporters (in moments of candor) as a wretched excess. Evidence that things were getting out of hand occurred when a *Money* magazine article announced, correctly, "Even a Rockefeller can get a school loan at 9 percent interest." The final straw was an article in *Better Homes and Gardens* recommending GSL funds as a possible source of assistance for home remodeling.[19]

The major problem facing federal officials was escalating costs. Federal expenditures for elementary and secondary education increased from $2.4 billion in 1968 to $6.7 billion in 1981.[20] Appropriations for higher education jumped from less than $500,000 to $6.3 billion during the same time period.[21] Indeed, when President

Reagan was inaugurated, higher education was one of the fastest-growing components of the federal budget, the product of the liberalized eligibility provisions enacted in 1978, which, in effect, ended means testing for guaranteed student loans.

Confronted by this evidence and encouraged by its own predilections for reducing the federal government's presence in American society, the Reagan administration set an ambitious agenda for reforming federal aid to education. According to the 1980 Republican platform, the administration would

> restore common sense and quality to education . . . replace the crazy quilt of wasteful programs with a system of block grants . . . support deregulation by the federal government of public education . . . encourage the elimination of the Department of Education . . . restore prayer in public schools . . . halt forced busing . . . enact tuition tax relief into law . . . clear away the tangle of regulation that has driven up college expenses and tuition.[22]

Upon taking office, the administration moved to give shape and structure to its agenda. Led by David Stockman, director of the Office of Management and Budget, the administration laid out a series of guidelines to help identify areas for budget cuts, including the following:

- preserving the social safety network of programs for the needy
- reducing subsidies to middle- and upper-income groups
- reducing overhead and personnel costs to the federal government
- applying sound economic criteria to subsidy programs
- consolidating categorical grant programs into block grants

Only one education program—Head Start—was to be preserved as part of the administration's safety net.[23] Almost all other education programs were targeted for varying degrees of policy changes or budget reductions. Some of the proposed modifications were adopted in the Omnibus Budget Reconciliation Act of 1981, some are still under consideration, and some have been abandoned. It is, however, to the initial budget proposals and their resolution that we first turn our attention.

The 1982 Budget: Request and Reconciliation

Responsibility for submitting the fiscal year 1982 budget fell to the outgoing Carter administration. On January 15, 1981, President Carter submitted a budget requesting $17.0 billion in appropriations for education programs for fiscal year 1982, $2.4 billion more than he had requested for 1981. While the budget generally preserved existing programs, it did propose a substantial reduction in impact aid and a tightening of eligibility for guaranteed student loans.

Proposals to cut impact aid were not new—every president for the past two decades has suggested reducing expenditures for this program, uniformly without success. Reduction in the GSL program was a new idea but one that was clearly necessary. After eligibility was broadened in the Middle Income Student Assistance Act, federal program costs rose from $500 million in 1978 to $2.5 billion in 1981. Unless checked, the volume of loan guarantees was expected to reach $10 billion in 1982.[24]

The Carter administration outlined a series of changes designed to reduce outlays. It proposed (1) limiting loans to a student's remaining financial need after all other financial assistance and the expected family contribution had been calculated, (2) eliminating the in-school interest subsidy, and (3) creating a new program of unsubsidized loans for parents.[25]

Upon taking office on January 20, 1981, the Reagan administration abandoned the Carter budget. Deep budget cuts were requested for almost all areas of social policy, and education was no exception. For fiscal year 1982 the administration proposed spending $13.0 billion at the Department of Education, $4.0 billion less than Carter had requested. In addition, the revised budget called for widespread rescissions in the fiscal year 1981 budget—reductions that would be felt by educational institutions in the 1981–1982 school year.[26] The suggested changes—and the eventual results—for both elementary/secondary and higher education are briefly described in the following sections.[27]

Elementary/Secondary Proposals. The centerpiece of the administration's 1982 budget was a plan to consolidate many categorical programs into block grants. The budget outlined the administration's ideas, but it was not until late April 1981 that the details became available. The administration suggested consolidating forty-four elementary and secondary programs into two packages totaling $4.4 billion. The bill would have repealed seven laws, including Title I of the ESEA and most of the Education for All Handicapped Children Act. It also abolished most planning and evaluation provisions, fiscal controls, program regulations, and reporting requirements. In addition, longstanding fiscal requirements that many state and local officials found onerous (such as maintenance of effort) were to be eliminated. Finally, there were no required advisory committees or procedural mandates for program planning or administration.

The bill required that benefits be directed to one or more of the groups of students with special needs served under existing legislation—educationally deprived and handicapped students, students involved in desegregation, adults lacking basic education, neglected and delinquent children, and migrant youth. Funds were to be used only for the same activities as under existing programs. It is significant, however, that the proposal did not require that services be provided for any one or all of these groups—merely that one or more of them benefit.

The Reagan plan was divided into two parts: Title I, Financial Assistance to Meet Special Needs; and Title II, Financial Assistance for Improvement of School Resources and Performance. Title I was allocated $3.8 billion, the vast majority of it to be distributed directly to local school districts. Title II, which provided $565 million to the states, consolidated thirty-eight small categorical programs into a single award. Funds under this title were to be used to encourage academic excellence through effective instructional and management practices, improve student achievement, increase opportunities for educational services for students with special needs, and strengthen state oversight and management functions.

Other suggested changes would have reduced federal aid to education even further. For example, the Reagan administration accepted the Carter administration's recommendations to cut impact aid and eliminate the Youth Conservation Corps. A 15 percent reduction from the Carter administration's request was proposed for vocational education.

Budget reductions in other departments would also significantly have affected federal support for education. The administration proposed to eliminate the public service employment programs of the Comprehensive Employment and Training Act (CETA), for example, and to reduce eligibility for the food stamp and child nutrition programs. Although these are not technically education programs, they do have an important effect on elementary and secondary schools, especially in urban areas.

Elementary/Secondary Reconciliation Results. The Omnibus Budget Reconciliation Act of 1981 made several major changes in the structure and administration of federal education programs. Perhaps the most dramatic were the redesign of Title I of the Elementary and Secondary Education Act and the consolidation of many small categorical programs into a single block grant. Both were adopted when, as part of the reconciliation act, Congress created the Education Consolidation and Improvement Act (ECIA) of 1981. Although the ECIA was clearly consistent with the administration's interest in block grants, it included none of the major programs the administration wanted to consolidate, nor did it eliminate as many regulatory provisions as were suggested.[28]

Chapter I of the ECIA basically continues Title I of the ESEA by providing financial assistance to state education agencies (SEAs) and local education agencies (LEAs) for the special needs of educationally deprived children. The new law, however, eliminates most regulatory requirements except those related to fiscal accountability. It states:

> The Congress declares it to be the policy of the United States to continue to provide financial assistance to state and local educational agencies to meet the special needs of education- ally deprived children . . . but to do so in a manner which will eliminate burdensome, unnecessary, and unproductive paperwork and free the schools of unnecessary federal su- pervision, direction and control. . . . Congress . . . finds that federal assistance [for education] will be more effective if education . . . personnel are freed from overly prescriptive regulations and administrative burdens which are not neces- sary for fiscal accountability and make no contribution to the education program.[29]

Like Title I of the ESEA, Chapter I requires local school systems to (1) use federal aid as a supplement to state and local resources, (2) ensure comparable services to recipient and nonrecipient attend- ance centers, (3) maintain fiscal effort and keep records for audits and program evaluation, (4) consult with parents and teachers about the design and implementation of programs, and (5) provide services to private school students. Yet Chapter I gives school systems substan- tially greater leeway in administration and in interpreting legislative intent than Title I. There are fewer reporting requirements, compara- bility is defined less stringently, and schools are given greater flexibil- ity in selecting student beneficiaries.

A second and even greater departure in the reconciliation act from the status quo was the consolidation of grants authorized under Chapter II of the ECIA. Although it did not include as many programs as the administration had requested, it consolidated some twenty- nine categorical grants into one simplified program. The programs affected included parts or all of Titles II, III, IV, V, VI, and IX of the ESEA; the Alcohol and Drug Abuse Education Act; the Teacher Corps Program of the Higher Education Act; Follow Through; training of precollege science teachers by the National Science Foundation; and the Career Education Incentive Act.

The provisions of Chapter II are grouped into three program subchapters (basic skills development, educational improvement and support services, and special projects) and two general subchapters (the secretary of education's discretionary fund and general provisions). The SEAs and LEAs are to determine specific educational needs and priorities among the program subchapters. States must design a formula for distributing Chapter II funds with the assistance of an advisory committee appointed by the governor.

Chapter II requires both states and school districts to submit applications for funds for a period not to exceed three years. The law includes a bypass procedure to ensure that private school students are served.[30] In addition, the application requirements include assurances of systematic consultation with parents, teachers, and school administrators about program planning and implementation and maintenance of the records required for audits and program evaluation. Finally, plans must describe the allocation of funds among the three program subchapters. Despite this last provision, states and local education agencies have almost complete discretion in deciding how to spend the funds.

Legislative change, however, did not end with the ECIA. The reconciliation act also revised several other programs that Reagan had sought to modify, including child nutrition, CETA, impact aid, and vocational education. Funding for child nutrition programs was reduced, chiefly by lowering income eligibility limits for students receiving federally subsidized meals. Public service jobs authorized by CETA (Titles II-D and VI) were eliminated, and funding for several other CETA programs, such as youth training, was reduced. Impact aid funding for part B students (children whose parents either live or work on federal property, but not both) was eliminated after fiscal year 1984, and appropriations for the program were reduced from $682 million in fiscal year 1981 to $456 million in fiscal year 1982. Finally, funding for the Vocational Education Act was reduced, but not nearly as much as the administration had urged.[31]

Higher Education Proposals. The administration's higher education proposals were less dramatic than those in elementary/secondary education, in part because they did not urge a fundamental restructuring of the programs. In addition, the most important proposals—to tighten eligibility for guaranteed student loans—were merely adopted from the Carter administration's budget.

Eligibility changes were also requested for the Pell grants. The administration proposed to direct Pell grants more specifically to the "truly needy," to increase the amount of discretionary income that families must contribute to meeting college costs, and to require a

$750 self-help contribution from a student before he or she could receive a Pell award.

Changes were also proposed in noneducation programs with higher education provisions. Social security benefits to college students whose parents received social security were to be eliminated. This program, begun in 1965 at a cost of $165 million, was projected to cost $2.0 billion in 1981, making it the third largest student assistance program. The administration argued that benefits under the program often went to middle- and upper-income students because eligibility was not tied to financial need. Moreover, since the size of the student's award was tied to the parent's social security entitlement, the higher the parent's earnings, the higher the student's benefit. Phasing out of this program had been encouraged, unsuccessfully, by Presidents Carter and Ford.

Higher Education Reconciliation Results. The Omnibus Budget Reconciliation Act of 1981 contained one of the administration's two main proposals for curbing the GSL program. As the president urged, Congress established a needs test, limiting GSL loans to the amounts needed to cover educational costs. But the test applied only to students from families with incomes over $30,000 a year, not to all borrowers as the administration had wanted. The suggestion to eliminate the in-school interest subsidy had little support and was not seriously considered. But Congress did impose a 5 percent origination fee on each new guaranteed loan, so that a student needing a $2,000 loan would have to pay a fee of $100.[32]

Congress also imposed appropriations limits on the Pell grant program for the first time. The Department of Education was authorized to modify Pell grant regulations so that the appropriations ceiling would not be exceeded. This is an important change, because Pell grants had been an entitlement not subject to appropriations battles. In addition, the act set authorization levels for the campus-based student aid programs (college work-study, supplemental educational opportunity grants, and national direct student loans) at their fiscal year 1980 levels for the next three years, effectively foreclosing growth in them through 1984.

Finally, social security benefits for students were eliminated. No new recipients were to be added after June 1982. For students still in the program, benefits would be reduced by 25 percent annually until all benefits end in fiscal year 1985.

Further 1982 Budget Reductions. On September 24, 1981, President Reagan proposed additional budget cuts to keep the federal deficit from growing. (Unbelievable as it seems now, the administration then projected a $22.9 billion deficit in fiscal year 1983 and a balanced budget in fiscal year 1984.) The centerpiece of the proposal was a 12 percent across-the-board cut in discretionary nondefense programs. The administration also proposed to reform several entitlement programs and to revise the tax code to "eliminate abuse . . . and enhance tax collections."[33] One change was the elimination of the in-school interest subsidy from the guaranteed student loan program.

Congress rejected the changes in the guaranteed student loan program and, in November 1981, agreed to reduce domestic discretionary programs by 2 percent. The White House found Congress's cuts insufficient, and the president vetoed the measure. Eventually Congress and the White House agreed on a continuing resolution that reduced domestic spending by nearly $4 billion, largely by imposing a 4 percent across-the-board reduction on most domestic programs, including education.[34]

Nearly a year later Congress overturned this reduction when it enacted a supplemental appropriation. This measure, passed over President Reagan's veto, rejected the administration's request for fiscal year 1982 rescissions and added substantial funds for education programs, especially student assistance.[35]

The 1983 Budget

For fiscal year 1983 the administration recommended $10.0 billion in appropriations, $3.0 billion less than it originally proposed in 1982. The most visible proposal in the 1983 budget was the request to abolish the Department of Education, create a much smaller Foundation for Educational Assistance, and distribute many education programs to other cabinet agencies. The administration also called for reductions in appropriations for almost all education programs. Among elementary/secondary programs, budget cuts were proposed for Chapter I (a reduction of $870 million from the March 1981 request for the fiscal year 1982 budget), Chapter II ($130 million), Indian education ($30 million), impact aid ($40 million), education of the handicapped ($45 million), and vocational and adult education ($219 million).

Substantial changes were recommended for postsecondary education. The administration proposed to cut Pell grants from $2.4 billion to $1.4 billion. The maximum award was to be reduced from $1,800 to $1,600, a reduction of 12 percent at a time when college costs were climbing 10 to 15 percent annually. The administration proposed to eliminate supplemental grants, national direct student loans, and state student incentive grants and requested an 18 percent funding cut in the college work-study program.

Modifications were again proposed to cut federal outlays for the guaranteed student loan program. The 1983 version called for increasing the origination fee from 5 to 10 percent, applying needs analysis to all GSL borrowers (rather than just those with family incomes above $30,000), and eliminating graduate and professional students from the program. The administration suggested that graduate students borrow under the auxiliary loans to assist students program (with the infelicitous acronym ALAS), which carried a 12 percent interest rate and did not offer the in-school interest subsidy. It justified the change by asserting that graduate and professional students frequently have high earnings prospects and would have little difficulty repaying the higher debts. Unfortunately, in most states the ALAS program, which had been authorized by the Omnibus Budget Reconciliation Act of 1981, had not yet begun to lend money to graduate or professional students. The suggestion to eliminate these students from the GSL, therefore, threatened to leave many without a source of education loans.

In contrast to the 1982 budget proposals, the administration's 1983 budget met with very little success. The proposal to abolish the Department of Education was not seriously considered. The suggestions for the GSL program were met with an outcry from college and university groups and received little attention on Capitol Hill. Eventually Congress enacted a continuing resolution for fiscal year 1983 that set spending for student aid programs at a level almost identical with the fiscal year 1982 appropriations. A similar funding level was set for the major elementary and secondary school programs.

The 1984 Budget

In 1984 the administration continued its efforts to reduce the federal presence in education. As in previous budgets, the administration proposed to reduce funding for education, recommending total appropriations of $13.1 billion, substantially below the 1983 appropriations of $15.4 billion.

Among specific programs, the administration urged small reductions in ECIA Chapters I and II, special education, rehabilitation, and educational research and statistics. Major cuts were suggested for Indian education, impact aid, vocational and adult education, and bilingual education. The 1984 budget also previewed five proposals to be submitted later: tuition tax credits, elementary and secondary education vouchers, mathematics and science block grants, education savings accounts, and the removal of education from cabinet status.

Some major changes in federal policy were suggested. In student aid, for example, the administration proposed to spend the same amount on Pell grants and campus-based student aid as in 1983 ($3.6 billion) but called for major changes in the way it was distributed. Pell grants would be replaced by a new program of self-help grants. Funding for the program would increase from $2.4 billion (1983 appropriation) to $2.7 billion. College work-study funds were to be boosted to $850 million (an increase of 44 percent). At the same time, however, the administration called for eliminating supplemental grants, state incentive grants, and new contributions to national direct student loans.

The guaranteed student loan program was again on the fiscal chopping block. Under the 1984 proposals, the origination fee for graduate and professional students would increase from 5 percent to 10 percent, and all students would be required to prove financial need before receiving loans.

The administration also proposed a program of education savings accounts, allowing families with incomes up to $40,000 to save $1,000 annually for future college costs. Unlike individual retirement accounts (which were the conceptual model for the program), there would be no tax deduction for the money saved each year. But interest and dividends earned by the accounts would not be taxed.[36]

The 1984 budget also called for the creation of a tuition tax credit for parents with children in private, nonprofit elementary and secondary schools. Tax credits had, of course, been a subject of debate and controversy for many years. Congress had come close to approving them on several occasions, and the 1980 Republican platform had featured them prominently. Strictly speaking, Reagan's proposal in the 1984 budget was not new: The idea had initially been advanced in the summer of 1982.

Under the plan parents would receive a tax credit for up to 50 percent of tuition costs paid to private, nonprofit elementary and secondary schools. The maximum credit would be $100 per child in 1983, rising to $300 in 1985 and beyond. A full credit would go to families with adjusted incomes of $40,000 or less. The credit would be reduced for families with incomes between $40,000 and $60,000. The administration estimated that 2.4 million families would use the credit and that the cost (lost tax revenue) would be $245 million in 1984 and $753 million in 1986.[37]

Finally, the 1984 budget also suggested a modest block grant to enable states to increase the number of mathematics and science teachers and to honor outstanding teachers.

In October 1983 Congress enacted the fiscal year 1984 budget for the Departments of Labor, Health and Human Services, and Education. This marked the first time since fiscal year 1979 that Congress had managed to pass an appropriation bill for these agencies. In general, the 1984 budget maintained or slightly increased funding in nominal dollars for the major education programs. The one exception was the guaranteed student loan program, where lower interest rates and substantial carry-over of fiscal year 1983 funds—not policy changes—allowed a reduction in federal appropriations.

The administration's new initiatives generally received scant attention. The student aid proposals, for example, went nowhere on Capitol Hill. Representative John Erlenborn (Republican, Illinois) agreed to introduce the bills "as a courtesy," and the administration was unable to find a Senate sponsor. The education savings account was greeted with some interest, but most educators and policy makers believed the proposed benefits did not provide a sufficient stimulus to saving. More generous bills also received little attention, however, suggesting that interest in the idea was, at best, lukewarm. There was almost no support for the proposed GSL revisions.

Tuition tax credits did attract attention and, eventually, were decisively rejected. As in previous discussions, opponents charged that tax credits would be inefficient and regressive and would weaken the public schools, while supporters argued that tax credits would enhance education choice and improve education quality. On November 16 the Senate tabled the administration-backed bill on a 59–38 vote.[38] The lopsided vote in the Republican-controlled Senate, coupled with inaction on the measure in the House of Representatives, seems likely to bury the program for the foreseeable future.

One successful initiative was the suggestion of a mathematics-science block grant. The proposal itself generated little interest, but it was seen as evidence that the president would sign a relatively small bill aimed at mathematics and science education.

The 1985 Request

The Reagan administration's fiscal year 1985 budget request of $15.5 billion constitutes a sharp break from previous submissions. In 1981 the administration requested $13.5 billion; in 1982, $13 billion; in 1983, $9.9 billion; and in 1984, $13.1 billion. In each of these years the Congress appropriated substantially more than the administration asked for: $14.7 billion in 1982, $15.4 billion in 1983, and $15.4 billion in 1984.

The level line represented by those appropriation figures is no accident. It reflects a congressional decision to provide level funding of the federal role in education, at least in nominal terms. Acquiescence in level funding, however, means that the real rate of spending decreases as inflation continues. To that extent the Reagan administration can claim that it has been partially successful in cutting education funding. Nevertheless, the press releases issued with the education budget pointed out that the largest education budget in history was being proposed.

Although that is not strictly true—Carter's revised 1981 request asked for $300 million more than Reagan's 1985 request, for example—it is likely that the Congress will enact the Reagan budget, perhaps with additions of its own, producing what would be the largest education budget ever enacted, if not the largest requested. Even so, the 1985 budget continues to slow the rate of growth: In real dollars, it constitutes a decline of about 5 percent from the amount appropriated in 1984.

Moreover, the 1985 request continues the earlier pattern of attempting to cut discretionary programs such as libraries, which remain at zero funding as they have in earlier Reagan budgets. At the same time, however, one significant program change was proposed, a quarter-billion increase in Chapter II. Although this change has no effect on means-tested programs, it constitutes a major shift in administration policy.

Means-tested higher education programs are targeted for significant change as well. The administration again proposed the Pell grant self-help initiative first advanced in the 1984 budget. In addition, the ceiling on Pell grants would be raised from $1,800 to $3,000. Funding for the work-study program would be increased sharply, while funding for the other student aid programs would be sharply cut. Finally, the 1985 budget again proposes to make GSLs subject to a means test for all families. Despite this and several other suggested changes, the cost of the program was estimated to increase rather sharply.

In sum, the 1985 budget represents a significant break with the first three years of administration policy. Because of this, it is tempting to describe the 1985 budget as an election year budget. But it is not clear that such a description is accurate or useful. The education establishment will not be wooed into the Reagan camp by level funding: Their antagonism to Reagan's education policy may be moderated but not transformed into support.

The 1985 budget does not satisfy the far right either. An election year budget for the far right would be one that "keeps the faith" and continues to propose substantial cuts, as a symbol of the administration's commitment to its earlier purposes.

Politically, by seeking the level that Congress has indicated it will support, the 1985 budget means that acrimonious debate will be avoided.

Other Education Initiatives: Regulatory Reform and Excellence

As we have noted, the Reagan administration has advanced several new initiatives designed to modify federal aid to education. Some of these, such as student aid and tax credits, have already been discussed, and others are not relevant to means-tested programs, but two general initiatives merit attention.

Revising excessive federal regulation was one of the Reagan administration's most cherished goals. In education, the administration has made several moves to reduce regulations that are relevant to the federal safety net. The first was taken within two weeks of the president's inauguration. On February 2, 1981, Secretary Terrel Bell withdrew the bilingual education regulations proposed by the Carter administration in August 1980. The regulations—which would have greatly increased the range of services local school districts would be required to provide—were widely criticized by state and local officials and were an easy target for the Reagan administration. Yet, despite repeated promises to the contrary, the administration has never prepared regulations to replace the "informal guidelines" laid out by the U.S. Office of Education in 1974, which continue to guide federal policy.

The administration also proposed to revise the complex regulations that govern the Education of All Handicapped Children Act. This measure is without question the most detailed and prescriptive federal education statute, and federal funding covers only a small portion of the total costs. In August 1982 the administration published regulatory changes designed to "reduce paperwork and regulatory detail." [39] The changes were greeted with a storm of criticism, and in November 1982 Secretary Bell withdrew some of the most controversial provisions. [40] A year later the department announced that it had abandoned any effort to modify the regulations. [41]

Yet another major regulatory initiative was the attempt to abolish the longstanding Internal Revenue Service guidelines barring discriminatory private schools from obtaining or retaining tax-exempt status. The administration's effort—which was regarded as both a violation of federal law and bad public policy—was met with widespread disbelief and anger. After much political controversy the proposal was abandoned, but the Reagan administration had managed to embarrass itself through the regulatory process.

134

Each of these regulatory areas—bilingual education, special education, and private schools—dealt with issues where federal efforts have been deemed vital to protect the interests of disadvantaged citizens. None of the administration's proposals can be regarded as either successful or consistent with its stated intention of maintaining a safety net for those in need. Moreover, two of them—special education and private schools—are undoubtedly the administration's greatest embarrassments in education policy.

By contrast, perhaps the administration's greatest success in education has been calling attention to the sad state of the nation's schools. In August 1981, in an event that attracted little notice, Secretary Bell appointed the National Commission on Excellence in Education and instructed it to examine educational issues at the elementary, secondary, and postsecondary levels, paying special attention to high-school-age youth.

Eighteen months later, in April 1983, the commission released its findings. The report took the form of an open letter to the American people. Its lofty rhetoric gave the news media a field day. The commission warned:

> The educational foundations of our society are presently being eroded by a rising tide of mediocrity that threatens our very future as a Nation and a people. What was unimaginable a generation ago has begun to occur—others are matching and surpassing our educational attainments.
>
> If an unfriendly foreign power had attempted to impose on America the mediocre educational performance that exists today, we might well have viewed it as an act of war. As it stands, we have allowed this to happen to ourselves. . . . We have, in effect, been committing an act of unthinking, unilateral educational disarmament.[42]

The report's primary criticism centered on the decline of the schools, and it urged a strengthening of academic requirements. The commission also made several recommendations designed to make teaching a "more rewarding and respected profession."

The report met with widespread acclaim. Policy makers, educators, and the public all found themselves in basic agreement with the commission's findings and recommendations. The report set off a rush to examine specific issues in more detail and to design programs and policies to address the problems. Congressional hearings on the state of education were initiated.

President Reagan praised the report. He told the commission members that he would "continue to work in the months ahead for passage of tuition tax credits, vouchers, educational savings accounts, voluntary school prayer, and abolishing the Department of Education," a promise that some believed was inconsistent with the report. In the weeks that followed, the president made several speeches about education in which he repeatedly suggested that merit pay for teachers was an essential step toward improving educational quality.

A cascade of other studies and reports on education were issued in the summer and fall of 1983.[43] All echoed the theme of the Commission on Excellence in Education: The schools are in trouble and urgently need attention. There is something of an irony here: The problems facing America's schools have been recognized for several years, and many states have taken steps to improve education quality by instituting stiffer graduation requirements, basic skills programs, and minimum competency testing. Yet, despite these efforts, it was the report of the commission on excellence that made education a subject of vigorous national debate and discussion.

Effect of the Reagan Administration's Changes

The effect of the administration's policy changes and budget cuts on state governments, local schools, and postsecondary institutions is not revealed by recapping the budgetary changes of the last three years. Unfortunately, it is not possible to assess this component of the education equation at this time. Most of the changes mandated in 1981 did not take effect until the 1982–1983 school year, and there is scant research evidence available now. The information that is available, however, provides some important clues.[44]

At the elementary/secondary level, the most far-reaching changes have taken place in response to the Education Consolidation and Improvement Act. Chapter I of the ECIA has reduced the administrative problems facing state and local school districts, but budget cuts have also reduced the resources available. Since Chapter I funds go primarily to poor school districts, the decline in support means that supplemental programs to aid low-income and minority youth are most likely to be affected. The administrative burden has also been eased under Chapter II of the ECIA, but the distribution of federal education money has been altered. Initial studies suggest that urban school districts now receive lower federal revenues while small school districts that did not get federal categorical funds previously do so now.

School districts that received substantial amounts of money under the Emergency School Assistance Act (ESAA)—such as Cleveland, St. Louis, Detroit, and Buffalo—have been especially hard hit by the elimination of funds for this program. Indeed, there is some congressional interest in reestablishing a program to help school districts desegregate their classrooms. Reductions in impact aid have had a serious effect on a small number of school districts—such as Yorktown, Virginia, and West Point, New York—that were heavily dependent on the program.

It is difficult to determine how individual districts are responding to the Chapter I and Chapter II programs, but some generalizations are possible. Some districts apparently fear that federal auditors will descend and examine Chapter I spending under the same criteria that governed Title I and have thus relied on the more stringent Title I regulations in designing programs.

Similarly, a fear that the administration planned to eliminate Chapter II through the budget process left some school districts hesitant to launch programs that they might have been forced to terminate later. As a result, many school districts initially spent these funds on purchases (such as microcomputers) that would not require local resources if federal funds disappear. Given the administration's proposed increase in Chapter II funding in the 1985 budget, districts will modify their spending patterns accordingly.

There is little evidence that states or local school districts have increased their own expenditures specifically to make up for federal budget cuts. Most schools are apparently shifting resources, if possible, or simply doing less in these program areas. Some states have recently moved to increase spending on education, but largely in response to perceptions of diminished education quality and not to federal reductions. California, Mississippi, Tennessee, Arkansas, Florida, and Pennsylvania have enacted far-reaching statutory changes or are seriously considering doing so. But there are limits to what states can do with existing revenue sources, and changes requiring large infusions of new money will be difficult to design and enact.

There is little doubt that the number of postsecondary students receiving federally sponsored student aid has fallen. That was, after all, the purpose of the budget cuts. It is certain that the income ceilings on the Pell grants and GSLs have reduced the number of middle-income beneficiaries. There is also some evidence that participation by low-income students in higher education has been affected. The National Association of Independent Colleges and Universities, for example, found a dramatic decline in the number and proportion of low-income students attending private colleges and universities between 1978–1979 and 1981–1982, a decline it attributes to increasing college costs and decreasing federal aid. Similarly, a study for the National Association of State Universities and Land Grant Colleges found reduced enrollment at historically black colleges and attributed it to reductions in federal aid to students.

Despite their importance, these findings must be regarded as preliminary. More extensive studies will continue to shed light on the effects of the programmatic and budgetary changes.

Assessing the Reagan Record

Judging the Reagan administration's education efforts is only slightly less complicated than describing what it has attempted to do. The administration has moved on many fronts, making simple judgments impossible. Moreover, the assessment of various events depends in part on the perspective of the analyst. Despite these difficulties, it is important to evaluate whether it has achieved what it set out to accomplish.

At one level, that of budget policy, it is easy to measure what the administration has accomplished. President Reagan made no secret of his wish to reduce federal domestic spending by eliminating some programs and slowing the growth of others. In education, the administration devoted considerable effort to reducing expenditures.

A review of the budget history between 1980 and 1984 suggests that the administration has indeed managed to hold federal education spending relatively constant. In current dollars the total federal education appropriations moved from $14.1 billion in fiscal 1980 to $14.7 billion in 1982 and $15.4 billion in 1984, an increase of 9 percent (see table 6–1).

But these aggregate numbers tell only part of the story. A substantial portion of federal education spending is devoted to the relatively uncontrollable costs of the guaranteed student loan program. The GSL is an entitlement, and the appropriations needed to fund the program depend on a number of fluctuating factors, including interest rates, the number of participants, and the costs of postsecondary education. Because it is an entitlement, anyone who is eligible has a right to participate. Thus the program is not subject to annual appropriations controls.

As we have noted, GSL costs grew rapidly in the late 1970s and early 1980s. Table 6–2 illustrates this growth and its effect on the entire Department of Education budget. Between 1980 and 1983, GSL appropriations increased by nearly 100 percent, before falling off in 1984. This increase had a major effect on total spending for the department. The major postsecondary education programs showed a 23 percent appropriations increase from 1980 to 1984, a jump almost entirely attributable to GSL costs. By contrast, the major elementary and secondary programs showed virtually no change between 1980 and 1984. Total spending for the Department of Education grew by 8.9 percent over this period; but when GSL spending is eliminated, the increase was a very moderate 4.9 percent.

138

In real terms, federal education spending is lower (in every category except GSL) than it was in 1980. The real (after-inflation) drop in elementary/secondary programs was 20.6 percent. For postsecondary programs, the decline was a moderate 3.2 percent. The change in postsecondary programs includes, obviously, the growth in the GSL program. If this program were excluded or if the elimination of social security benefits for college students were included, federal aid would show a sharp decline.

When federal education spending is measured without the GSL program, it shows a decline of 17.7 percent. When the GSL program is included, total appropriations for the Department of Education show a drop of 14.5 percent over the four-year period.

Yet in any presidency the record must reflect a more comprehensive list of successes and failures than budget policy alone. Perhaps the clearest success of the Reagan administration is not generally seen as a part of education policy but is in an area in which the administration asserted it would make a major difference: reducing inflation. When Secretary Bell came into office, he repeatedly cited reducing inflation as the single most important thing the federal government could do to help education. The point was so obvious and so clearly correct that little attention was paid to it. Critics, however, offered another interpretation: that the administration was emphasizing inflation to keep the public's mind off budget cuts.

There was that element in the administration's position, but reducing inflation was genuinely important. The galloping inflation of the late 1970s drove up the cost of everything from pencils to school buildings. At the same time, there is strong circumstantial evidence that high rates of inflation can easily wipe out earlier salary gains, a problem particularly threatening to schoolteachers and university faculty, whose salaries are not especially market sensitive in the short run. In short, by reducing inflation, the administration has helped establish a more stable fiscal climate for state, local, and institutional education.[45]

The reduction in inflation benefits some federal programs directly. The decline in interest rates, for example, has reduced the funds needed for the guaranteed student loan program, and any further decline in interest rates would reduce budget outlays.

Among specific education issues, the successes are less easily identifiable. The administration has met part of its objective of reducing the education budget, despite the refusal of Congress to cut it as sharply as proposed. As table 6–2 shows, between 1980 and 1984 the federal education budget (excluding the GSL program) increased by less than 5 percent. In real (after-inflation) dollars, it fell by 17.7 percent.

TABLE 6-1

MAJOR BUDGET REQUESTS AND FINAL APPROPRIATIONS, U.S. DEPARTMENT OF EDUCATION, FISCAL YEARS 1980–1985
(thousands of dollars)

	1980 Appropriation	Carter request (Jan. 1980)	FY 1981 Reagan request (March 1981)	FY 1981 Appropriation
Elementary/secondary programs				
ECIA Chapter I	3,215,593	3,514,772	2,636,028	3,104,317
ECIA Chapter II	742,896[a]	632,258[a]	491,977	523,485[a]
Impact aid	755,000	567,000	648,500	681,750
Indian education	75,900	81,782	81,680	81,680
Handicapped education	1,049,025	1,102,050	834,112	1,025,231
Rehabilitation services	932,620	965,875	943,552	958,749
Vocational and adult education	901,841	899,241	674,430	781,639
Libraries	79,448	86,655	86,665	84,405
Bilingual education	191,463	189,089	134,822	161,427
Postsecondary programs				
Pell grants	2,157,328	2,970,000	2,820,000	2,604,000
Supplemental grants	370,000	370,000	370,000	370,000
Work-study	550,000	555,000	555,000	555,000
Direct loans (all parts)	300,800	200,800	200,800	200,800
State incentive grants	76,750	76,750	76,750	76,750
Guaranteed student loans	1,609,344	2,233,751	1,847,026	2,535,470
Other programs				
Special institutions[d]	191,932	208,977	208,977	208,977
Research and statistics[e]	84,061	88,997	84,061	74,561
Other	838,546	834,021	775,238	779,502
Total	14,122,547	15,577,018	13,469,618	14,807,743

	FY 1982			
	Carter request (Jan. 1981)	Reagan request (March 1981)	Reagan request (Sept. 1981)	Appropriation
Elementary/secondary programs				
ECIA Chapter I	3,830,272	2,811,818	2,474,400	3,033,969
ECIA Chapter II	684,616[a]	563,366	518,643	470,941
Impact aid	326,000	326,000	286,880	456,200
Indian education	101,816	81,096	71,364	77,852
Handicapped education	1,215,235	890,350	783,508	1,068,580
Rehabilitation services	1,010,716	724,406	861,000	952,171
Vocational and adult education	901,241	719,393	633,925	742,186
Libraries	92,988	66,042	58,117	80,080
Bilingual education	209,000	143,810	126,553	138,058
Postsecondary programs				
Pell grants	2,752,000	2,486,000	2,187,680	2,419,040
Supplemental grants	400,000	370,000	325,600	355,400
Work-study	555,000	555,000	484,000	528,000
Direct loans (all parts)	311,000	311,000	273,680	193,360
State incentive grants	76,750	76,750	67,540	73,680
Guaranteed student loans	2,345,576	1,773,846	2,409,669	3,073,846
Other programs				
Special institutions[d]	253,137	253,137	228,424	228,500
Research and statistics[e]	97,396	70,947	62,433	61,979
Other	1,806,459	780,191	672,478	775,807
Total	16,969,202	13,003,152	12,525,894	14,729,649

(Table continues)

TABLE 6-1 (continued)

MAJOR BUDGET REQUESTS AND FINAL APPROPRIATIONS, U.S. DEPARTMENT OF EDUCATION, FISCAL YEARS 1980-1985
(thousands of dollars)

	FY 1983		FY 1984		FY 1985
	Reagan request (Feb. 1982)	Appropriation	Reagan request (Feb. 1983)	Appropriation	Reagan request (Feb. 1984)
Elementary/secondary programs					
ECIA Chapter I	1,942,000	3,200,394	3,013,969	3,480,000	3,480,000
ECIA Chapter II	433,000	479,420	478,879	479,420	729,000
Impact aid	286,880	540,200	455,000	585,000	496,630
Indian education	51,119	69,185	1,243	68,780	68,780
Handicapped education	845,668	1,119,402	1,110,252	1,239,445	1,214,495
Rehabilitation services	650,000	1,045,347	1,031,727	1,121,400	1,091,660
Vocational and adult education	500,000[b]	823,661	500,000[b]	838,475	838,475
Libraries	0	130,320	0	86,880	0
Bilingual education	94,534	138,057	94,534	139,365	139,200

Postsecondary programs					
Pell grants	1,400,000	2,419,040	2,663,800[c]	2,800,000	2,800,000
Supplemental grants	0	355,400	0	375,000	0
Work-study	397,500	590,000	850,000	555,000	850,000
Direct loans (all parts)	2,500	193,360	4,000	180,860	4,000
State incentive grants	0	60,000	0	76,000	0
Guaranteed student loans	2,484,631	3,100,500	2,047,100	2,256,500	2,840,677
Other programs					
Special institutions[d]	228,421	228,500	248,810	232,200	241,465
Research and statistics[e]	63,392	64,203	56,978	56,978	62,978
Other	570,893	865,297	571,147	808,177	627,589
Total	9,950,538	15,422,286	13,127,439	15,379,480	15,484,949

NOTE: 1984 appropriation includes PL 98–139 and 1984 second continuing resolution.
a. Antecedent programs.
b. Proposed consolidations.
c. Proposed self-help program.
d. Includes federal support for American Printing House for the Blind, National Technical Institute for the Deaf, Gallaudet College, and Howard University.
e. Includes the National Institute of Education and the National Center for Education Statistics.
SOURCE: U.S. Department of Education, budget documents, selected years.

TABLE 6-2

Change in Federal Education Appropriations, Fiscal Years 1980–1984
(thousands of dollars)

	1980	1981	1982	1983	1984
Major elementary/secondary programs[a]					
Appropriations					
Current dollars	7,943,786	7,402,683	7,020,037	7,545,986	8,038,765
Constant (1980) dollars	—	6,766,621	6,051,756	6,220,928	6,309,863
Increase (decrease) since 1980 (%)					
Current dollars	—	(6.8)	(11.6)	(5.0)	1.2
Constant (1980) dollars[b]	—	(14.8)	(23.8)	(21.7)	(20.6)
Major postsecondary programs[c]					
Appropriations					
Current dollars	5,064,222	6,342,020	6,643,326	6,718,300	6,243,360
Constant (1980) dollars	—	5,797,093	5,727,005	5,538,582	4,900,597
Increase (decrease) since 1980 (%)					
Current dollars	—	25.2	31.2	32.7	23.3
Constant (1980) dollars	—	14.5	13.1	9.4	(3.2)
Other education programs					
Appropriations					
Current dollars	1,114,539	1,063,040	1,066,286	1,158,000	1,097,355
Constant (1980) dollars	—	971,700	919,212	954,658	861,346
Increase (decrease) since 1980 (%)					
Current dollars	—	(4.6)	(4.3)	3.9	(1.5)
Constant (1980) dollars	—	(12.8)	(17.5)	(14.3)	(22.7)

Total federal spending[d]					
Appropriations					
Current dollars	14,122,547	14,807,743	14,729,649	15,422,286	15,379,480
Constant (1980) dollars	—	13,535,414	12,697,973	12,714,168	12,071,806
Increase (decrease) since 1980 (%)					
Current dollars	—	4.9	4.3	9.2	8.9
Constant (1980) dollars	—	(4.2)	(10.1)	(10.0)	(14.5)
Guaranteed student loans					
Appropriations					
Current dollars	1,609,344	2,535,470	3,073,846	3,100,500	2,256,500
Constant (1980) dollars	—	2,317,614	2,649,867	2,556,059	1,771,193
Increase (decrease) since 1980 (%)					
Current dollars	—	57.5	91.0	92.7	40.2
Constant (1980) dollars	—	44.0	64.7	58.8	10.1
Total federal spending less GSL[e]					
Appropriations					
Current dollars	12,513,203	12,272,273	11,655,803	12,321,786	13,122,980
Constant (1980) dollars	—	11,217,800	10,048,106	10,158,109	10,300,613
Increase (decrease) since 1980 (%)					
Current dollars	—	(1.9)	(6.9)	(1.5)	4.9
Constant (1980) dollars	—	(10.4)	(19.7)	(18.8)	(17.7)

a. Includes ECIA Chapter I, ECIA Chapter II, impact aid, Indian education, handicapped education, rehabilitation services, vocational and adult education, libraries, and bilingual education. Appropriations for specific programs found in table 6–1.
b. Real change measured by changes in GNP deflator, fourth quarter to fourth quarter. See Office of Management and Budget, midsession review of the budget.
c. Includes Pell grants, supplemental grants, work-study, direct loans, state incentive grants, and guaranteed student loans.
d. Includes all Department of Education appropriations.
e. Includes all Department of Education spending less appropriations for guaranteed student loans.

SOURCE: Authors, based on data in table 6–1.

The administration can also claim victory in the creation of the Chapter II block grant and the reduction of regulatory provisions governing Chapter I. In neither case was Congress willing to go as far as the administration proposed, but the administration's efforts were the impetus for a significant change in public policy.

Thus the administration has been successful in its quest to give more flexibility to states and local school districts. There is no question that administrative requirements placed on states and local schools have been reduced through ECIA Chapters I and II, but the effect clearly is that the states pay for discretion. Those programs with the most flexibility—Chapter II, vocational education, impact aid—have been hit hardest by budget cuts. Interestingly, it is the big means-tested programs—Title I (now Chapter I), Pell grants, and guaranteed student loans—that enjoy the most vigorous congressional support and that appear to be most resistant to the administration's efforts to change.

Some moderate change has also occurred in the direction of federal aid to education. By reducing or eliminating the regulatory requirements that formerly governed Title I and by creating the Chapter II block grant, the administration has moved the federal government one step closer to general aid to education. The outcome is ironic, because, as we suggested earlier, for many years the strongest support for general aid has come from the National Education Association (NEA). The groundwork is well laid if at some time the NEA finds a friend in the White House.

Finally, as noted earlier, the administration can clearly call the Commission on Excellence in Education a major success. Its report has forced the American public to take a more serious look at the education system than any other event in recent memory.

Yet, just as there are some successes, there are also failures. Clearly the federal deficit is one. Just as reducing inflation has helped education, the huge federal deficit has hurt it. The deficit almost certainly cost the Reagan administration favorable congressional action on tuition tax credits. The Democratic Senate in 1978 gave more support to tuition tax credits than the Republican Senate in 1982, even though President Carter opposed them and President Reagan supported them. The budgetary effect of the proposal clearly weighed heavily on the minds of several senators who voted against its passage.

More specifically, there are a number of areas where the Reagan administration sought significant changes and failed to achieve them. Regulatory reform, for example, has proved elusive. Block grant proposals in vocational and adult education and in special education were not seriously considered. The proposal to restructure student aid was largely ignored. The promised constitutional amendment to permit school prayer was rejected by the Senate. Tuition tax credits suffered an embarrassing defeat. And, perhaps most conspicuous, the Department of Education still stands.

What the administration achieved was accomplished in the first six months of the term, and there has been little movement since. Many of its most important goals—tax credits, school prayer, regulatory reform, abolishing the department—are increasingly unlikely. By any scorecard, it has lost more battles than it has won.

Yet merely listing accomplishments and shortcomings is not completely fair. No administration can achieve all it proposes. To a large extent, the secret of political success (and historical recognition) is the ability to develop a small number of ideas and bring them to fruition. President Reagan has certainly done that with tax and expenditure policy. He has not done it with education. His administration's success so far can best be characterized as a triumph of "less of the same," a consequence of budget policy ("cut, squeeze, trim"), not of education initiatives. The education policies it pursued often went in different directions. Moreover, it missed important opportunities to restructure or rationalize the federal presence in education.

The most important was the opportunity to design programs to strengthen the education of poor and minority youngsters, precisely the population most in need of help and the population to which the Republican party needs to reach out. Particularly with accusations that the administration takes from the poor and gives to the rich, a strategy to help the poor and minorities was desirable. That had been the focus of the federal education strategy for two decades, and it would have been to the administration's credit and advantage to have forged a Republican strategy for that population.

Tuition tax credits were not such a strategy (even though they were means tested), because most of the poor earn too little to enjoy the benefit of a credit against income taxes. In any case, tuition tax credits could not pass, given the budgetary realities of the administration's other decisions. If the administration wanted to invest time and money in private school issues, it should have focused on the disadvantaged. For about the same price as tuition tax credits (approximately $2 to $4 billion),[46] the administration could have proposed full funding of Title I (now Chapter I); as a condition of supporting full funding, it could have required that the money follow the child, just as Pell grants do in higher education. Using a popular program as the basis for approaching a new constituency (with a program that is philosophically consistent) would at least have raised the debate to the appropriate level.

A conservative approach to education is one that extends the benefits of choice to those who do not currently enjoy it—liberty as well as equity for the poor. The intellectual groundwork has already been well prepared. The research findings (funded in large measure by the federal government when President Carter was in office) are powerful, and even if they do not persuade those opposed to aid to private education, they provide a point of departure for serious discussion.[47] One possible device might have been a program of education vouchers, or entitlements, to help the poor attend either private schools or public schools out of their neighborhood attendance zones. Lip service was paid to the idea in the form of a weakly supported proposal to create a program of Chapter I vouchers; but the idea and ideas like it were not fully developed, nor did the administration do its homework on Capitol Hill.

Part of the reason the administration has been unable to accomplish more of its objectives or identify new targets of opportunity is that it lacks the confidence of the education community. The Reagan administration has done little to conceal its hostility toward a federal role in education, and, not surprisingly, most education interest groups regard its efforts skeptically. Ordinarily the collision between ideology and practical politics produces an implicit understanding that allows the political and budgetary agendas to be recast. In the Reagan administration this had not been the case in the first three years. It showed little willingness to compromise positions and lacked the outside support necessary to turn its policies into reality.

A Summing Up

The conclusion that must be drawn is that although the Reagan administration has had budgetary policies, it never really had an overarching education policy. There were campaign slogans and stump speeches, and there were isolated ideas, but there was no coherent and consistent education policy. Not even within the context of budget policy—which had the virtue of being direct if severe—was there education policy. The sole purpose was to cut the budget. Once the decision to make major cuts in education had been made, it was possible to imagine a set of education policies that would have rationalized the expenditure of whatever money was left. But that did not happen.

Reagan campaigned against the Department of Education, against the federal role, against federal intrusiveness. His attachment to local control was so complete that he was accused of being a romantic; his opposition to the education establishment was so deep that he had no friends among them—no debts to pay, no obligations to honor.

148

That he did not punish them, that he did not pursue his campaign rhetoric with more vigor, is itself a commentary on the real nature of the Reagan administration's interest in education. It was not great. In truth, beyond the battle of the budget the administration cared little—it cared not enough to do much, up or down.

So education under President Reagan—in spite of grand rhetoric to the contrary—changed a little but not much. Today, three and one-half years into the Reagan administration, any mandate for change, or any political opportunity to change, has evaporated. In basic outline the federal role in education looks very much as it did under Presidents Johnson, Nixon, Ford, and Carter. The 1985 education budget exemplifies this: It reflects the Reagan administration's recognition—however reluctant—that a modest federal role in education is here to stay.

Notes

1. It is true that most state school finance systems take into account the relative wealth of local districts, but only cursorily. That was the reason for the spate of school finance lawsuits in the 1960s and 1970s. Legislative redress having escaped school finance reformers, they turned to the courts. California's landmark Serrano v. Priest decision is the best known.

2. The program is now known as Chapter I of the Education Consolidation and Improvement Act (ECIA).

3. In fairness to supporters of these proposals, it should be noted that elimination of denominational and nondenominational prayer in public schools had been a federal constitutional issue; similarly, the principal objection to favorable tax treatment of private school tuition had been constitutional. The recent Supreme Court decision in Mueller v. Allen appears to have finally settled the issue of what type of tax credit program will pass constitutional muster.

4. For a somewhat more detailed review of the history of federal aid to education, see Terry W. Hartle and Richard P. Holland, "The Changing Context of Federal Education Aid," Education and Urban Society, vol. 15, no. 4 (August 1983), pp. 408–31. See also two reports by the Advisory Commission on Intergovernmental Relations, Intergovernmentalizing the Classroom: Federal Involvement in Elementary and Secondary Education, and The Evolution of a Problematic Partnership: The Feds and Higher Education (Washington, D.C.: Advisory Commission on Intergovernmental Relations, 1981).

5. For a comprehensive review of federal aid to vocational education, see U.S. Department of Education, The Vocational Education Study: The Final Report (Washington, D.C., 1981).

6. Public Law 78–346, enacted June 22, 1944.

7. Public Law 815 provided funds for construction and Public Law 874 provided funds for operation of schools in areas affected by federal installations.

8. Public Law 85–864, 72 Stat. 1580, enacted September 2, 1958.

9. The Vocational Education Act is Public Law 88–210, 77 Stat. 403, enacted December 18, 1963. The Higher Education Facilities Act is Public Law 88–204, 77 Stat. 363, enacted December 16, 1963.

10. Public Law 89–10, 79 Stat. 27, enacted April 11, 1965. For an extended discussion of the enactment and implementation of this law, see Stephen K. Bailey and Edith K. Mosher, *ESEA: The Office of Education Administers a Law* (Syracuse, N.Y.: Syracuse University Press, 1969).

11. Public Law 89–329, 79 Stat. 1219, enacted November 8, 1965.

12. The Higher Education Amendments of 1972, Public Law 92–318, 86 Stat. 235, enacted June 23, 1972, are a major landmark in federal education policy. For an extensive discussion of the law, see Thomas Wolanin and Lawrence Gladieux, *Congress and the Colleges* (Lexington, Mass.: D.C. Heath, 1976). See also Chester E. Finn, Jr., *Education and the Presidency* (Lexington, Mass.: D. C. Heath, 1977).

13. See Finn, *Education and the Presidency.*

14. Public Law 94–142, 89 Stat. 773, enacted November 29, 1975.

15. Public Law 94–482, 90 Stat. 2081, enacted October 1, 1976.

16. Public Law 95–566, signed November 1, 1978.

17. Public Law 96–374, signed October 3, 1980.

18. For an analysis of the problems confronting the National Institute of Education, see Chester E. Finn, Jr., "What the NIE Cannot Be," *Phi Delta Kappan*, February 1983, pp. 407–10.

19. The vast expansion in student borrowing after the Middle Income Student Assistance Act should not obscure the fact that the program did exactly what it was designed to do: it provided loans of convenience for families with children in college. That the idea was probably bad public policy and that budget costs quickly spun out of control are clearly important, but the law did what the Carter administration and Congress intended.

20. Twentieth Century Fund, *Making the Grade* (New York: Twentieth Century Fund, 1983), p. 65.

21. Department of Education budget documents.

22. Republican National Convention, *Republican Party Platform*, July 14, 1980, Detroit, Michigan.

23. Head Start is an $800 million program providing education and socialization services to disadvantaged preschool children. Not everyone considers it an education program. Indeed, Head Start is administered by the Department of Health and Human Services, not the Department of Education. For a more complete discussion of changes in Head Start and other social service programs, see Michael F. Gutowski and Jeffrey J. Koshel, "Social Services," in John L. Palmer and Isabel V. Sawhill, eds., *The Reagan Experiment* (Washington, D.C.: Urban Institute Press, 1982), pp. 307–28.

24. Office of Management and Budget, *Budget of the United States of America, 1982* (Washington, D.C., 1982), p. 214.

25. Interest on federal student loans is not charged to students during the period they are in school but is paid by the federal government. Federal payment of this interest is known as the in-school subsidy.

26. Most federal education programs are forward funded; so the budget for

fiscal year 1982 (which would begin on October 1, 1981) contained funds for the 1982–1983 school year. Rescissions in the FY 1981 budget, however, would have reduced funds for the 1981–1982 academic year. The rescissions would have reduced federal education appropriations for fiscal year 1981 by $2.1 billion below the Carter budget request.

27. Material on the president's budget requests for 1982, 1983, and 1984 is drawn primarily from U.S. Office of Management and Budget, *Budget of the United States*, selected years. Other sources include Paul M. Irwin et al., "Impact of Budget Changes in Major Education Programs during the Reagan Administration," Education and Public Welfare Division, Congressional Research Service, Library of Congress, July 19, 1983; Angela Giordano-Evans, "Education: FY 81 and FY 82 Funding Issues," Education and Public Welfare Division, Congressional Research Service, Library of Congress, July 15, 1982; Angela Giordano-Evans, "Education: FY 83 and FY 84 Funding Issues," Education and Public Welfare Division, Congressional Research Service, Library of Congress, November 2, 1983; Angela Giordano-Evans, "Overview and Analysis of the Reagan Administration's Budget Requests for Programs Administered by the Department of Education," Education and Public Welfare Division, Congressional Research Service, Library of Congress, June 24, 1983; American Council on Education, "Student Aid Cuts in the Reagan Administration," Washington, D.C., June 6, 1983 (photocopy); and U.S. Congress, House of Representatives, Committee on Education and Labor, Subcommittee on Postsecondary Education, *Staff Report and Fiscal Year 1984 Budget Analysis of Programs under the Jurisdiction of the Subcommittee on Postsecondary Education*, 98th Congress, 1st session, April 1983.

28. For more detailed summaries of changes enacted in the Omnibus Budget Reconciliation Act of 1981, consult the following sources: K. Forbis Jordan and Paul M. Irwin, "Education Consolidation and Improvement Act of 1981," Education and Public Welfare Division, Congressional Research Service, Library of Congress, August 1981; June O'Neill and Margaret Simms, "Education," in Palmer and Sawhill, *The Reagan Experiment*, pp. 329–60; and David S. Osman, "Summary of Amendments to the Guaranteed Student Loan (GSL) Program under the Omnibus Budget Reconciliation Act of 1981," Education and Public Welfare Division, Congressional Research Service, Library of Congress, September 1981.

29. Education Consolidation and Improvement Act of 1981, Chapter I, sec. 552.

30. Bypass provisions allow the U.S. secretary of education to arrange for direct services to private school students if any state department of education is unable or unwilling to provide them. Bypass provisions have been exercised in Missouri and Virginia, where state constitutional provisions limit the states' ability to serve pupils in private schools.

31. For general information about the provisions of the Omnibus Budget Reconciliation Act, see "Reconciliation Roundup," *Congressional Quarterly Weekly Report*, vol. 39, no. 33 (August 15, 1981), pp. 1461–520; see also *Review: 1981 Session of the Congress*, American Enterprise Institute Legislative Analysis, no. 31 (Washington, D.C., 1983).

32. Osman, "Summary of Amendments to the GSL Program."

33. Dale Tate, "New Reagan Budget Cuts Face Stiff Fight," *Congressional Quarterly Weekly Report*, vol. 39, no. 39 (September 26, 1981), pp. 1819–21.

34. Harrison Donnelly, "Weekend Contest Produces Three-Week Funding Accord; Government Shutdown Ends," *Congressional Quarterly Weekly Report*, vol. 39, no. 48 (November 28, 1981), pp. 2324–27.

35. See American Council on Education, "Student Aid Cuts," p. 3. See also Evans, "Overview and Analysis of Budget Requests."

36. For additional information see U.S. Office of Management and Budget, *Major Themes and Additional Budget Details, Fiscal Year 1984* (Washington, D.C., 1983), pp. 96–97.

37. For more details see ibid., pp. 98–99.

38. The Reagan administration expected the vote to be much closer. Vice President Bush was present on the Senate floor to cast a tie-breaking vote as president of the Senate. Obviously his presence was not necessary. For more information see Tom Mirga, "Senate Defeats Tax-Credit Bill by Twenty-One Votes," *Education Week*, November 23, 1983, p. 1.

39. Proposed Rules: "Assistance to States for Education of Handicapped Children," *Federal Register*, vol. 47, no. 150 (August 4, 1982), pp. 33836–60.

40. Modification of Notice of Proposed Rulemaking: "Assistance to States for Education of Handicapped Children," *Federal Register*, vol. 47, no. 213 (November 3, 1982), pp. 49871–72.

41. Statement reported in *Education Week* interview with Madeline Will, November 15, 1983.

42. National Commission on Excellence in Education, *A Nation at Risk* (Washington, D.C., 1983), p. 5.

43. Other major studies include Twentieth Century Fund, *Making the Grade;* National Science Board Commission on Precollege Education in Mathematics, Science, and Technology, *Educating Americans for the Twenty-first Century* (Washington, D.C.: National Science Foundation, 1983); and Ernest Boyer, *High School* (New York: Harper and Row, 1983).

44. Information about the initial effects of the Reagan administration's budget and policy changes is drawn from a variety of sources. See, for example, American Association of School Administrators, *Impact of Chapter II of ECIA on Local Education Agencies* (Arlington, Va.: AASA, March 1983); American Council on Education, "Student Aid Cuts"; Anne H. Hastings and Ted Bartell, *The Effects of Chapter II Consolidation on the Administration and Paperwork Requirements for Local School Districts* (McLean, Va.: Advanced Technology, June 1983); Irwin et al., "Impact of Budget Changes in Major Education Programs"; Virginia Hodgkinson and Julianne Still Thrift, "Recent Trends in Financial Aid to Students Attending Independent Colleges and Universities" (Washington, D.C.: National Association of Independent Colleges and Universities, August 1982); Richard K. Jung and Ted Bartell, *Fiscal Effects of the Chapter II ECIA Block Grant on the Largest School Districts and Cities* (McLean, Va.: Advanced Technology, May 1983); Michael Knapp et al., *Cumulative Effects of Federal Education Policies on Schools and Districts* (Menlo Park, Calif.: SRI International, 1983); Mary Moore et al., *The Interaction between Federal and Related State Education Programs* (Washington, D.C.: Educational Testing Serv-

ice, 1983); and House of Representatives, Committee on Education and Labor, *Staff Report and Fiscal Year 1984 Budget Analysis.*

45. William H. Wilken, "Teacher Benefits Take Rising Share of School Budgets," *School Cost Management,* vol. 1, no. 14 (October 31, 1983), p. 7.

46. Estimating the cost of a tuition tax credit program is notoriously difficult. Obviously, the amount of the credit and eligibility requirements will affect the cost. There are, however, more fundamental problems. One difficulty is that there is no way to determine how many people would take advantage of such a program. Indeed, a 1982 telephone survey for the Department of Education to assess likely participation found that many parents were unfamiliar with the idea of tax credits for educational purposes. It is thus not possible to say what percentage of families would use tuition tax credits. A second problem is that it is impossible to determine how many people have access to private schools. Even if it were possible to determine the percentage of families that *would* use a tax credit, it is not clear that all of them *could* use it. Any attempt to estimate the budgetary cost, therefore, must be made very carefully. For a more complete discussion of the problems, see School Finance Project, *Private Elementary and Secondary Education* (Washington, D.C.: Department of Education, 1982).

47. See especially James S. Coleman, Thomas Hoffer, and Sally Kilgore, *High School Achievement* (New York: Basic Books, 1982).

7

Employment versus Training in Federal Manpower Programs

Sean Sullivan

The Job Training Partnership Act (JTPA), which went into effect in October 1983, reflects a definite shift in philosophy with respect to federal employment and training policy. The Reagan administration makes no bones about its distaste for make-work jobs programs of the kind described in various exposés of abuses under JTPA's predecessor, the Comprehensive Employment and Training Act (CETA). Although the new act is principally the work of Senator Dan Quayle of Indiana, it has been adopted as the administration's manpower policy, with a clear emphasis on training ("employment" is gone from the title as well as from the program).

Early History

The first important contemporary federal manpower training program was the Manpower Development and Training Act (MDTA) of 1962. Funded initially at $100 million, it was designed to train and retrain workers displaced by technological change. In 1963 funding was added to train the unskilled and those with educational deficiencies. For the next decade MDTA funded both institutional and on-the-job training, with "skills centers" set up for the disadvantaged who could not afford regular institutional training. By 1973 spending had grown to $358 million—not a staggering sum and the smaller part of federal manpower outlays.

What had happened in the meantime was the Johnson administration's declaration of war on poverty with the passage of the Economic Opportunity Act of 1964 (EOA). It created an array of programs to train and employ the disadvantaged, including the Neighborhood Youth Corps for poor teen-agers, the Job Corps for environmentally deprived youths, the Work Experience and Training Program to make welfare recipients self-supporting, and the Community Action Program for poor neighborhoods. By 1967 total funding for these programs exceeded $700 million; the Job Corps was the centerpiece, although it came under increasing criticism for high costs and low benefits and its funding was decreased in succeeding years. Amendments to the legislation in 1967 revamped the Job Corps program, and its performance improved (it improved again after 1969 when the program was moved from the Office of Economic Opportunity to the Labor Department).

These four Johnson administration programs received continued funding into the 1970s with outlays in 1973 totaling $730 million—about the same as in 1967. Amendments to other manpower legislation redirected training toward the handicapped and other disadvantaged groups; in 1965, for example, lower-income people became eligible under the vocational rehabilitation program. By 1973, then, a hodgepodge of programs made up the federal manpower training "system," which the Nixon administration decided to streamline.

The Comprehensive Employment and Training Act

It is sometimes forgotten that CETA was the creation of a Republican administration seeking to rationalize what had become a set of overlapping and uncoordinated employment and training programs into a comprehensive—and comprehensible—system. The Comprehensive Employment and Training Act of 1973 consolidated nine programs into one federal grant-in-aid program. About a third of CETA's initial $1.4 billion went to training-related programs and most of the rest to public service employment and summer jobs for youth, even though the emphasis was meant to be on training the structurally unemployed rather than on employing the cyclically unemployed. Job creation became dominant during the sharp recession of 1974-1975; spending for public service jobs was increased to the point where they accounted for nearly half of CETA's $2.8 billion budget in 1975. And despite the end of the recession in 1976, the Carter administration created 350,000 additional public service jobs in 1977.

Titles II-D and VI of CETA authorized public service employment (PSE) to provide transitional, federally subsidized public service jobs to enable their holders to move into permanent, unsubsidized jobs—generally in the private sector. Title II-D was designed to deal with chronic structural unemployment by giving economically disadvantaged people PSE jobs and related training and job placement services to enable them to move into either unsubsidized employment or other training programs. Title VI was a countercyclical measure to alleviate severe cyclical unemployment through temporary public service jobs for workers who would, presumably, return to private sector jobs when the economy improved. But the cyclical employment aspect of PSE came to dominate the program during the severe recession that began in 1974, shortly after CETA was passed. Even after recovery, income maintenance remained the dominant element of the program, and training the structurally unemployed never assumed the importance intended for it when the act was passed.[1] Given the political ease of doing something visible about high unemployment and the subsequent difficulty of undoing it once it is done because of the constituencies created and served, this may not be surprising. In any event, job creation came to overshadow training under CETA.

The public service employment program was much more visible than the training component of CETA. It was supposed to create new jobs for the economically disadvantaged, but it was criticized for abuses as many cities rehired laid-off municipal workers who could scarcely have qualified as "economically disadvantaged," that is, on welfare or with incomes below the official poverty level. (In 1978 an average of 16 percent of the total municipal workforce was reported to be on the CETA payroll.)[2] Congress reacted to these criticisms by tightening eligibility requirements for PSE participants to focus the program better on the disadvantaged. These changes decreased the size of the eligible population substantially and significantly increased the proportion of disadvantaged participants (table 7-1).

Although the changes retargeted assistance and doubtless reduced the potential for abuse, PSE became an even larger component of CETA; appropriations in 1978 were more than twice those of 1975, while funding for training grew only about 20 percent over the same period. But the program's reputation was permanently tarnished, and it was an easy candidate for elimination when the Reagan administration decided to restructure the federal training system.

TABLE 7-1

Economically Disadvantaged PSE Participants, 1976–1980
(percent)

	1976	1977	1978	1979	1980
Public assistance recipients	13	16	19	20	25
Recipients with incomes below the poverty level	45	60	78	86	93

Source: Laurie Bassi, "CETA—Did It Work?" *Policy Studies Journal*, vol. 12, no. 1 (September 1983), p. 108.

CETA was a huge program, spending about $60 billion over its eleven-year existence. During its peak in 1979 its $10.3 billion appropriation made up 2 percent of total federal spending; more than half of it, or $6.2 billion, went for public service employment. Between PSE and Trade Adjustment Assistance (discussed later), the federal government was spending the lion's share of its training and employment dollars on income maintenance. This provoked much of the criticism of CETA because jobs programs do not have the longer-term payoffs that can come from training. The distinction is between providing temporary employment and enhancing permanent employability. Garth Mangum, in his study of CETA, concluded that programs that help increase employability are superior to those that primarily create jobs.[3] Although the cost-benefit ratios shown in table 7–2 need not be accepted as precise, on-the-job training appears to be the activity with the highest payoff, followed by the Job Corps and classroom training (benefits are generally measured as increased earnings after completion of the program). Work experience had negative results, and no ratio could be calculated for public service employment, which did not generally lead to permanent employment.

TABLE 7–2

ENROLLMENTS AND OUTCOMES OF CETA COMPONENTS,
Fiscal Year 1980

Component	Enrollment (thousands)	Annual Cost per Participant (dollars)	Average Length of Stay (months)	Benefit-Cost Ratio, 1976–1978
Classroom training	750	8,046	5.1	1.14
On-the-job training	181	6,088	4.3	2.18
Public service employment	870	9,030	11.3	NA
Work experience	400	5,311	4.9	negative
Job Corps	95	13,193	6.2	1.39
Summer youth employment	705	743[a]	NA	NA

NA = not applicable.
a. Ten weeks.
SOURCE: Robert Taggart, published in Garth L. Mangum, "CETA as a 'Second Chance' System for Disadvantaged Youth," in Robert E. Taylor, Howard Rosen, and Frank C. Pratzner, eds., *Job Training for Youth* (Columbus, Ohio: National Center for Research in Vocational Education, 1982).

Transition to the New Employment and Training Regime. The Reagan administration won the consent of Congress to do away with the PSE program in 1981, arguing that it had failed to provide skills training or to benefit the long-term unemployed. The Carter administration's request of $9.6 billion for CETA in fiscal 1982 was slashed to $3.5 billion, and funding was eventually cut further to $3.0 billion.

The elimination of public service employment cut some 325,000 people from the CETA rolls and did away with the largest program—in dollars—in the federal employment and training budget, saving $3.7 billion from 1980 budget levels. PSE outlays were 39 percent of total CETA expenditures in 1980. They had dropped from 50 percent of the total in 1979 because of a decline in the numbers served under the Title VI countercyclical program but were slated to rise again in 1981 under the Carter budget proposals.

The Reagan administration in its 1981 budget revisions reduced grants to states and localities by cutting work experience—which was largely a stipend program—in favor of classroom and on-the-job training. In the 1983 budget the administration sought to prohibit stipends altogether and replace CETA with a block grant to the states. Instead, Congress passed the Job Training Partnership Act (JTPA), to become effective at the start of the 1984 fiscal year, and funded CETA at $3.7 billion during its phase-out year. Although the administration did not get its prohibition on stipends, it came close: Stipends are virtually eliminated under JTPA. Grants to states and localities were cut by about $1.0 billion from 1981 to 1982 and another $600 million from 1982 to 1984. The cuts chiefly came from severely restricting the payment of stipends, so that the share of the budget going to grants for training increased from about a third to almost one-half over the five-year period shown in table 7-3.

Provisions of the Job Training Partnership Act

The Job Training Partnership Act allows all the activities that went on under CETA except public service employment while sharply limiting income maintenance payments for wages, allowances, and stipends as well as administrative costs. During CETA's last year 82 percent of Title II funds were spent on wages, stipends, support services, and administration and only 18 percent on training. Under JTPA 70 percent of all training funds must be spent on training. Of the remaining 30 percent, 15 percent is to be used for supportive services to trainees and for any wages and allowances, and the other 15 percent is allocated to administration.

The 70 percent of funds targeted for training includes half the costs of work experience that is linked to training. Work experience, as

TABLE 7–3

OUTLAYS FOR EMPLOYMENT AND TRAINING, Fiscal Years 1980–1984
(millions of dollars)

Activity	1980	1981	1982	1983	1984
Grants to states and localities for training and work experience[a]	3,238	3,381	2,374	2,291	1,784
Dislocated workers[b]	7	8	7	26	230
Job Corps	470	540	570	563	610
Public service employment[c]	3,697	2,399	108	0	0
Summer youth employment[d]	721	769	679	750	647
Work Incentive (WIN) program	395	381	235	289	273
Older workers[e]	235	263	269	274	319
Other national programs	737	603	412	294	312
Total	9,500	8,344	4,654	4,487	4,175

a. For 1980–1983, CETA Titles II-B and C, IV-A, VII; for 1984, JTPA Title II-A.
b. For 1980–1982, Trade Act only; for 1983–1984, Trade Act and JTPA Title III.
c. CETA Titles II-D, VI.
d. For 1984, net of savings realized from establishing a differential minimum wage for summer youth employment; no change in number of youths served.
e. For 1984, outlays are from 1983 authority.
SOURCE: Office of Management and Budget.

distinct from classroom or on-the-job training, means putting people in work environments and supporting them while they learn what it is like to function in a job; it is not training in specific job skills. Also included in the training funds are the full costs of youth "tryout" employment under specific conditions. Still, the definition of "training" under JTPA is much more restrictive than the notions of it that were accepted under CETA.

The half of the nontraining funds that do not go to cover administrative costs may be spent for a variety of supportive services needed to enable those who are eligible to participate in training. These services include transportation, health care, special services and materials for the handicapped, child care, meals, temporary shelter, financial counseling, and other expenses determined to be reasonable. Also to be covered by this 15 percent of funds are the other half of the costs of work experience linked to training, the full cost of work experience that is not linked to training, and all needs-based payments (stipends or allowances) necessary to enable eligible people to participate in training—the necessity of such payments to be determined under local formulas or procedures. Given that stipends consumed nearly half the training funds under CETA, the JTPA limitation constitutes a substantial cutback.

Exceptions to the 15 percent limit must be granted under specified conditions, which include above-average unemployment rates in the service delivery area, disproportionate numbers of people from groups that require exceptional supportive services, costs of necessary child care or transport that exceed specified limits, and substantial numbers of trainees enrolled in training programs for nine months or more. These exceptions were put in the act to encourage greater service to people who could benefit the most from training but who can least afford the extra costs of child care, transport, or long enrollment periods in training programs.

Cutting back stipends raises more questions than eliminating public service jobs. Some fear that lack of stipends will limit the participation of male heads of households and out-of-school youths who are not on welfare in training programs of any duration,[4] while others worry that it will shift the emphasis from the hard-core unemployed toward the recently unemployed.[5] But some people in the training establishment argue that stipends draw people who want the money rather than the training; 70001 Ltd., a leading nonprofit trainer of high school dropouts, pays no stipends. Of course, JTPA provides for limited payment of stipends, and Job Corps enrollees will continue to receive allowances while in training.

Training is the chief activity the Reagan administration wants to support, and it argues that real funding for this purpose will actually increase despite an overall reduction in employment and training budgets. By stressing training over income maintenance and by ending public service employment, the administration estimates that JTPA will provide more training in 1984 than was provided in 1983 during the transitional year under CETA. The block grant request of about $1.8 billion for 1984 will fund one-third more service-years of training than in 1983, according to the Office of Management and Budget. The administration points out that elimination of stipends for classroom trainees enabled the same number of people to be served in 1983 as in 1982 for $360 million less.

Although JTPA wipes out public service jobs, it continues the Summer Youth Employment Program (SYEP), which is not much different except for being much smaller than PSE. Summer jobs have largely provided spending money rather than training for disadvantaged youths. Failing to provide much supervision or direction, they have been accepted even by opponents of make-work programs as a means of keeping these mostly inner-city youths "off the street" (although funding formulas under JTPA will allocate fewer dollars to inner cities than those under CETA). Later, "enriched" versions of SYEP, however, such as the Career Exploration Program operated by the Opportunities Industrialization Centers, have tried to provide career education and counseling, job referral, and placement assistance. These enriched programs showed positive effects on school enrollment and later employment for participants.[6]

Funding for summer youth employment is to be maintained at about the same level in 1984 as in 1983, when it was the same as in 1980 (table 7–3 shows lower numbers for 1984 because of an offset for savings to be realized from a yet unpassed differential minimum wage for youths in this program). Although there were fluctuations in 1981 and 1982, funding for summer jobs for youths has remained fairly constant over the five years from 1980 through 1984. Funds may be used for remedial education, work experience, counseling, and other activities designed either to give employment to those who are eligible or to prepare them for it. It may also be used for supportive services to enable them to participate. SYEP is funded under Title II-B of JTPA separately from the training grants under Title II-A. SYEP funds authorized under part B may be used for wages and supportive services according to local training plan standards without, of course, being subject to the 30 percent limit on nontraining expenditures for regular programs under part A. The 1984 funding will serve about the same number of youths as in 1983.

Programs for Indians and other Native Americans as well as for migrant and seasonal farmworkers are continued under JTPA, and a new program for veterans is added; these are all national programs under Title IV. Funding for Indians and other Native Americans and for migrant and seasonal farmworkers is set by formula in the act as a percentage of Title II-A funds and is a little more than $60 million for each group in 1984. This is less than in 1983 and will fund fewer service-years. The Veterans' Employment Program request is less than $10 million for the first year.

The Job Corps is to continue under JTPA, providing the same number of slots in 1984 as it did in 1983. The $600 million requested for it in 1984 is actually more than was spent in the last year of the Carter administration. The Job Corps pays allowances to enrollees while they undergo training and absorbs the cost of their room and board as well because it is a residential program that keeps trainees an average of six months and provides remedial education and social services as well as vocational skills training. Its resulting high cost brought it under criticism in earlier studies,[7] but in recent years all but its severest critics have acknowledged it as a relative success story within the disappointing overall performance of the federal employment and training system. It has even been shown to have been cost effective,[8] partly because it has brought about a reduction in crime by the youths who have enrolled in it. It is, then, at least a modestly successful combination of training and income maintenance or redistribution for some of the more seriously disadvantaged youths in our society. The Job Corps is a holdover—the only one—from the antipoverty programs of the Johnson administration and predates CETA by a full decade. This makes it the senior member of the revamped training and employment system under JTPA, a distinct national program that has shown considerable staying power.

The renewed emphasis on training under JTPA is shown in its new Title III Dislocated Worker Assistance Program. This program supplants training under the Trade Adjustment Assistance program, which was authorized as part of the 1974 Trade Act. Although TAA was intended to provide job retraining for workers displaced by import competition, it became almost entirely an income maintenance program for large numbers of automobile workers and others who were certified as eligible when they lost their jobs during the 1979–1980 recession. Spending for TAA exceeded $3 billion for 1980 and 1981 combined, but only $9.7 million of that amount was authorized for training.[9] A large-scale income maintenance program for laid-off manufacturing workers who cannot be counted among those for whom the safety net is woven was an easy target for the Reagan administration, and it has been cut back drastically. Equity alone argues against a program that singles out for special treatment workers who have become unemployed for one particular reason. But for congressional support for a program with strong political constituencies, the administration would probably have scrapped TAA entirely.

The 1984 funding request for dislocated workers is $230 million, a ninefold increase over the modest 1983 start-up amount in response to the growing number of structurally unemployed workers created by the severity of the most recent recession. With state matching funds, this will provide an estimated 48,000 service-years of training, job search, and related assistance.

The Reagan administration argues that JTPA not only will provide more real training than CETA with fewer dollars but also will better serve those whose lack of basic skills makes them unemployable, namely, the poor. Together with the new program for dislocated workers, JTPA's training grants are aimed directly at the problem of structural unemployment, which CETA's massive public service jobs program arguably failed in large part to address.

Ninety percent of JTPA funds are reserved for low-income people who are officially designated as "economically disadvantaged." The basic eligibility criteria are essentially unchanged from those of CETA. Participants must either receive or belong to a family that receives cash welfare payments or food stamps or belong to a family whose income is less than 70 percent of the lower living standard designated as the Office of Management and Budget's poverty guideline. Although the basic criteria for determining the economically disadvantaged correspond closely, CETA varied the specific criteria for different kinds of training whereas JTPA applies the same criteria to all local training programs except for the new category of dislocated workers. The abuses under CETA's public service employment program have already been cited—the widespread use of public service jobs to reemploy laid-off municipal workers who were decidedly not the disadvantaged—and before the 1978 amendments its training components were also much less focused on the economically disadvantaged group. After 1978, however, CETA served its intended target group much better, and the classroom and on-the-job training components became more cost-effective methods of improving participants' postprogram earnings. The PSE and work experience programs, however, were not cost-effective methods of doing this, which supports the Reagan administration's position that federal funds are better spent on training than on employment.[10]

A study by the National Commission on Employment Policy found that about 21 percent of CETA Title II–B and C enrollees in 1981 were receiving payments from Aid to Families with Dependent Children (AFDC).[11] Services to people on welfare may increase under JTPA because its performance standards emphasize reduced welfare dependency as a specific goal, giving program operators more credit for serving welfare recipients than for serving other clients. The act also requires that welfare recipients be served in proportion to their share of eligible persons in each service delivery area who are sixteen or older. The intent of this provision is not to impose strict quotas but to attempt to focus the program better on a group that can certainly use more help than it received under CETA.

School dropouts constitute another group of disadvantaged persons that may benefit from JTPA, since it requires that, like welfare recipients, they be served in proportion to their share of eligible persons sixteen or older in each service area. With respect to youths more generally, JTPA requires that at least 40 percent of funds be spent on disadvantaged sixteen- to twenty-one-year-olds. This compares with 48 percent of total CETA funds in 1979, when $4.5 billion was spent on youths, although $1.1 billion of it went for public service employment. While dropouts may be better served because of the specific incentives created for program operators, it is unclear how the target population of youths as a whole will fare. Again, the virtual elimination of stipends means that more of the 40 percent of total funds will go for training.

Up to 10 percent of participants in all regular adult and youth programs under Title II-A may be eligible regardless of income if they have met other barriers to employment. This category includes displaced homemakers, school dropouts, teen-age parents, handicapped persons, older workers, veterans, offenders, alcoholics, addicts, and people with limited English-language ability. At least in principle this does not constitute a significant change, since even under the public service employment program in 1980 fewer than 10 percent of the participants were not economically disadvantaged.

Unemployment Compensation and Training

Unemployment compensation is an important income maintenance device that has been somewhat at odds with the assumed purpose of manpower policy, which is to provide training or placement assistance to the structurally unemployed. CETA and JTPA were designed to serve the disadvantaged. Trade Adjustment Assistance and unemployment insurance were established for the benefit of an entirely different group—workers who have been laid off from jobs that in many cases paid well enough to make them middle-class citizens. Although TAA was at least originally conceived as a training as well as an income maintenance program, even though it never did much training, unemployment insurance has never tried to be anything but an income maintenance program. It has been designed not to support the search for a new job but to maintain the worker awaiting recall to a previous one. In periods of especially severe unemployment, such as the recent recession, unemployment benefits are extended beyond the normal twenty-six weeks, Congress approving thirteen-week extensions at a time. The Reagan administration has not led the charge for extending benefits but has fallen quickly in line whenever prevailing congressional sentiment has favored doing so.

What this administration has tried to do, however, is to change the law to make the unemployment insurance system into something more than purely an income maintenance program. As the law is presently constructed, it threatens laid-off workers who decide to undergo retraining with loss of unemployment benefits—creating an obvious disincentive to do anything more than wait for the benefits to be exhausted before considering enrolling in training. Two proposals to Congress would change this situation. One would allow states to use part of their unemployment insurance tax receipts for training the unemployed and helping them to relocate. The other would entitle unemployed workers who are eligible for supplemental federal benefits to vouchers that would allow employers hiring them to claim a tax credit. Passage of either—certainly of both—of these provisions would mark a significant change in the rationale for unemployment insurance, away from pure income maintenance toward support for the development of employability.

Conclusions

Although the Reagan administration is continuing various special income maintenance programs that were legislated for particular categories of workers, such as lumber workers affected by restrictions on logging in the new Redwoods National Park, there have been big changes in the federal manpower system. With the end of public service employment, the era of jobs programs has passed, at least for now. While some will decry the new regime's insistence that federal dollars be spent on training instead of job creation, others will welcome it and will not mourn the passing of a program that consumed billions of dollars without noticeably denting structural unemployment in the United States. Nevertheless, after the 1978 CETA amendments focused PSE more on the economically disadvantaged, it provided temporary income to large numbers of low-income people even though it did not train them for permanent income gains.

The Trade Adjustment Assistance (TAA) program, which has been virtually scrapped, was a middle-class welfare program that never served the safety net population. There is little that can be said for income redistribution of this kind by anyone but the unions whose members it benefited.

The remaining leg of the income support stool has been shortened, as stipends and allowances paid to those in training programs have been severely restricted if not eliminated. This may have some effect on the ability of certain groups of eligible persons to participate in training, but it is defended on the ground that more dollars should be spent on actual training.

Finally, although the eligibility criteria are essentially the same for JTPA as for CETA, the Reagan administration promises to enforce them more tightly so that the program does a better job of serving those who are economically disadvantaged. The early abuses of PSE will certainly not be repeated, but it remains to be seen whether those who are eligible will actually be better served under JTPA.

An analysis by the Congressional Budget Office of reductions in outlays for fiscal years 1982–1985 for various human resource programs shows larger percentage cuts in employment and training—60 percent—than in any other category. The dollar cuts are larger than in health care (Medicare and Medicaid) by more than a third and even slightly larger than in social security. There will clearly be much less income maintenance and redistribution than before with the major changes noted, and there may be some fraying of the safety net with the end of public service jobs and the limiting of stipends. It remains to be seen whether a stronger emphasis on training will help JTPA's clientele more than reduced income support will hurt it, as the administration argues. And the proposed budget savings may be reduced by increased costs of other federal programs, such as welfare, food stamps, and Medicaid, caused by the elimination of PSE.[12]

Notes

1. Pat Choate and H. William Tanaka, "Special Report on Human Capital and National Economic Development," House Wednesday Group, July 6, 1983.

2. James Bovard, "Busy Doing Nothing: The Story of Government Job Creation," *Policy Review* (Heritage Foundation), Spring 1983.

3. Garth L. Mangum, "CETA as a 'Second Chance' System for Disadvantaged Youth," in Robert E. Taylor, Howard Rosen, and Frank C. Pratzner, eds., *Job Training for Youth* (Columbus, Ohio: National Center for Research in Vocational Education, 1982).

4. Charles Tetro of Training Development Corporation, cited by Harvey Shapiro, *Across the Board* (New York: Conference Board, 1983).

5. Shapiro, *Across the Board*.

6. Andrew Sum, "A Summary of Selected Key Findings from the Youth Knowledge Development Effort under YEDPA," Center for Labor Market Studies, Northeastern University, November 1981.

7. Choate and Tanaka, "Special Report."

8. Mangum, "CETA as a Second Chance."

9. Choate and Tanaka, "Special Report."

10. Laurie J. Bassi, "CETA—Did It Work?" *Policy Studies Journal* (Florida State University), vol. 12, no. 1 (September 1983).

11. Janet W. Johnston, *The Allowances and Stipend Issue in Federally Financed Training Programs* (Washington, D.C.: National Commission on Employment Policy, 1982).

12. Congressional Budget Office, "Effects of Eliminating Public Service Employment," Staff Working Paper, Washington, D.C., June 1981.

PART TWO

Contrasting Views
of Current Policy

8

The Safety Net from the Reagan Administration's Perspective

Kenneth W. Clarkson

Few subjects create more intense feelings or more rigid moral and political posturing than social assistance spending, either in general or for specific programs such as food stamps, Aid to Families with Dependent Children (AFDC), or similar federal programs. This paper is intended to clarify the issues and contribute to more informed discussions of social assistance programs. First the legacy of excessive growth in federal spending on social programs inherited by the current administration is investigated. The need for reform in many of the specific programs in the so-called social safety net is then addressed.[1] Next overall changes in the safety net and related federal programs since 1981 are discussed. Finally some overlooked but positive aspects of individual safety net reforms instituted by the Reagan administration are examined.

Legacy of Excessive Growth in Social Programs

It should come as no surprise to informed students of federal budget policy that the development of a full-scale social insurance system, consisting of retirement income for the elderly, disability protection for most workers, and a comprehensive medical care system for elderly and low-income citizens, accounts for much of the real expansion in government spending over the past two decades. In 1963, before these major social programs were created or enlarged, average federal social insurance benefits for a retired couple were $6,500 in constant 1983 dollars. By 1983 they had risen more than 50 percent in real after-inflation dollars to approximately $10,000 per retired couple. The social welfare contract also financed approximately $1,700 for each Medicaid beneficiary and $2,200 for each Medicare recipient in that year. A total of 54 million elderly and lower-income citizens receive income and medical care protection today, up from 19 million in 1963. In real terms, the social contract rose from 2.7 percent of gross national product (GNP) in 1963 to 6.8 percent in 1981.[2]

169

TABLE 8-1

SHARE OF GNP GOING TO SOCIAL SERVICES, 1970 AND 1981

(percent)

Budget Component	GNP Share 1970	1981	Percentage Change, 1970–1981
Entitlements			
Social contract	4.0	6.8	70
Other[a]	2.0	3.3	65
Subtotal	6.0	10.1	68
Nondefense discretionary	4.1	5.5	34
National defense and security	8.3	5.5	−34
Other			
Net interest	1.5	2.4	60
Remainder	0.3	0.1	−67
Total	20.2	23.6	17

a. Includes military retirement pay.

SOURCE: Office of Management and Budget, Budget of the United States Government, Fiscal Year 1984.

Social contract spending, however, was not solely responsible for this dramatic government growth. Most of the growth in the federal sector as a percentage of GNP between 1963 and 1970 could be traced to gradual programmatic increases in the social contract, but this trend changed in 1970.[3] In addition to a sudden expansion after 1970 of the share of GNP spent for the social contract, which increased 70 percent (from 4.0 percent in 1970 to 6.8 percent in 1981, the final year of the Carter administration), other entitlements also grew rapidly (see table 8-1). In 1970 those other entitlements, such as means-tested programs and federal retirement and disability programs, experienced rapid growth rates similar to those for social contract spending. Their share of GNP, which was about 2.0 percent in 1970, rose to 3.3 percent in 1981. Other nondefense real federal government spending, less directly linked to social spending, also rose during this period, but more slowly. Its share of GNP rose from 4.1 percent in 1970 to 5.5 percent in 1981. As the table indicates, between 1970 and 1981 entitlements and nondefense discretionary spending rose from 10.1 to 15.6 percent of GNP. Overall government expenditures did not rise as rapidly, however, reflecting a decline in the share of resources devoted to national defense and international security programs. Excluding social contracts, government spending in 1981, for example, was 16.8 percent of GNP, a mere 0.3 percentage point above its 1963 level.[4]

The Need for Reform

Although the expansion of social spending was undertaken with the good intention of helping the needy, it failed to achieve that goal in any permanent fashion. The percentage of the U.S. population considered impoverished (as measured by *pretransferred* incomes), for example, after declining more than twelve percentage points in the two decades before 1970, rose in the 1970s to the level that existed before 1960.[5] Thus half the percentage of families whose incomes had risen above the poverty level during the 1950s and 1960s fell below that level during the 1970s. Even more important, by the time the Reagan administration came to office, the major means-tested programs associated with the social safety net proved to be so deficient in design and coordination that they were fraught with errors and abuses, poorly targeted, and often irreparable even with highly effective management within the existing program structure.

Poor Recipient Incentives: The Case of Public Assistance. For more than two decades social analysts have noted that high effective tax rates on in-kind benefits discourage participation in the work force. What is less well recognized but equally understandable is that simultaneous reductions in multiple in-kind benefits (such as food stamps, public housing, and Medicaid) to public assistance recipients when their earned income rises often effectively deter participation in the work force or expanded work effort. Provisions were therefore written into law to offset such disincentives and to encourage work. The primary changes were the earned income disregard—a portion of earned income excluded in determining eligibility and benefits—and specific deductions for work-related expenses.

These attempts to design programs that would both provide minimum benefits to families with no earned income and still maintain high disregards for earned income as work incentives, however, have proved largely ineffective and enormously expensive. If average benefits were reduced by 25 percent of earned income for a family of four currently receiving $6,000 in benefits, for example, the family would theoretically continue to be eligible for benefits until it reached an earned income of $24,000 per year. Such high benefits would be unacceptable to taxpayers and to Congress. Consequently, relatively high benefit reduction rates for earned income (that is, low income disregards) have become necessary.

171

The Reagan administration also discovered that benefits, particularly for in-kind transfers, were uncoordinated. While some families achieved relatively high combined benefits as measured by the market value of the transfers, others remained below the poverty level.

The administration's review of these public assistance programs revealed significant work disincentives and inequities, mostly resulting from the combined effects of lower earned income benefits and higher market values of transferred benefits. In 1981, for example, only 12.6 percent of AFDC families and 17.7 percent of food stamp recipients aged eighteen to fifty-nine worked at all during the year.[6] But at the same time, welfare recipients who did join the labor force were able to keep many of their benefits and thus were much better off than other low-income workers who had not participated in welfare programs. In the 1970s, moreover, the disparities increased. The overall inequities arising from social welfare programs designed in the 1960s and 1970s are well illustrated by the following example, which accompanied the fiscal year 1983 budget.[7]

• An average welfare family of four in 1970 would have received AFDC, Medicaid, and school lunch benefits equivalent to $7,548 in 1980 dollars. Ten years later their inflation-adjusted benefits (including food stamps in 1980) would have increased to $8,124 in 1980 dollars.

• By contrast, a working nonwelfare family of four with exactly the same after-tax income in 1970 would not have done nearly as well. If their income rose with national average earnings, their after-tax income in 1980 would have been $7,224, a 4 percent decline in real terms. The family's income would have been 11 percent below that of a nonworking welfare family.

• If the head of the welfare family had gone to work in the same occupation as the head of the nonwelfare family, the welfare family would have been even better off. The combined effects of earnings disregards in cash and in-kind assistance programs and the earned income tax credit would have given the working welfare family after-tax income including benefits of $11,076—an amount 53 percent higher than that received by the family that supported itself through work alone.

Thus those who receive benefits and subsequently join the labor force are much better off than those who have not participated in welfare programs.

Errors and Abuses. When the Reagan administration took office, poor program design included overcomplex regulations and inadequate coordination among related welfare programs. These factors contributed to significant errors and waste in means-tested programs. In addition, the programs were evidently not administered efficiently or economically. In 1981, for example, states improperly paid an estimated $3.5 billion in AFDC, food stamps, and Medicaid benefits.[8] In the food stamp program alone, about one of every ten dollars was spent on overpayments or on payments to ineligible families. Further, about one-third of this total was directly linked to the complex deductions and exclusions used to determine benefits and eligibility.[9] The Health Care Financing Administration found that approximately one-half billion dollars of insurance payments that could have been obtained in 1980 from private health insurers for Medicaid coverage had not been collected.[10] States also failed to require parents who had left their families and had been ordered by a court to make support payments to meet their responsibilities. In 1981 alone the states neglected to collect about $1 billion in court-ordered payments for AFDC recipients.[11] In the school lunch program, the inspector general of the Agriculture Department and the General Accounting Office estimated that up to one-half billion dollars was overpaid in 1980 as a consequence of invalid applications for free and reduced-price lunches and inflated meal counts.[12]

Poorly Targeted Benefits. The combination of poorly designed programs and associated errors and abuses often made the distribution of existing resources inefficient. An analysis of Current Population Survey (CPS) data for March 1981, before the Reagan administration's legislative changes were implemented, shows that a substantial fraction of benefits went to households that were raised above the poverty level as a result of those programs, while many poor households received nothing. This inequity was particularly glaring for the working poor. Some 6.7 million wage-earning families with cash incomes below 150 percent of the poverty-level income received no AFDC, food stamps, Medicaid, or housing benefits, while 12.7 million households that received AFDC or Supplemental Security Income (SSI) had total cash income and benefits greater than 150 percent.[13]

In all, approximately 36 percent of income-tested benefits, or $16.9 billion, went to more than 23 million households whose total cash benefits and other cash income placed them above the poverty line.[14] This survey does not separately measure earned income and transfers, so that it is not possible to determine how much of the transfers were in excess of the poverty level. But it was surely substantial. Households whose cash benefits and other income placed them above 150 percent of the poverty level received more than $8.3 billion

TABLE 8–2

SAFETY NET BENEFITS PROVIDED TO HOUSEHOLDS WITH INCOME
ABOVE 150 PERCENT OF POVERTY LEVEL, 1981
(percent)

Program	Cash Income with Cash Benefits above 150 Percent of Poverty		Cash and In-Kind Income with All Benefits above 150 Percent of Poverty	
	Recipients	Benefits	Recipients	Benefits
AFDC	14.2	10.7	29.0	26.9
SSI	33.2	26.8	62.5	61.4
Food stamps	15.1	8.1	30.2	24.5
Free and reduced-price school lunch	25.9	23.3	34.9	32.5
Medicaid (insurance value)	27.5	26.2	46.2	53.3
Public housing benefits	10.6	5.7	38.3	46.7
Section 8 rent subsidy	12.5	7.0	45.9	54.0
One or more of the benefits above	28.6	17.5	42.4	42.1

NOTE: Includes households in which at least one person receives benefits from the program listed.
SOURCE: Office of Management and Budget, *Major Themes and Additional Budget Details, Fiscal Year 1984*, pp. 27, 28.

in means-tested cash benefits. Such inaccurate targeting becomes even more apparent when the market value of in-kind benefits, such as food stamps and the insurance premium value of Medicaid, is included in the definition of income. In the CPS survey, these in-kind transfers constituted approximately two-thirds of the total federal resources for means-tested benefits.[15] When they are included, approximately 83 percent of the total benefits, about $39.2 billion, went to households whose cash and in-kind incomes placed them above the poverty line. Furthermore, approximately $20 billion, or 42 percent, went to households with total incomes and benefits above 150 percent of the poverty level.

Table 8–2 shows the percentages of beneficiaries and benefits going to households above 150 percent of the poverty level for each of these means-tested programs. Counting cash incomes only, participation rates ranged from 11 percent for public housing to 33 percent for SSI; counting cash and in-kind benefits, the range was from 29 percent for AFDC to 63 percent for SSI. A smaller fraction of dollar benefits went to such households: the corresponding ranges were 6 to 27 percent and 24 to 61 percent.

Inaccurate targeting of transfer payments is further revealed by comparing the pretransfer and posttransfer poverty gaps, measured as the amount of means-tested expenditures necessary to raise all persons above the poverty threshold. In 1981 the pretransfer poverty gap was $50.1 billion measured in 1982 dollars. In 1981, after about $81 billion in 1982 dollars was spent on means-tested benefits, including in-kind transfers, the poverty gap was $25.6 billion.[16] This remainder illustrates the failure to direct welfare benefits to those most in need.

Overall Changes in the Safety Net and Related Programs

Despite the widespread perception that the Reagan administration has significantly cut safety net and related programs, overall federal spending in these areas has not changed appreciably since 1981. Table 8–1 reveals that 10.1 percent and 5.5 percent of GNP went for entitlement programs and nondefense discretionary spending respectively in 1981. Although the fraction of GNP devoted to nondefense discretionary spending is expected to drop by 1.3 percentage points to 4.2 percent in 1984, more than half that decline will be offset by an increase in the share going to entitlements: Spending on entitlement programs in 1984 is expected to increase to 10.8 percent of GNP. Overall spending for each of the major categories discussed earlier, as well as the 1981–1984 changes, appears in table 8–3.

Totaling the costs of the four major social functions of government provides another measure of the social safety net and its related programs. These functions are (1) income security, (2) health, (3) education, training, employment, and social services, and (4) veterans' benefits and services. In 1981 the federal government spent $345.5 billion, or 52.6 percent of total federal outlays, on these functions. By 1984 they will cost an estimated $424.0 billion, half the total budget.[17] Many federal programs in these four categories, however, are not directed primarily to low-income households. Furthermore, for a more precise evaluation of changes in the safety net, we must look beyond aggregate spending for these programs.

Defining the Safety Net. Determining the extent of changes in the safety net requires a clear definition of the specific federal programs it should encompass. My analysis is limited to programs designed for persons who are regarded as truly needy. Because beneficiaries with substantial assets and outside income often qualify for social security,

TABLE 8–3

FEDERAL BUDGET SHARE OF GNP, 1981 AND 1984

(percent)

Budget Component	GNP Share		Change in GNP Share, 1981–1984 (percentage points)
	1981	1984	
Entitlements			
Social contract	6.8	7.6	0.8
Other[a]	3.3	3.2	−0.1
Subtotal	10.1	10.8	0.7
Nondefense discretionary	5.5	4.2	−1.3
National defense and security	5.5	7.2	1.7
Other			
Net interest	2.4	3.0	0.6
Remainder	0.1	0.5	0.4
Total	23.6	25.7	2.1

a. Includes military retirement pay.

SOURCE: Office of Management and Budget, *Budget of the United States Government, Fiscal Year 1984.*

civil service, or veterans' pensions, those programs are excluded by this definition of the safety net. Because unemployment insurance and Medicare are not means tested, they are also excluded by this definition. The SSI program, however, whose benefits generally go to low-income individuals, is included in the definition. With one exception, I restrict the definition of basic safety net programs to those that are means-tested entitlements. The exception is the inclusion of housing assistance programs, because they are included in the annual March CPS, which is used to measure poverty status.[18] Under these guidelines, then, the programs included in the definition of the basic safety net are AFDC (with child support enforcement), SSI, food stamps, child nutrition, Medicaid, and housing assistance.[19] This definition permits an analysis of some of the consequences of program changes for indigent recipients.

Changes in Outlays for the Basic Safety Net Programs. The changes in the safety net programs are analyzed in table 8–4. In 1981, the final year of the Carter administration, the federal government spent $54.2 billion for AFDC, SSI, food stamps, child nutrition, Medicaid, and housing assistance.[20] If legislative changes after July 31, 1983, are ig-

TABLE 8-4

OUTLAYS FOR BASIC SOCIAL SAFETY NET PROGRAMS, 1981 AND 1984
(billions of dollars)

| | | | Carter Budget, 1984 | |
Program	Baseline 1981	Reagan Budget 1984	No policy changes	With policy changes
AFDC	8.5	8.3	9.5	8.9
SSI	7.2	8.0	7.5	7.5
Food stamps	11.3	12.3	14.3	13.7
Child nutrition	3.4	3.4	4.8	4.3
Medicaid	16.9	21.3	22.7	23.4
Housing assistance	6.9	10.1	10.6	10.6
Total	54.2	63.4	69.4	68.4

SOURCES: Congressional Budget Office, "Major Legislative Changes in Human Resources Programs since January 1981," August 1983; and Office of Management and Budget, *Budget of the United States Government, Fiscal Years 1982* and *1983*.

nored and February 1983 economic assumptions are used, the total expenditures for these programs in 1984 are estimated by the Congressional Budget Office (CBO) at $63.4 billion.[21] Thus the increase for these programs between 1981 and 1984 is $9.2 billion, or approximately 17 percent. Expressed in constant 1983 dollars, the 1981 expenditures of $54.2 billion would be $59.6 billion.[22] Because the number of recipients also changed between 1981 and 1984, the overall effect on participants' real income cannot be determined from this table.

The CBO provides a different interpretation of the changes in these programs. Using the Carter administration 1981 current services expenditures as a baseline and assuming no policy changes, the CBO projects 1984 expenditures for these programs totaling $69.4 billion, as shown in column 3 of table 8-4.[23] The currently projected expenditures for these programs by 1984 constitute a $6.0 billion reduction from that total. For reasons discussed earlier, we cannot tell if recipients who remain on these programs are worse off because of reduced overall funding. More important, the CBO current service estimates assume that no policy changes would have been made in these programs if the Carter administration had continued in office beyond 1981. This is an important omission, because the last Carter budget proposed approximately $1 billion in cuts for the basic safety net

TABLE 8–5

TARGET EFFICIENCY OF MEANS-TESTED BENEFITS, 1981 AND 1982
(billions of 1982 dollars)

	Total Benefits	Amount of Benefits Reducing Poverty	Target Efficiency (percent)
1981			
Cash	16.9	11.6	69
In-kind	32.9	13.0	40
Total	49.8	24.6	49
1982			
Cash	16.5	12.1	73
In-kind	32.6	14.6	45
Total	49.1	26.7	54

NOTE: Included are only benefits reported for AFDC, SSI, food stamps, free and reduced-price school lunches, Medicaid, and housing assistance. Target efficiency is the percentage of expenditures going to reduce the poverty gap.

SOURCE: Calculated from Census Bureau, Current Population Survey (CPS), March 1982 and March 1983.

programs by 1984. The effect of its proposed reductions is shown in column 4 of the table.[24] The CBO estimates also assume that Congress would not have initiated any changes affecting the programs' aggregate expenditures.

Effects on Recipients of Changes in Safety Net Programs

I now turn to the effects of legislative changes since 1981 on beneficiaries of needs-tested programs. Legislative and agency changes adopted during the Reagan administration were designed to (1) improve targeting of benefits to the needy, (2) improve program design and structure, and (3) reduce errors and waste. First, it must be determined whether the targeting of benefits has improved and whether programs have become more efficient, as measured by the Target Efficiency Index (defined as the percentage of means-tested benefits used to reduce the degree of poverty). The CPS survey shows that from 1981 to 1982 the Target Efficiency Index rose 10 percent, as the percentage of total benefits that went to reducing or eliminating the poverty gap rose from 49 to 54 percent (see table 8–5). The improved targeting of benefits occurred despite the modest decline in means-tested benefits from 1981 to 1982. Thus, while total benefits fell from

$49.8 billion to $49.1 billion in constant dollars, the benefits used to reduce poverty rose from $24.6 billion in 1981 to $26.7 billion in 1982 (in constant 1982 dollars). The retargeting of benefits also affected participation in these programs. From 1981 to 1982 the proportion of poor receiving assistance rose by 1 percent. At the same time, the number of nonpoor beneficiaries fell by 6 percent.[25]

The safety net also appears to be more effective, as a result of the Reagan administration's changes, in protecting people during recessions. From 1981 to 1982, when real per capita GNP fell 2.8 percent, the number of nonelderly poor increased 9.6 percent. During previous recessions, however, the number of poverty-level households rose more steeply. In the 1979–1980 recession, when real per capita GNP fell 1.4 percent, the number of nonelderly poor rose 13.4 percent. In the 1973–1975 recession, while real per capita GNP fell 3.6 percent, the number of nonelderly persons classified as poor rose 15.0 percent.[26]

I now turn to the consequences of legislative changes in some individual safety net programs.

Cash Assistance. The AFDC program provides cash benefits to low-income families with children. It is jointly financed by the states and a federal grant based on a formula. Qualifying income and benefit levels are established by the states. The Reagan administration's major changes in the AFDC program include efforts to target assistance to those in greatest need and to refine eligibility criteria.

Each state is now required to end eligibility for families with incomes above 150 percent of its standard of need. In addition, income and resources available to a family unit but not previously counted by AFDC must be included as income to the family. Thus the income of stepparents who live in the same household is now counted as AFDC family income. Many deductions and exclusions that previously permitted some families with substantial income to participate in the AFDC program have been reduced and standardized. Under prior law, recipients could exclude the first $30 of monthly earnings plus one-third of the remainder of each month's earnings from income used to determine benefits. Under current law, the $30 and one-third earnings disregard is limited to a four-month transitional period. Other changes were designed to improve administration of the program by requiring stricter accounting procedures and recovery of overpayments to recipients. States may also establish community work experience programs in which recipients receive training and work experience while performing useful services to the community.

In addition to these changes, Congress enacted several proposals

179

strengthening the child support enforcement program. Under these changes, deductions are made from the federal income tax refunds of parents who do not meet court-ordered support payments. The deductions reimburse states that have made higher AFDC payments in the absence of support from those parents.

Recent evidence indicates that these reforms are converting AFDC to a more responsibly managed program of last resort for those who must temporarily rely on governmental income support. The changes also illustrate how redesigning the program can motivate additional work effort among aid recipients with earnings. A study prepared by the Research Triangle Institute of North Carolina demonstrated that AFDC reforms have had a substantial effect on AFDC families with earnings.[27] Approximately 28 percent of AFDC families with earnings in 1980 were not on AFDC one year later. A year after the reforms were implemented in 1981, 55 percent of AFDC cases with earnings were no longer on the program. In addition, analyses show a 65 percent probability that an AFDC case would close within a year for 1981 earners compared with a 33 percent probability for 1980 earners. At the same time, the 1981 changes had little effect on AFDC cases in which families did not have earnings at the time of implementation. Some 76 percent of these cases were participating in AFDC a year after implementation in 1981, an amount not significantly different from the 83 percent for AFDC nonearners in 1980. Finally, it is estimated that real AFDC benefits per recipient remained level between 1981 and 1983.[28] In contrast, during the four-year Carter administration, real AFDC benefits per recipient fell 10 percent while prices rose 45 percent.

Legislative changes in Supplemental Security Income (SSI), which provides cash benefits to low-income aged, blind, and disabled persons, were minor in both 1981 and 1982 when compared with changes in other means-tested programs. They included prorating the first month's benefits and linking cost-of-living adjustments to those in social security. In the social security amendments of 1983, these changes were more than offset by an increase in SSI benefits of up to $20 per month for single parents and up to $30 per month for married couples. Overall, changes in the SSI program are projected to increase outlays in 1983 and beyond.

Unemployment compensation, though not a means-tested entitlement, is often regarded as a vital component of the social safety net. Under this program, laid-off workers who are covered by their employers are eligible to receive cash assistance to help offset lost wages for up to twenty-six weeks. Regular benefits are determined by the states and are funded through state payroll taxes. Workers are also eligible for up to thirteen additional weeks of extended benefits funded by the federal government if the unemployment rate in their state is above a specified level. In states with high unemployment rates, workers are able to collect up to fourteen more weeks of unemployment payments after their extended benefits expire. Reforms include raising the minimum or "trigger" unemployment levels for extended benefits and prohibiting payment of extended benefits to persons who have worked less than twenty weeks. Overall payments for unemployment compensation rose from $16.0 billion in 1981 to $29.5 billion in 1983—a 28 percent increase when adjusted for the number of unemployed.[29]

Food Stamps. The food stamp program provides vouchers (coupons) redeemable for food to low-income persons. Standardized benefits vary with net income after exclusions and deductions. Eligibility standards were tightened in 1981 by the establishment of a gross income limit at 130 percent of the poverty-level income. Other reforms prohibited participation by union strikers unless they were eligible before striking and required that children living with their parents file as part of the same household. Periodic income reports, with the first month's benefits prorated and retrospective accounting required, also helped reduce abuses. Other changes included postponing adjustments for inflation, establishing a separate nutrition assistance grant for Puerto Rico, instituting a sanctions system to penalize states for high administrative errors, and creating a workfare option that allows states to require recipients to earn their benefits through training and jobs. Many of these changes, however, including the gross income cap and deductions for medical expenses, do not apply to the elderly.

Much of the available evidence supports the perception that the food stamp program is a major component of the safety net. From 1980 to 1982 participation in the program, excluding Puerto Rico, rose from 19.2 million to 21.6 million recipients.[30] Efforts have been made to retarget food stamp benefits. Data in table 8–6, calculated from the annual March CPS, indicate that more food stamp recipients are now coming from families with incomes below the poverty line. In 1981, for example, 65.4 percent of families participating in the program had cash incomes below the poverty line. By 1982 the percentage of families in this category had increased to 71.3 percent. Federal funding of the food stamp program has also been redesigned to increase the average real purchasing power of participants. The average federal bonus rose from forty-five cents per meal in 1981 to fifty-four cents per meal in 1983, an increase of 20 percent, while food prices rose only 6 percent.[31] Contrary to some beliefs, there is substantial evidence that

TABLE 8-6
SHARE OF ALL FOOD STAMP RECIPIENTS WITH FAMILY INCOME BELOW POVERTY THRESHOLDS, 1980–1982
(percent)

Family Income	1980	1981	1982
Less than 50 percent of poverty threshold	21.5	23.4	28.0
Less than 100 percent of poverty threshold	63.1	65.4	71.3
Less than 130 percent of poverty threshold	76.8	78.3	83.7

SOURCE: Tabulations from CPS, March 1981, 1982, and 1983.

the Reagan administration's efforts to retarget benefits, redesign incentives, and improve management procedures in the food stamp portion of the social safety net have actually improved delivery of goods to the truly needy.[32]

Child Nutrition. Child nutrition programs, which provide both cash and commodity assistance, include the national school lunch program, the national school breakfast program, the summer feeding program, the child care feeding program, and a number of smaller programs. Most of the federal funding of these programs is directed toward subsidized meals for children in schools, although some meal assistance is provided for child care facilities and other institutional settings.

The administration's changes in the child nutrition programs target assistance more selectively to needy children, reduce duplication in the federal subsidies, and improve administration of the programs. Subsidies for nonneedy students have been reduced, for example, and the special milk program has been removed from schools that also participate in other federal meal subsidy programs. Several procedural changes have decreased fraudulent claims and established eligibility for federal subsidies more accurately. In addition, the summer feeding program has been directed to areas where lower-income households are concentrated.

Although the total dollars for child nutrition programs have remained fairly constant, participation in the programs has declined somewhat, partly because of declining school enrollment: some 46.8 million children enrolled in schools in 1981 and only 45.5 million in 1983.[33] In addition, schools with high tuitions were excluded from the program by law in 1981. Other declines in participation are more difficult to explain. Participation in the free lunch program for students with family incomes less than 130 percent of the poverty level, for example, fell from an average of 10.6 million meals per day in 1981 to 10.4 million in 1983.[34] The largest decline, however, occurred for students whose family incomes exceeded 185 percent of the poverty threshold, or $17,210 for a family of four in 1983.

These programs are successfully retargeting assistance to the most needy recipients, the percentage of meals served in the free and reduced-price categories having increased from 48 percent in 1981 to 52 percent in 1983.[35] Federal funding for the child care food program rose from $327 million in 1981 to $342 million in 1983, but increasing food costs caused a decline of 3 percent from the 546.5 million meals served in 1981. Retargeting of benefits also occurred in the school breakfast programs, where the percentage of free and reduced-price meals rose from 86.9 percent to 90.4 percent from 1981 to 1983. In sum, tightened eligibility requirements and other administrative changes have brought about small declines in participation and a retargeting of benefits to the most needy children.

An analysis of child nutrition funding would not be complete without an examination of the special supplemental food program for women, infants, and children (WIC), which, though not formally an entitlement, provides supplemental foods to low-income pregnant and postpartum mothers and to infants and young children. Benefits in this program consist of specific items, such as milk, cheese, fruit juice, and eggs. Funding for the WIC program comes from the federal government, but states are permitted to choose an income eligibility standard between 100 and 185 percent of the poverty-level income. Total funding for the WIC program rose from $888 million in 1981 to an expected $1.13 billion in 1983, an increase of approximately 27 percent. At the same time, program participation also rose, from 2.1 million in 1981 to an expected 2.5 million in 1983, two-thirds of whom are infants and children.[36]

Medicaid. The Medicaid program provides matching grants to states to finance medical care of low-income families and individuals. About 80 percent of Medicaid recipients also receive either AFDC or SSI benefits. States receive open-ended matching payments, ranging from 50 to 78 percent of program costs, for the medical expenditures of these low-income individuals.

Legislation in 1981 reduced federal Medicaid grants to states by 3 percent in 1982, 4 percent in 1983, and 4.5 percent in 1984. These reductions could be offset, however, by states that reduced their error rates or rates of benefit growth. Additional changes permitted the states to mandate copayments from recipients and to recoup the cost of benefits from recipients who died in institutions by placing liens on their assets. Although it is too early to assess the overall effect of these changes, some early evidence of states' responses is available from the April report of the Intergovernmental Health Policy Project. Its survey showed that many states were forced to control growth in spending that had occurred before the reforms. Although some of the changes did reduce benefits to recipients, the reforms have allowed states to increase services and add beneficiaries. Specifically, the report finds that

> perhaps the most striking difference between the two years (1981 and 1982) is that even in the face of continued fiscal stress, a substantial number of States acted in 1982 to add new services, reinstate previously eliminated benefits, lift existing restrictions on access, or even increase payments to providers. . . . Also in contrast to 1981, 1982 marked the beginning of a gradual shift in the focus of cost-containment activities away from the traditional short-term strategies, e.g., limitations on eligibility and services, reductions in provider payments, etc., to a concentration on more long-range, structural reforms in the organization, financing and delivery of Medicaid services.[37]

At the same time Medicaid costs continue to rise rapidly. Total expenditures were $16.9 billion in 1981 and rose to $19.3 billion in 1983.[38]

Housing Assistance. Most federal housing assistance is provided through public housing programs and Section 8 subsidies for new construction and existing housing. Subsidies were limited to families with incomes below 80 percent of the median (roughly 150 to 160 percent of the poverty-level income) in their area who also paid a monthly rent that was typically 25 percent of their adjusted incomes.

The Reagan administration's reforms lowered the qualifying income to 50 percent of median income in the area and increased the rents paid by subsidized housing tenants from 25 to 30 percent of their adjusted incomes. Legislative changes also redirected funds appropriated for construction and other purposes to individual rent subsidies. Between 1981 and 1983 the number of families receiving housing subsidies increased about 13 percent, from 3.30 million in 1981 to 3.72 million in 1983. Overall housing assistance for the needy is expected to rise from $6.9 billion in 1981 to $9.4 billion in 1983, an increase of 36 percent in just two years.[39]

Conclusions and Future Reforms

When viewed in their entirety, reforms in the social safety net programs have certainly not been as severe as some critics have claimed. Nor has funding for these programs been cut drastically. Benefits totaling $20 billion went to families whose total cash and in-kind benefits exceeded 150 percent of the poverty-level income in 1981. Some of these resources—though the precise amount is unknown—could still be redirected or saved without significantly harming the truly needy. In fact, less than one-third of that amount was actually redirected for fiscal year 1984; and, despite the improvement in targeting, almost one-half of the total expenditures designed to reduce the poverty gap fail to do so.[40] These comparisons also signal that additional reforms are feasible without significantly lowering the social safety net.

In the future a comprehensive, compassionate approach to federal assistance for needy families will increasingly demand a responsible, cost-effective method of delegating tax funds. The current administration's attempts to identify qualified beneficiaries more accurately, to redesign programs, and to target benefits to specific populations all reflect a desire to establish a more effective basic social assistance safety net. With congressional and popular support, these changes will do much to improve the situation of those in need.

Notes

1. There is no generally accepted definition of the social safety net. This paper addresses a number of measures, ranging from aggregate spending for all social programs to spending for programs that are explicitly measured in the Current Population Survey (CPS).

2. See Office of Management and Budget (OMB), *Budget of the United States Government, Fiscal Year 1984*, pt. 3, for an expanded discussion of the changes in social contract spending.

3. Social contract programs constituted 2.7 percent of GNP in 1963 and grew to 4.0 percent by 1970. The proportion of GNP used by the federal government rose from 19.2 percent in 1963 to 20.2 percent in 1970. Data reported in the rest of this section are provided in or calculated from OMB, *Budget of the United States Government, Fiscal Year 1984*, pt. 3.

4. Ibid., pp. 3–7.

5. It is interesting to note that in 1970 the decline in the percentage of population regarded as poor, as measured by pretransferred or earned income, came to an end. See Charles A. Murray, *Safety Nets and the Truly Needy: Rethinking the Social Welfare System* (Washington, D.C.: Heritage Foundation, 1982).

6. Department of Health and Human Services, Social Security Administration, "Aid to Families with Dependent Children: Quality Control Findings,

October 1980–March 1981"; and U.S. Department of Agriculture, Food and Nutrition Service, "Preliminary Report: Characteristics of Food Stamp Households," August 1981.

7. Adapted from OMB, *Major Themes and Additional Budget Details, Fiscal Year 1983*, p. 38.

8. U.S. Department of Agriculture, Food and Nutrition Service, "Semiannual Summary Report of Food Stamps Quality Control Reviews, October 1980–March 1981"; Social Security Administration, "Aid to Families with Dependent Children: Quality Control Findings, October 1980–March 1981"; and Department of Health and Human Services, Health Care Financing Administration, "Medicaid Quality Control Report for October 1980–March 1981."

9. Food and Nutrition Service, "Semiannual Summary Report."

10, Department of Health and Human Services, Health Care Financing Administration, Region X, and Washington State Department of Social and Health Services, "Third Party Liability in the Medicaid Program: A Seattle Case Study," October 1981; and Maximus, Inc., Final Report on "Evaluation of the Cost Effectiveness of the Collection of Third Party Liability by State Medicaid Agencies," August 1981.

11. Census Bureau, *Current Population Reports*, Series P-23, no. 124, "Child Support and Alimony," 1981.

12. General Accounting Office, "Analysis of a Department of Agriculture Report on Fraud and Abuse in Child Nutrition Programs," CED-81-81, 1981.

13. Calculated from U.S. Bureau of the Census, Current Population Survey (CPS), March 1982.

14. OMB, *Major Themes and Additional Budget Details, Fiscal Year 1984*, p. 27.

15. These programs include AFDC, SSI, food stamps, Medicaid, school lunches, and public housing or rent subsidies. Data are calculated from Census Bureau, CPS, March 1982.

16. U.S. Congress, House of Representatives, Committee on Ways and Means, Subcommittees on Oversight and on Public Assistance and Unemployment, statement of David A. Stockman, 98th Congress, 1st session, November 3, 1983, p. 18.

17. If offsetting receipts and interest payments are ignored, the share of the federal budget for these four functions was 57.1 percent in 1981 and is expected to be 55.2 percent in 1984.

18. The CPS is also used to publish various Census Bureau series, including *Money Income of Households, Families, and Persons in the United States; Characteristics of the Population below the Poverty Level;* and *Characteristics of Households and Persons Receiving Selected Noncash Benefits.*

19. Child nutrition excludes special supplemental feeding programs for women, infants, and children (WIC) for two reasons. First, participation in WIC is not reported separately in the CPS, and, second, persons who earn up to 185 percent of poverty-level incomes may still participate in the program. The chosen definition, of course, does not imply that the poor are not also helped by programs that are excluded, nor does it imply that these programs fail to alleviate poverty. Some of these programs, such as manpower and education, which are primarily designed to alleviate the long-run poverty

problem, are treated elsewhere in this volume.

20. OMB, *Budget of the United States Government, Fiscal Year 1983.*

21. Congressional Budget Office, "Major Legislative Changes in Human Resources Programs since January 1981," August 1983, pp. 24, 34, 47.

22. The conversion to constant dollars is based on the August 1983 consumer price index relative to the index for 1981.

23. These projections also use February 1983 CBO economic assumptions.

24. Carter's proposed budget cuts for the basic safety net programs are based on 1981 economic assumptions. See OMB, *Budget of the United States Government, Fiscal Year 1982,* pp. 235, 252.

25. Calculated from CPS, March 1982 and March 1983.

26. The percentage changes in the number of poor persons in nonelderly households, excluding those headed by females, showed a similar pattern. In 1981–1982 the increase was 12.7 percent, during the 1979–1980 recession it was 17.6 percent, and in the 1973–1975 recession it was 18.7 percent. See Stockman, statement before House Ways and Means Subcommittees on Oversight and on Public Assistance and Unemployment, p. 17.

27. Department of Health and Human Services, Social Security Administration, "Final Report: Evaluation of 1981 AFDC Amendments," Research Triangle Institute Report, North Carolina, April 15, 1983.

28. Reported in Stockman, statement before the House Ways and Means Subcommittees on Oversight and on Public Assistance and Unemployment, p. 23.

29. Average unemployment during fiscal year 1981 was 7.8 million, and total payments were $16.0 billion. For fiscal year 1983 payments were approximately $29.5 billion, and average unemployment was 11.3 million.

30. U.S. Department of Agriculture, Food and Nutrition Service, Fact Sheets. In 1982 Puerto Rico was given a block grant to provide food assistance to the needy, and accurate participation levels have not been available since June 1982.

31. Calculated from data provided in Food and Nutrition Service, Fact Sheets, and CPI data for 1981 and 1983. For 1983 the bonus for the lowest-income families was about seventy cents per meal per person. Families at the thirty-seventh percentile for food expenditures spent eighty-nine cents per person per meal.

32. Future improvements in the food stamp program are still quite possible. Error rates—payments to ineligible persons as well as overissuance or underissuance of food coupons to participants—remain high. See the final report of the President's Task Force on Food Assistance for additional information on the food stamp program.

33. Food and Nutrition Service, Fact Sheet, 1983.

34. Ibid.

35. Ibid.

36. Ibid. For more information on WIC and other child nutrition programs, see "Perception and Reality in Nutrition Programs" in this volume. A recent General Accounting Office study of the WIC program found insufficient evidence for making any general or conclusive judgments about WIC's overall

effectiveness. See U.S. General Accounting Office, Report to the Committee on Agriculture, Nutrition, and Forestry, "WIC Evaluations Provide Some Favorable but No Conclusive Evidence on the Effects Expected for the Special Supplemental Program for Women, Infants and Children," Report No. PEMD-84-4, January 1984.

37. George Washington University, Intergovernmental Health Policy Project, "Recent and Proposed Changes in State Medicaid Programs: A Fifty State Survey," April 1983.

38. OMB, *Budget of the United States Government, Fiscal Years 1983 and 1984.*

39. OMB, *Budget of the United States Government, Fiscal Year 1983*; and Congressional Budget Office, "Major Legislative Changes in Human Resources Programs since January 1981," August 1983.

40. Calculated from table 8–4.

9

Shredding an Already Tattered Safety Net

Tom Joe

The Center for the Study of Social Policy has been involved in a series of analyses of the sweeping changes made by the Reagan administration in the nation's domestic human service programs. These analyses form the basis for this paper. My attention is focused on the programs of last resort—those that provide assistance to low-income persons when other means of support are unavailable.

I begin by considering the basic question posed in this book: Has a "safety net" in fact been maintained for these "truly needy" people? In short, I do not think that it has. I then consider a number of claims that the administration has made on behalf of its policies and proposals: that better targeting of benefits has been achieved; that cost savings have been realized; that program administration has been simplified. In each case, I conclude that the administration's claims are greatly exaggerated, if not completely erroneous.

Has a "Safety Net" Been Maintained to Protect the "Truly Needy"?

What Is the "Safety Net"? To answer the question whether the safety net has been maintained, it is first necessary to define the term "safety net." The concept of the safety net as introduced by President Reagan has been flawed from its inception.

First, the definition was circular. The administration designated certain programs as constituting a safety net and participants in those programs as the "truly needy." It is thus simply by definition that the net protects the truly needy.

Second, the definition is based not on human needs or decency but on political vulnerability. Programs such as social security, Medicare, and veterans' benefits, which make up 95 percent of all funds in the "safety net" but mainly serve people above the poverty line, have been spared the budget knife. But programs that serve only the poor—Aid to Families with Dependent Children (AFDC), Medicaid, and food stamps—have been severely cut.

Third, the circular definition of the "truly needy" neglects many who are indisputably needy—the working poor, the homeless, the deinstitutionalized mentally ill, to name a few—but who are not on the rolls of any government program. In sum, the very concept of the safety net as defined by the Reagan administration may be meaningless.

Are Benefits Excessive? The administration has claimed that individual income assistance benefits have been excessive—despite abundant evidence to the contrary. A quick glance at these programs shows that both the benefits and the percentage of federal expenditures devoted to assistance programs are far from excessive.

At the low end of the scale, the maximum AFDC benefit for a family of three in Mississippi is $96 per month. In two-thirds of the states, AFDC payments provide an income that is less than 65 percent of the poverty threshold. Moreover, AFDC benefits, unlike social security benefits, are not indexed to inflation. Thus, in constant dollars, the median state benefit for a four-person AFDC family fell 36 percent between 1970 and 1983.[1]

Adding the value of food stamps to the AFDC grant still does not raise benefits to the poverty level. Food stamps average only forty-three cents per person per meal. In Mississippi, even with food stamps, the average family on AFDC remains at 45 percent of the nationally defined poverty standard. In Pennsylvania, with benefits just above the median, the combined value of AFDC and food stamps raises a three-person family to only 77 percent of the poverty threshold.[2] Evidently the administration considers these subpoverty benefits to be excessive.

The administration also claims that public assistance expenditures have grown too rapidly. But in fact such expenditures as a proportion of the total federal budget have risen only slightly. Outlays have also remained relatively stable when inflation is taken into account, as AFDC and Supplemental Security Income (SSI), the major cash benefit programs, illustrate. In constant 1983 dollars, federal AFDC expenditures grew from $6.8 billion in 1970 to $8.8 billion in 1983. SSI expenditures (in constant dollars) increased from $8.5 billion in 1975, when the program began, to $8.7 billion in 1983. Similarly, the proportion of the total federal budget spent on public assistance and social services grew only slightly, from 2.7 percent in 1970 to 3.1 percent in 1980, and then dropped back to 2.7 percent in 1983. It is not the means-tested entitlements but the universal social insurance programs, such as social security and Medicare, that have consumed the greatest portion of federal social expenditures.[3]

The administration's contention that these benefits are excessive begs a more important question: To what extent is poverty tolerable to this administration, in both economic and human terms? I would argue that the administration's tolerance of destitution is far too high and that we should not put the burden on future taxpayers to pay the consequences. In short, we cannot afford escalating poverty.

How Have the Poor Been Affected by the Budget Reductions? Despite the inadequate benefits and minimal program growth, the Reagan administration has brought about severe reductions in major programs designed to help the poor. The effects of the massive budget cuts have been direct and immediate. The plight of America's poor has deepened. Not only are more Americans (34.4 million) poor than in any other year since 1964, but the "poverty gap"—the money required to raise the poor to the poverty threshold—has doubled (in constant dollars) in the past decade. In 1982 the gap amounted to $43 billion.[4] Although it is difficult to quantify the particular effects of the administration's program changes, one thing is certain: At a time when the recession created economic hardship for tens of millions of families, the administration limited eligibility for major assistance programs and reduced their benefits.

Preliminary studies reveal some of the effects of the budget cuts. Sheldon Danziger and other researchers at the Institute for Research on Poverty found that the poverty rate among working AFDC recipients in Wisconsin doubled after the program changes were implemented.[5] Similarly, a series of studies in Michigan, New York City, and Georgia sponsored by the Ford Foundation found that the poverty rate among working AFDC families rose after the budget cuts from 19 percent to 45 percent in New York City, from 18 percent to 42 percent in Michigan, and from 70 percent to 79 percent among a sample of families in Georgia.[6] It appears that the administration not only has increased poverty but has made already poor people even poorer.

In addition to deepening poverty, the budget cuts have had several other effects:

• The cuts have created a financial disincentive to work for AFDC recipients. An analysis by the Center for the Study of Social Policy showed that in half the states working AFDC recipients with average earnings will have less disposable income than nonworking recipients.[7] In Mississippi a mother with two children earning only $150 per month is now ineligible for supplementary AFDC payments because

191

her income places her above the "truly needy" category. Moreover, for each extra dollar a recipient earns, she loses at least ninety-nine cents in benefits. Thus the new policies discourage work for new applicants and penalize those who want to increase their work effort.

• Under the new policies, AFDC benefits are no longer available during the first six months of pregnancy to women with no other children. This new rule ignores the critical importance of adequate prenatal care. Yet without such assistance expectant mothers will not be able to provide adequately for their children. At least two states, Michigan and California, have chosen to continue these benefits at state expense because they recognize the importance of the investment from a human as well as an economic standpoint.

• The 1982 budget cut maternal, child health, and crippled children's services by 30 percent. These cuts were accomplished by placing a number of programs in a maternal and child health block grant. The Children's Defense Fund estimates that during 1982 the cuts led to the closing of 120 community health centers and loss of services for 1.26 million people.[8]

• Food programs for children suffered severe cuts in the Omnibus Budget Reconciliation Act of 1981. Funding for school lunches fell 30 percent, for school breakfasts 20 percent, for the child care food program 30 percent, for special milk 80 percent, and for summer feeding 50 percent. More recently the administration has proposed a block grant covering school breakfasts, the summer food program, and the child care food program, with an additional cut in funds of close to 30 percent; and it has tried to cut and even to abolish the women, infants, and children supplemental food program (WIC). Congress has resisted these proposals.

Because of the links among human service programs that aid the disadvantaged, the budget cuts have caused particular hardship for many low-income individuals and families. The real "safety net" is a patchwork design of multiple categorical programs for specific needs. Food stamps will buy only food, Medicaid provides certain health care services, the school lunch program offers free and reduced-price meals for students in school, and housing assistance helps pay rent. Because eligibility for these programs is intricately linked, cuts in one have automatic and direct effects on others. A family that has lost its AFDC benefits because of the recent cuts in that program, for example, automatically loses Medicaid coverage unless it is eligible for a "medically needy" program (offered in only thirty-one states). At the same time other cuts may mean that such a family will receive less low-income energy assistance and be asked to pay a larger portion of its income for rent under public housing. Thus in considering hardship caused by the president's Economic Recovery Program, it is essential to recognize that poor recipients are feeling the adverse effects of multiple cuts rather than of single, isolated ones.

The Fairness Issue. The administration's budget reductions not only have created severe hardship for the disadvantaged but, assessed with the rest of the administration's policies, are grossly unfair. The poor have suffered disproportionately. At the same time the administration was cutting social programs, it provided tax cuts that have widened the gap between rich and poor. An analysis by the Urban Institute shows that while a four-person family whose income was half the median income would receive a $263 increase in disposable income under the tax cut, a family of the same size making twice the median income would receive a $2,630 increase.[9] Thus the family with a gross income four times that of the less affluent family would receive a tax break ten times as large.

Estimates by the staff of the *National Journal* of the combined effects of the tax cuts and benefit reductions show that incomes of families in the lowest income quintile have been reduced by an average of $70 while incomes of more affluent families in the second, third, fourth, and fifth quintiles have increased by $30, $280, $650, and $2,040 respectively.[10] Moreover, the administration's budget cuts have reduced income support to the working poor on the apparent theory that these families should be "weaned" from welfare dependency, while at the same time the administration offered substantial tax breaks to the affluent.

Fairness requires distributing burdens in proportion to resources, something that the administration's policies clearly fail to do. The unfairness is pervasive. For example, the administration has strongly supported natural gas deregulation, which has already led to rising gas prices. Sixty percent of poor families rely on gas for heat. At the same time appropriations for the low income energy assistance program were cut from $1.85 billion in FY 1981 to $1.75 billion in FY 1982, and the administration has sought still further cuts, albeit unsuccessfully. For fuel prices to be forced up by one set of policies while energy aid for the poor is kept down by other policies is certainly unfair.

Similarly in the legal arena, less government means fewer legal demands on corporations. But the poor have seen their lawyers, those funded by the Legal Services Corporation, come under an intense attack by the administration. Although the president was unsuccessful in his bid to eliminate the corporation, its funds have been cut about 25 percent. Because of the cut, 20 percent of legal services offices around the country were closed, and 28 percent of lawyers funded by the corporation lost their jobs. Even before any of the cuts, legal services programs were inadequately staffed and funded to meet the needs of their client population. Now that situation is much worse, and it is the poor who will suffer most. They will in many instances be unable to challenge policy decisions that are sharply curtailing social programs.

Are Benefits Better Targeted?

The Reagan administration has offered several arguments in an attempt to defend and rationalize its budget cuts. One of the most frequent is the assertion that benefits were poorly targeted and went to many families who were not poor. The Office of Management and Budget (OMB) has claimed, for example, that 83 percent of the benefits in seven programs went to households with incomes above the poverty level in 1981 and 42 percent to those with incomes above 150 percent of the poverty threshold.[11] These figures are taken from Census Bureau data, but they are used incorrectly in several blatant distortions of fact. There is, in fact, much less of a targeting problem than the administration argues.

The most serious shortcoming of the census data is that they include the assistance benefits as part of income. The numbers reflect incomes *after* the benefits are obtained rather than the more accurate pretransfer income used by most economists. To use these statistics as the administration has done not only distorts the data but leads to false conclusions about the magnitude of benefits going to nonpoor families. By contrast, Robert Plotnick found that in 1974, 84 percent of all AFDC, SSI, and general assistance cash payments and 73 percent of all in-kind benefits went to people below the poverty standard.[12] Plotnick believes that these proportions have remained relatively stable over the past decade, indicating that the vast majority of means-tested benefits do go to the poor.

A related problem is that the census data do not indicate how much of the benefit is required to lift the recipient family to the poverty level or to 150 percent of it. If benefits are sufficient to put a family even one dollar above the poverty line, for example, the entire amount of benefits is counted as going to a family "above poverty." This is grossly misleading as an indicator of poor targeting.

But a more fundamental flaw in the administration's argument is that Congress *intended* to provide some benefits to individuals and families with incomes above the poverty level. Such benefits are not mistargeted or somehow wasted, as the administration seems to believe. Consider the following examples:

194

- In the thirty-four states with "medically needy" programs, individuals or families are entitled to Medicaid benefits when their incomes exceed AFDC eligibility standards or even the poverty level if their medical expenses are high. Such individuals or families might well show up in the Census Bureau's data as receiving Medicaid even though their household incomes exceed 150 percent of the poverty threshold because, when medical costs are paid, their disposable income falls below the poverty line.

- A blind elderly person living with her daughter's family may receive SSI even though the daughter's family has an income above 150 percent of the poverty threshold. SSI is intended as a cash benefit for low-income elderly, blind, and disabled persons, regardless of the income of the household in which the recipient lives.

These are reasonable benefits for "nonpoor" households, not examples of poor targeting. The administration's use of census data to support its claim that its budget cuts have not hurt the needy is a gross misrepresentation of the facts. The figures they quote are inaccurate, distorted, or entirely misleading.[13] As a result, the Office of Management and Budget has lost a good deal of credibility among members of Congress and the research community.

Is There Evidence of Cost Savings?

In some sense of the word, the federal government has "saved" money through its budget cuts. Upon scrutiny, however, the savings are better characterized as (1) cost shifts to state and local governments, (2) shortsighted savings that simply postpone costs through failure to invest in human capital, or (3) highly speculative figures.

When funds for basic human needs are reduced, the needs do not disappear. People do not stop needing medical care or food; instead, the needy turn to other sources. Thus many of the federal "savings" are actually shifts in costs to state and local governments. Because of the vertical structure of the categorical human service programs—from the federal government through the states to one or more layers of local government—the costs of particular programs are often shared by each level. This system allows considerable leeway for shifts in costs among levels of government—specifically, from the federal to state and local governments—which have indeed occurred in several areas.[14] Three examples are useful:

- Poor persons forced out of the Medicaid program must turn to state and local hospitals and clinics. Many working low-income people have lost their Medicaid eligibility because of budget cuts and policy changes but are not covered by private health insurance. They must increasingly be served by already overburdened county and municipal hospitals. Transfers from private hospitals to the Cook County Hospital in Chicago, a public institution, have increased from 125 to 400 patients per month since federal and state Medicaid cuts were imposed. Thus the county is picking up many of the costs of the Medicaid cuts.[15]

• Many AFDC families turn to general assistance programs, which give cash support to the indigent. Most such programs are sponsored by local governments, although some get state aid. In New York the number of families transferring from AFDC to general assistance rose by 65 percent between November 1981 and April 1982—as the Omnibus Budget Reconciliation Act was implemented.

• Similarly, a nationwide study by the Center on Budget and Policy Priorities found a "dramatic increase in the number of people coming to soup kitchens and food pantries. . . . Nearly one-third of the programs doubled in size." As the center further noted, "Nine out of ten agencies also reported that a significant proportion of the people they had served were those whose food stamps had run out."[16]

In these cases, there are no real "savings"—only a shift of costs from the federal government to the states and counties.

In addition to costs shifts, some of the administration's "savings" are myopic dollar savings that will inevitably entail greater costs because of a systematic failure to invest in human capital. Cuts in child nutrition, maternal and child health, education, and other vitally important services mean that two or three decades into the future—indeed, for the foreseeable future—society will be faced with increased costs for welfare, criminal justice, unemployment, disability, ill health, and other problems. Prevention today is surely less expensive than correction tomorrow. One study has shown that each WIC dollar will save $3 in future health care costs by reducing the number of low-birthweight and handicapped babies. As George Will has written about the WIC program:

> Breaking the poverty cycle and enhancing equality of opportunity require recognizing that by [the age of] five many children have suffered irreparable diminishment of intelligence and social competence. . . . It is cheaper to feed the child than jail the man. Persons who do not understand that are not conservative, just dim.[17]

Moreover, the administration's savings estimates are highly speculative. Not only do they fail to include increased costs to state and local agencies and increased long-term expenditures, but they fail to consider the interdependence of the programs affected. Savings in one program may be offset by increases in others. Because food stamp benefits are tied to the amount of AFDC received, for example, the cost of food stamps rises as AFDC benefits decline. The administration failed to take this into account when projecting its initial budget savings from the AFDC cuts.

In addition, state and local officials have used their discretion in regard to many of the entitlement programs to take actions that have countered the effects of the federal cuts. The administration's savings estimates did not anticipate such offsetting actions. For example, when the federal government imposed a new eligibility ceiling for AFDC at 150 percent of the state need standard, many states realized they could offset this provision by raising their need standards, which remain a state responsibility by law. Although this action would not increase payments to recipients, it would ensure that recipients could earn higher wages and still qualify for AFDC and would negate the federal intention of reducing eligibility for working recipients. Ten states took this action deliberately to avoid having thousands of earners terminated and to prevent increased future payments to recipients who might quit their jobs and return to AFDC at a higher grant level after being terminated. Another thirteen states raised their need standards as a routine adjustment. Twenty-three states thus failed to achieve all the savings intended by the federal budget cutters.

Moreover, two states modified the way they calculate AFDC benefits to avoid reducing payments to recipients with earnings. This action increases in those states both the number of working families eligible for AFDC and the amount of benefits paid to the working poor. Acting in direct response to the new federal rules that reduce benefits to this group, both states operated on the theory that spending the relatively small amount of money needed to sustain the working poor is preferable to paying them higher grants if they quit work and return to AFDC.

Another complexity overlooked by federal budget designers concerns the return of those terminated from AFDC. Because the target of the AFDC cuts was the working poor, much of the intended savings will be offset by recipients who return to the rolls and receive higher grants. If a working mother with earnings of $175 who receives $200 in AFDC is terminated, she is likely to find that she cannot support her family on $175 per month. She may be forced to quit her job and return to the welfare rolls, where she will receive $300 per month plus Medicaid. This action increases expenditures by $100. Analyses conducted by the Center for the Study of Social Policy indicate that the return of a single recipient to the AFDC rolls in Georgia offsets the federal cost savings from five terminations.[18]

In summary, the administration seems to have taken a fairly myopic view of budget savings. To assess the real savings from the AFDC cuts, we must not only subtract the increased costs or lack of savings due to return rates, state actions taken to counteract the federal changes, and shifts in other human service programs. We must also ask the difficult question whether any sums left are really "savings" in the long run or merely short-term reductions that will compound problems in the future.

Is There Evidence of Increased Administrative Efficiency?

Because the policy changes enacted in the human service arena were driven by the budget process, little thought was given to the administrative complexity of the new rules. The tension that is always present in the implementation of federal policies because of the inevitable gap between policy making and practice seems to have been exacerbated by the sweeping changes enacted in the past three years. In 1981 the budget reconciliation process was used to allow the president's entire budget to be adopted by Congress with virtually no debate about substantive consequences. The need to reduce entitlement spending was accepted, and how the programs should be reduced received little if any attention from policy makers. In short, the administrative problems posed by the new laws were ignored.

Substantial confusion and increased administrative burdens have been created by certain changes. Policies were enacted with little thought about the administrative consequences for already complex programs, and several provisions have caused considerable difficulty.

Schools serving free or reduced-price lunches to children, for example, now have to document a household's income and its participation in food stamps. This requirement has placed a cumbersome new burden on the local schools and agencies that administer school food programs, many of which are ill equipped to handle it.

AFDC recipients must now complete monthly reports to the local welfare office. This requirement has created more paperwork for caseworkers and confusion for clients. Many recipients have lost their eligibility by failing to complete the forms, but their reinstatement rate has been high. This situation clogs up the appeals systems and creates additional administrative burdens.

Moreover, the 1981 budget bars payments to an AFDC family with over $1,000 in assets. A number of states have declined to enforce this provision vigorously because they lack the administrative resources needed to investigate family assets in detail. As one state official said, "One of the ironies of all the Reagan revisions is that they put more strings on the welfare program, but they don't give us the money to administer all the changes. You have to pony up the money yourself."

In summary, the new federal policies brought with them increased administrative complexity rather than ease. State and local administrators are now both bearing the brunt of the federal government's inattention to procedural issues and being forced to pick up an increasing share of support for the poor.

Have Federal Funds Been Monitored to Ensure Their Use for Intended Purposes?

If the federal government is to be accountable for its actions, it must acquire the data necessary to determine the effects of its budget and policy changes. Because sweeping changes were enacted in 1981 and 1982 in many entitlement programs and because the plight of low-income families and other disadvantaged clients of these programs is a national concern, the government must act responsibly to ensure that its efforts have had positive effects. To carry out its responsibility, it must obtain information on which to base an objective and thorough evaluation of its actions.

Instead of maintaining the national data bases necessary to collect such information, this administration has eliminated many essential information-gathering operations. It appears that the administration is not interested in learning the effects of its actions, for it has virtually wiped out many of the large-scale surveys that provide the only information available on client populations. The Census Bureau, for example, has had to cut back on several surveys at the very time the nation is undergoing significant demographic and economic changes. The Bureau of Labor Statistics has ceased production of its lower living standard index. The Panel Study on Income Dynamics, which provides national data on families, with a particular emphasis on low-income families, received no federal funds for the first time in fourteen years. And the threat of extinction hangs over several other data-gathering projects. The Census Bureau's Survey of Income and Program Participation, for example, a source of data on participants in multiple entitlement programs, had been terminated but was recently given a reprieve.

In the name of deregulation, the federal government has ceased requiring states to report on the use of their funds. State reporting requirements for the low-income energy assistance program, for example, have been substantially reduced. States are not bound to any plan and can disburse the money as they see fit. States are also not required to report on their use of funds disbursed through the several block grants.

The withdrawal of support for research and survey data can only worsen the federal government's capacity to defend its programmatic strategies and budget cuts. Moreover, the withdrawal leaves the government without any basis for modifying its policies or for assessing their effects. In short, the federal government cannot be accountable if it halts collection of the data needed to assess the effects of its policies and programs.

Summary

The facts presented here lead to several conclusions about the effects of recent budget cuts and policy changes on the poor. First, although these new policies may save a little money for the federal government, they do so at great cost to the most vulnerable groups in our society. Moreover, few real long-term savings will be achieved. The cumulative effect of the federal changes in multiple human service programs appears to be harsh not only for welfare recipients but for the growing class of "new poor"—people suddenly without jobs or means to provide for their families. The policies enacted over the past three years are grossly unfair in two ways—to the dependent groups who must rely on public programs and in comparison with the minimal sacrifice being asked of the more affluent.

The only way truly to judge the effect of the Reagan administration is to examine the clients who rely on its programs and policies. Although much of the evidence is not yet in, preliminary information suggests that the poor are suffering because of a combination of factors. While a deteriorating economy and rising unemployment were causing hardship for millions, the administration's policies were cutting back the programs designed to help in times of economic distress. Its new policies, rather than shoring up marginal workers and the working poor, have made it increasingly difficult for them to move out of poverty. Instead of helping poor people pay their fuel bills with funds from a tax on windfall oil profits, the administration has forced the poorest of the poor to choose between heating and eating.

A second conclusion about these policies is that they will have adverse long-range consequences for the structure of our human service programs. The constriction of these programs makes them less flexible and less able to meet the range of needs in our society. The gaps in the "safety net," already large, are now enormous. AFDC, for instance, has been transformed from a program of aid for a wide group of poor families with children—including some with jobs at low wages and others without jobs—into a much narrower effort aimed primarily at nonworking families. As such, the program cannot now hope to increase work effort among the client population. The working poor have been left to fend for themselves. The programs are also becoming more difficult to administer, adding to the strain felt by fiscally distressed state and local agencies.

If the increased hardships being borne by the poor had actually reduced the federal deficit and thereby improved economic conditions, it could be argued that the budget cuts and policy changes were evil but necessary. But the deficit has reached record heights and is growing larger each month. Cutting the main programs for the poor has had virtually no effect on its size. Furthermore, as previous sections illustrate, many of the anticipated savings are no more than cost shifts to state and local governments or from one human service program to another. The rise in poverty statistics shows that the need is increasing; we cannot ignore it by pretending to save money in one part of a complex intergovernmental system.

Despite the obviously harsh consequences for people, programs, and budgets, the Reagan administration appears uninterested in the effects of its actions. Data collection has been severely curtailed or even eliminated at the very time it is needed most. As a result, government cannot be accountable for its actions. To remedy this, the federal government should provide financial assistance for states to conduct their own research and establish a mechanism for evaluating the effects of policy changes among the states. Lacking such a mechanism, the federal government is ignorant of the effects of its policy changes throughout the country.

In summary, the so-called safety net has not been maintained. The programs providing the main line of defense for the poor, though never adequate in the past, have been drastically reduced, leaving an already tattered safety net in shreds.

Notes

1. U.S. Congress, House of Representatives, Committee on Ways and Means, *Background Material and Data on Major Programs within the Jurisdiction of the Committee on Ways and Means*, February 21, 1984, p. 308, table 9.

2. Ibid., pp. 299–300, table 5.

3. Ibid., pp. 4, 10.

4. See Bureau of the Census, *Money Income and Poverty Status of Families and Persons in the United States: 1982*, P-60, no. 140.

5. Steven Cole, Sandra Danziger, Sheldon Danziger, and Irving Piliavin, "Poverty and Welfare Recipiency after OBRA: Some Preliminary Evidence

from Wisconsin" (Wisconsin: Institute for Research on Poverty, October 1983).

6. Center for the Study of Social Policy, "Working Female-headed Families in Poverty" (Washington, D.C., March 1984).

7. See Center for the Study of Social Policy, "Profiles of Families in Poverty: Effects of the FY 1983 Budget Proposals on the Poor" (Washington, D.C., February 1982).

8. See Children's Defense Fund, *A Children's Defense Budget* (Washington, D.C., 1983).

9. Charles Hulten and June O'Neill, "Tax Policy," in John Palmer and Isabel Sawhill, eds., *The Reagan Experiment* (Washington, D.C.: Urban Institute Press, 1982).

10. Joel Havemann, "Sharing the Wealth: The Gap between Rich and Poor Grows Wider," *National Journal*, October 23, 1982.

11. Office of Management and Budget, "Means-tested Individual Benefits," in *Major Themes and Additional Budget Details: FY 1984*, pp. 27–35.

12. Robert Plotnick, "Social Welfare Expenditures: How Much Help for the Poor?" *Policy Analysis*, vol. 5, no. 3 (1975), p. 284.

13. See, for example, Center for the Study of Social Policy, "OMB and Poverty Reform: Distorting the Meaning of Means-tested Benefits" (Washington, D.C., April 1983).

14. See Center for the Study of Social Policy, "Effects of Federal AFDC Policy Changes: A Study of a Federal-State Partnership" (Washington, D.C., March 1983).

15. "Medicaid Cuts Put Urban, Public Hospitals at the Crunch Point," *Washington Post*, August 19, 1982.

16. Center on Budget and Policy Priorities, "Soup Lines and Food Baskets" (Washington, D.C., May 1983).

17. *Newsweek*, December 20, 1982, p. 92.

18. See Center for the Study of Social Policy, "Working Female-headed Families in Poverty."

Contributors

EDWARD D. BERKOWITZ is associate professor of history and director of the Program in History and Public Policy at the George Washington University. He served on the staff of the President's Commission for a National Agenda for the Eighties and has been a policy analyst at the U.S. Department of Health, Education, and Welfare. The coauthor of *Creating the Welfare State*, he has written widely on social welfare history and policy.

KENNETH W. CLARKSON is professor of economics and director of the Law and Economics Center at the University of Miami. He served as associate director for human resources, veterans, and labor at the Office of Management and Budget during 1982 and 1983. He has been a member of the Advisory Council on Education Statistics of the U.S. Department of Education and a consultant to the President's Task Force on Food Assistance and has written more than fifty publications, including monographs on the food stamp and nutrition programs and on unemployment statistics.

DENIS P. DOYLE is resident fellow and director of Education Policy Studies at AEI. He was formerly director of planning and program coordination at the U.S. Department of Education and assistant director for education finance at the National Institute of Education. His paper "Education Policy for the 1980s and Beyond: A National Perspective" was recently published by the Center for National Policy. He has also written widely on education vouchers and tuition tax credits.

TERRY W. HARTLE is a research scientist and Washington liaison for the Educational Testing Service, specializing in issues of the finance and governance of education. His articles on education policy have appeared in several publications, including *Public Administration Review, American Political Science Review, Journal of Contemporary Studies*, and the *New Republic*.

G. WILLIAM HOAGLAND is deputy staff director of the U.S. Senate

Budget Committee. He previously served as administrator of the Food and Nutrition Service, as special assistant to the secretary of agriculture for food and nutrition policy, and as an analyst with the Congressional Budget Office in the field of income security policies.

TOM JOE is director of the Center for the Study of Social Policy in Washington, D.C. He previously served as special assistant to the under secretary of the U.S. Department of Health, Education, and Welfare and as a member of the senior staff of the California state legislature. He has also been a consultant to several federal government agencies, state governments, and foundations and has conducted studies of health policy, welfare reform, and other income security programs.

JACK A. MEYER is resident fellow in economics and director of the Center for Health Policy Research at AEI. He was formerly assistant director of the U.S. Council on Wage and Price Stability. His most recent book is *Passing the Health Care Buck: Who Pays the Hidden Costs?* He has also edited *Market Reforms in Health Care: Current Issues, New Directions, Strategic Decisions* and *Meeting Human Needs: Toward a New Public Philosophy*.

SEAN SULLIVAN is a senior analyst at AEI in the fields of health and employment. He recently served as executive director of the National Center for Occupational Readjustment and was formerly assistant director for pay monitoring at the Council on Wage and Price Stability. He has written widely on problems of youth employment and displaced workers.

JOHN C. WEICHER holds the F. K. Weyerhaeuser Chair in Public Policy Research at AEI. He has served with the President's Commission on Housing and as chief economist at the U.S. Department of Housing and Urban Development. He taught economics at the Ohio State University and was director of the housing and financial markets research program at the Urban Institute. Past president of the American Real Estate and Urban Economics Association, he has recently written *Housing: Federal Policies and Programs* and *Metropolitan Housing Needs in the 1980s*.

A NOTE ON THE BOOK

This book was edited by
Gertrude Kaplan and Ellen Dykes of the
Publications Staff of the American Enterprise Institute.
The staff also designed the cover and format, with Pat Taylor.
The figure was drawn by Hördur Karlsson.
The text was set in Palatino, a typeface designed by Hermann Zapf.
Hendricks-Miller Typographic Company, of Washington, D.C.,
set the type, and R. R. Donnelley & Sons Company,
of Harrisonburg, Virginia, printed and bound the book,
using paper made by the S. D. Warren Company.

SELECTED AEI PUBLICATIONS

Meeting Human Needs:
Toward a New Public Philosophy

JACK A. MEYER, Editor

Joblessness, illness, crime, poor housing—in coping with problems such as these, is there no alternative to inflexible, ineffective government programs? The authors of this volume see hope in approaches that combine greater private sector participation with reforms in government policy.

"There is a subtlety to the relations between state and society which [*Meeting Human Needs*] appreciates." *The New Republic*

"Sensible, grounded in reality, and focused on what can and does work. . . . Exciting." *Staff* (the congressional staff journal)

"A major new study . . . many types of private sector initiatives that have never been extensively studied before." *Urban and Social Change Review*

469 pp./1982/paper 1358-9 $13.95/cloth 1359-7 $34.95

Essays in Contemporary Economic Problems:
Disinflation

WILLIAM FELLNER, Project Director

The essays in the 1983–1984 edition of this continuing series describe and analyze the consequences of disinflation.

"A common thread runs through the papers in this volume—disinflation. Without minimizing its costs, they make clear the much greater cost of letting inflation run, as well as the quickly diminishing returns to expansionary fiscal and monetary policies." Henry C. Wallich, Board of Governors, Federal Reserve System

"The contributions of noted scholars collected in this volume provide valuable analytical insights into the impact of the disinflationary process on the economy of the United States, its implications for the future, and its lessons for public policy." Marina v. N. Whitman, Vice President and Chief Economist, General Motors Corporation

". . . continues to provide informative reading on a wide range of important issues for professional economists and policy makers." *Journal of Economic Literature*, on an earlier edition

330 pp./1984/paper 1364-3 $10.95/cloth 1365-1 $19.95

Making Economic Policy in Congress

ALLEN SCHICK, Editor

Several experts analyze how Congress attempts to reconcile its political and economic roles, identifying ways in which its machinery for economic policy making might be improved.

". . . notable for . . . consistent excellence in explaining the congressional economic role to the nonspecialist." *Library Journal*

282 pp./1984/paper 3535-3 $10.95/cloth 3534-5 $19.95

Market Reforms in Health Care: Current Issues, New Directions, Strategic Decisions

JACK A. MEYER, Editor

This volume examines proposals to improve incentives for providers and consumers to contain health care costs. Topics include Medicare and Medicaid reforms, private sector initiatives, trade-offs between cost and quality, and the fiscal effects and administrative feasibility of the new proposals.

". . . makes an excellent case for incentives and describes their potential benefit. . . . a measured view tempered by necessary *caveats.* . . . Federal and state as well as private solutions are defined and evaluated." *Journal of Policy Analysis and Management*

331 pp./1983/paper 2236-7 $10.95/cloth 2242-1 $19.95

Housing: Federal Policies and Programs

JOHN C. WEICHER

Weicher evaluates a number of proposals intended to make homeownership more accessible and concludes that most of them would subsidize families that can afford to buy homes and are already doing so in substantial numbers.

"A highly readable and well reasoned economic analysis of forty years of government housing programs . . . must reading for supply-side and non-supply-side economics advocates alike." *American Planning Association Journal*

161 pp./1980/3378-4 $6.25

• *Mail orders for publications to:* AMERICAN ENTERPRISE INSTITUTE, 1150 Seventeenth Street, N.W., Washington, D.C. 20036 • *For postage and handling, add 10 percent of total; minimum charge $2, maximum $10* • *For information on orders, or to expedite service, call toll free* 800-424-2873 • *Prices subject to change without notice* • *Payable in U.S. currency only* • *When ordering by International Standard Book Number, please use the AEI prefix—*0-8447.